Studies in Comparative Literature

No. 4
THE DRY MOCK

THE
DRY MOCK

A Study of Irony in Drama

ALAN REYNOLDS THOMPSON

"... the figure *Ironia*, which we call the *drye mock* ..."
THE ARTE OF ENGLISH POESIE (1589)

PORCUPINE PRESS
Philadelphia

First edition 1948
(Berkeley and Los Angeles: University of
California Press, 1948)

Reprinted 1980 by
PORCUPINE PRESS INC.
Philadelphia, PA 19107
By arrangement with The University of California Press

Library of Congress Cataloging in Publication Data

Thompson, Alan Reynolds, 1897-
. The dry mock.

    (Studies in comparative literature ; no. 4)
    Reprint of the ed. published by the University of
California Press, Berkeley.
    Includes bibliographical references and index.
    1. Drama—History and criticism. 2. Irony in
literature. I. Title. II. Series.
PN1680.T5   809.2′1   80-20927
ISBN 0-87991-507-2

Manufactured in the United States of America

Preface

A SCHOLAR's *work, also, is never done. One thing always leads to another. In a general study of dramatic theory published in 1942* (The Anatomy of Drama, *University of California Press) I dealt with irony only in passing.* But my attention had been drawn to it and my curiosity was teased by puzzling peculiarities of its effect on my emotions. I did not find these peculiarities satisfactorily explained in the studies of irony which I could obtain, and I cast about from time to time to explain them for myself. The problem suggested an essay, and the essay has expanded into a book. Whether my analysis will satisfy all readers, my examples will at least speak for themselves.*

There is of course no special kind of irony limited to plays. What is commonly called dramatic irony is found in novels, short stories, narrative verse, the movies, and, of course, life itself. Arbitrarily I restrict my theme to the field of my special interest, and in that field mainly to a few great writers. One must set up limits, for once one starts looking for an effect like irony he sees it everywhere, even as Sir Thomas Browne, once having set himself looking for quincunxes, found, as Coleridge said, "quincunxes in heaven above, quincunxes in earth below, quincunxes in the mind of man, quincunxes in tones, in optic nerves, in roots of trees, in leaves, in everything." Moreover, my

---

* In the second edition of this book (1946) I have incorported conclusions about irony which are devoloped at length in the present work.

[v]

intentions at the start were modest: I thought of a small book, an essay; and even now, when I find it swollen to a size much larger than I planned, I do no more than touch upon irony in literature outside the drama, and I merely suggest its wider uses. To treat fully the ironic sense in our time alone would involve nothing less than the spiritual predicament of modern man, yearning for faith in a world not made for his needs. I look down this vista now and then, but I do not explore it.

My indebtedness to earlier studies is fully acknowledged in the notes. If anyone unfamiliar with the literature were to ask which are the most useful of these works, I should, with hesitation over omissions, suggest the following. In the course of my discussion I disagree on occasion with them all, but without them, both for disagreement and for guidance, I could not have written this book.

J. A. K. Thomson, *Irony, an Historical Introduction* (London, 1926)
(Chiefly on meanings and uses of irony in Greek literature.)

Haakon M. Chevalier, *The Ironic Temper: Anatole France and His Time.* (New York, Oxford University Press, 1932)
(This, though a special study of France, has an excellent chapter on irony in general and the most nearly complete bibliography on irony available.)

David Worcester, *The Art of Satire* (Cambridge, Mass., 1940)
(This has two chapters on irony: "The Ally of Comedy" and "The Ally of Tragedy." It is lucidly and delightfully written.

G. G. Sedgewick, *Of Irony, Especially in Drama* (Toronto, 1934)
(These lectures survey "The Meanings and History of Irony," and examine in particular a few Greek tragedies and *Othello.* They are both entertaining and stimulating.)   A. R. T.

Acknowledgments

───────────────── ❧ ─────────────────

AMONG FRIENDS and colleagues at the University of California who have generously aided me I must thank particularly Mr. Henry Schnitzler, who read the book in manuscript and made very helpful suggestions. Professor L. A. Post, of Haverford College, Sather Professor of Classical Literature at the University of California in 1948, kindly read the manuscript and made useful suggestions. I regret that, as the book was then in press, it was impossible to make as much use of them as I should have liked. I should not have considered the manuscript complete had not my wife, Marie K. Thompson, gone through it with pencil in hand. And no editorial work could excel in skill and sympathetic understanding that done by my friend, Mr. Harold A. Small, Editor of the University of California Press.

Contents

Part One

EMOTIONAL DISCORD: THE NATURE OF IRONY

Aristodemus did not hear the beginning of the discourse, and he was only half awake, but the chief thing which he remembered was Socrates insisting to the other two that the genius of comedy was the same as that of tragedy, and that the writer of tragedy ought to be a writer of comedy also. To this they were compelled to assent, being sleepy, and not quite understanding his meaning. PLATO

The comical and painful are not objectively distinct. Every kind of humor can be matched by a kind of pain. Everything that is tragic may be comic if you contrive to take it playfully.

MAX EASTMAN

Irony acts as a counterpoise to the emotions raised by either tragedy or comedy. It furnishes an alternative scale of values which prevents the spectator from being altogether carried away by sympathy with the actors. DAVID WORCESTER

Martyrs are lacking in irony; it is an unpardonable fault, for without irony the world would be like a forest without birds; irony is the gaiety of meditation and the joy of wisdom.

ANATOLE FRANCE

CHAPTER I

The Forms of Irony

IRONY CAN BE viewed either as a special combination of things in the external world or as our feelings on seeing that combination. It can be viewed, in other words, as an objective cause or as a subjective effect. The simplest, or at least the crudest form of irony, for example, is illustrated by the sarcastic expression "Oh, yeah?" That locution combines a form of agreement with an implied denial; it says Yes and means No. But its effect is more than a simple recognition that "Oh, yeah?" means No. If that were all there were to the verbal situation, a person would merely accept the two words as a synonym for No, even as in learning German he accepts *Nein.* No emotion would be felt, or so little as to be negligible. But of course the expression is richly if not elegantly emotive. Even when we read the words and do not hear the jeering tone that labels irony in impolite conversation, they have a very different effect from a mere negative. The peculiar quality of the ironic contradiction, indeed, lies in its capacity to rouse a special sort of emotional response.

But this is viewing irony as emotional effect, and to do that is difficult, for all emotions are private experiences. We cannot really communicate them; we can only hint at them and hope that others, who have already had similar experi-

ences, will know what we mean. Our ways of hinting—
facial expression, gestures, vocal tones, words, even the fine
arts—are at best rough and uncertain. It is therefore convenient to view esthetic effects objectively and define them
in terms of their external causes. Such-and-such artistic
devices have been observed regularly to rouse emotions in
observers. Whether or not the emotions differ in all the observers is irrelevant to this approach. It may reasonably be
assumed that their likeness is greater than their difference.
At all events, their causes are phenomena of the external
world and therefore subject to the exact methods of science.
We are on sure ground if we disregard the effect, for we
can define and classify the cause. Hence most definitions of
irony are objective.

Thus the dictionary tells us that irony is the use of words
to signify the opposite of what they say (verbal irony), or
the feigning of ignorance, etc. (Socratic irony or irony of
manner), or a condition of affairs exactly the reverse of
expectation (dramatic irony, or the "irony of fate"). The
word is derived from the Greek *eiron,* meaning a dissimu-
lator. The seeming simpleton in Old Comedy who got the
laugh on his boastful antagonist was an *eiron.*[1] His manner
was ironical because it was the opposite of the truth, and
his speech was the irony of understatement, or litotes. Another type of irony, called Sophoclean, occurs when "a
speaker is made to use words bearing to the audience, in
addition to his own meaning, a further and ominous sense,
hidden from himself, and, usually, from the other person
on the stage."[2] The Greeks, however, never understood
irony in this sense, and the term originated with Bishop
Connop Thirlwall in 1833.

[1] For notes to chapter i see p. 261.

The dictionary is not very satisfactory in its distinctions between irony, sarcasm, and satire. It says that sarcasm is bitter and taunting reproach, but it might well add that sarcasm is a form of irony which has the qualities of "flesh-tearing" suggested by its etymology. As David Worcester wittily says, "When we dislike a writer's irony, we call it sarcasm."⁴ Again, the dictionary tells us of satire merely that it is the ridicule of folly. But irony is so often used as a satirical weapon, as for example by Swift, that casual speakers tend to confuse the terms. Mr. Worcester considers irony only as one of the forms of satire, along with invective and burlesque. Verbal irony, to be sure, is almost always offensive, but dramatic irony occurs often without any satirical implications. It would be far-fetched to say, for example, that Sophocles is attacking Oedipus with ridicule. The unhappy king is mocked by fate, or Apollo, but not by the author.

We may sum up and simplify this objective material by listing the forms of irony under three heads. The names I have given these three seem to me somewhat more accurate and less ambiguous than those customarily used. Under each head I offer a few examples; and since throughout the rest of this work I use dramatic illustrations, for the sake of variety I take these from nondramatic sources.

1. IRONY OF SPEECH (verbal irony). *The implication of what is said is in painfully comic contrast to its literal meaning.*

This irony ranges from crude sarcasm to profound philosophical observation or tragic utterance.

Job: "Doubtless ye are the people, and wisdom shall die with you!"⁵

Mark Twain: "The holy passion of Friendship is of so sweet and steady and loyal and enduring a nature that it will last through a whole lifetime, if not asked to lend money."[6]

Pitt, answering Walpole's sneer at his youth on entering Parliament: "The atrocious crime of being a young man, which the honourable gentleman has, with such spirit and decency, charged upon me, I shall neither attempt to palliate or deny; but content myself with wishing that I may be one of those whose follies may cease with their youth, and not of those who continue ignorant in spite of age and experience."[7]

Fielding's *Jonathan Wild* is called "the most sustained and consistent work of ironic narrative in all satire."[8] Jonathan, a highwayman, is constantly and solemnly called a Great Man. Here the verbal irony is built on the dramatic irony of a parallel between the criminal and the statesman.

Voltaire's Micromégas is a giant eight leagues tall from a planet of the star Sirius. On a visit to Saturn he is at first inclined to laugh at the puny size of its inhabitants. "But, since the Sirian was intelligent, he quickly realized that a thinking being could very well not be ridiculous for being only six thousand feet tall."[9]

France: "Arriving we know not from whence ... and successively invaded and conquered by four or five peoples from the north, south, east, and west, miscegenated, inter-bred, amalgamated, and commingled, the Penguins boast of the purity of their race, and with justice.... This idea that they belong to the best race in the world, and that they are its finest family, inspires them with noble pride, indomitable courage, and a hatred of the human race."[10] St. Maël, observing the Penguins fighting over the boundaries of their fields, says, "Do you see, my son, that madman who with his teeth is biting the nose of the adversary he has overthrown and that other one who is pounding a woman's head with a huge stone?" " 'I see them,' said Bulloch. 'They are creating law; they are founding property; they are establishing the principles of civilization, the basis of society, and the foundations of the state.' "[11]

2. IRONY OF CHARACTER (irony of manner). *A person's true character is shown to be in painfully comic contrast to his appearance or manner.*

A braggart who is really a coward or a windbag who is really a fool fits this formula, but he does so as victim, and the term is traditionally applied to the seeming simpleton, like Socrates, who shows him up. We find irony of character also in other than such satirical situations when a startling contrast of character is simply *exhibited,* as in the story from Saki quoted a little further on. But first let us take an illustration from Plato:

SOCRATES:... Speak out then, my dear Euthyphro, and do not hide your knowledge.

EUTHYPHRO: Another time, Socrates; for I am in a hurry, and must go now.

SOCRATES: Alas! my companion, and will you leave me in despair? I was hoping that you would instruct me in the nature of piety and impiety, so that I might have cleared myself of Meletus and his indictment. Then I might have proved to him that I had been converted by Euthyphro, and had done with rash innovations and speculations, in which I had indulged through ignorance, and was about to lead a better life.[12]

France: "If it is absolutely necessary for me to fight M. Brunetière, I suffer under many disadvantages.... Whilst he finds my criticism annoying, I find his excellent. I am thereby reduced to that defensive position, which . . . is considered bad by technicians. I hold M. Brunetière's strong constructive criticism in high regard. I admire the strength of the materials, and the grandeur of the plan. . . . . The ideas therein are developed with much method, and placed in a pleasing, imposing and novel order. Their heavy but certain advance recalls the famous manoeuvre of the legionaries marching shoulder to shoulder, protected by their shields, to the assault of a town. It was called the Tortoise."[13]

Saki: Ten-year-old Conradin hates his guardian, Mrs. de Ropp. "Thwarting him 'for his good' was a duty which she did not find particularly irksome." From a butcher boy he got a big polecat-ferret and hid it in the toolshed, praying to it as to a god: "Do one thing for me, Sredni Vashtar." Mrs. de Ropp, noticing his visits to the shed, gets the key and goes in, Conradin watching her the while from the dining room. She does not come out, but after a time the beast does, "with dark wet stains around the fur of jaws and throat." The maids go to hunt for their mistress. Conradin calmly makes tea, with much butter on his toast. He hears shrieks. " 'Whoever will break it to the poor child? I couldn't for the life of me!' exclaimed a shrill voice. And while they debated the matter among themselves, Conradin made himself another piece of toast."[14]

Note: The event in this story is so startling and horrible that it is likely to overshadow the irony of character and to suggest, at first glance, irony of events. But the event in itself is not ironical; the ironic "twist" of the ending is the grotesque contrast between the truth and the appearance of the child murderer.

3. IRONY OF EVENTS (dramatic irony). *Chance or fate in real life, the author in fiction, makes the outcome incongruous to the expectation, with painfully comic effect.*

This irony may be pointed up by speeches in which the victim expresses his expectation (Sophoclean irony). If we who observe know what is really going to happen, these speeches give a powerfully ironic effect. But their irony derives from the event, not from themselves, and they are innocent of irony if they stand alone. They thus differ from the verbal irony of our form 1, in which the speeches contain the incongruity. Since I shall deal with this type of irony at length later, I postpone illustrations. In the following examples the event contains the irony.

Voltaire's *Candide* is one long series of events that contradict the hero's expectation that all is for the best in the best of all possible worlds, and of explanations of these events which maintain the hero's faith. Thus Pangloss on his syphilis: "... it was a thing unavoidable, a necessary ingredient in the best of worlds; for if Columbus had not in an island of America caught this disease, which contaminates the source of life, frequently hinders generation, and which is evidently opposed to the great end of nature, we should have neither chocolate nor cochineal."

France, in *Penguin Island,* tells how a war arose directly as the result of an affair between the prime minister and the wife of a member of his cabinet. The injured husband cannot seek revenge direct, because he wants to keep his portfolio, so he instigates a whispering campaign against his wife's lover. This involves the nation in conflict with a neighboring empire. Too late the ministry is overthrown. "The very day of this fall the neighboring and hostile nation recalled its ambassador and flung eight millions of men into Madame Cérès' country. War became universal, and the whole world was drowned in a torrent of blood."[15] (Here the irony is one of disproportion rather than contradiction.)

The newspapers, at the time this book was being written, carried an item reporting that Negroes in two Northern cities had successfully protested against the performance of *Uncle Tom's Cabin* there, on the ground that it would be harmful to racial relations.

Viewed, then, as external cause, irony is a device generally but not always employed for satirical ends which uses contrast as its means. Its essential feature is a discrepancy or incongruity between expression and meaning, appearance and reality, or expectation and event. What we notice and then call irony is a striking discrepancy: one which is artfully arranged to draw attention to itself, or which, though occurring by chance, likewise compels our notice. Discrepancies are everywhere, but in normal usage we call them ironies only when, as the French say, they jump to the eyes.

So far, so good; and for ordinary critical purposes these definitions and distinctions should serve. Yet even after we have analyzed the mechanics of irony some puzzling questions remain unanswered. The chief of these is the relation of irony to comedy.

Irony arises from contrast; so also does comedy. The commonest mechanism of a joke is illustrated by a series of drawings by Cobean in the *New Yorker:* 1. Husband in chair buried behind newspaper; wife about to open her handbag on table. 2. She thrusts her hand into bag. 3. She removes ration book. 4. She thrusts her hand in. 5. She removes lipstick and compact. 6. She thrusts her hand in. 7. She removes handkerchief, key, and comb. 8. She thrusts her hand in. 9. She removes letters and loose coins and stares into bag. 10. Scowling, she thrusts her hand in. 11. With a smile of success she draws out a pistol. 12. Shoots husband.[16] Discrepancy between expectation and event! But we do not call it irony. It illustrates the way in which comedy builds up a psychic pressure in one direction, then suddenly releases it by offering something unexpected in another. There are other and more primitive sources of laughter, like tickling; but they are negligible in art, and this is fundamental. It operates even on a baby when he laughs at the sudden popping in and out of his father's head from behind a door. "Laughter is an affection arising from a strained expectation being suddenly reduced to nothing."[17]

This well-known observation of Kant's needs one or two qualifications, however. As Max Eastman points out, the effectiveness of a joke is heightened when its turn is not a mere reduction to nothing, but the presentation of an unexpected gratification.[18] And he is correct in insisting elsewhere on the existence of a playful mood as a condition for wholehearted merriment.[19] At the same time, laughter is increased when the mood has been oppressive in some fashion —embarrassed or oversolemn, for example—so that a joke affords release for more than one tension. In any case a sudden contrast is the central operative device of comedy.[20]

Irony involves the contrast but not the playfulness; its effect is the emotional discord we feel when something is both funny and painful. Without the discord a situation ironic in form is not ironic in effect, as we shall see. Hence in this study only those situations are considered ironic which both hurt and amuse at one and the same time.

This thesis needs demonstration, and the first doubt to assail a reader is likely to be whether amusement is always necessary to the more savage or tragic ironies. I shall consider *Oedipus the King* in the next chapter, and there will be many other illustrations to test the matter. But immediately we may consider the opinion of a student of irony, Edgar Johnson, who in the introduction to his anthology of satire insists that satire need not be comic and cites to prove his contention, in addition to Juvenal's direct invective (which is not ironical), the irony of Swift on the Yahoos and Aldous Huxley's on the Fifth Earl of Gonister. "Our illustrations prove, and it cannot be too emphatically stated, that satire does *not* have to arm or disguise itself with comedy."[21] His citation from Juvenal does not concern us, and is solemn enough to prove that satire of that sort need not amuse. But his citations of irony do concern us directly. Let us consider them.

Gulliver's description of European civilization, of which he is so proud, leads to the overwhelming conclusion of the King of Brobdingnag that men are "the most pernicious race of little odious vermin that nature ever suffered to crawl upon the surface of the earth." This in itself is not irony, but invective, and it certainly is not funny. The irony, and the amusement that causes it, arise from Gulliver's attitude. "I was forced to rest with patience while my noble and most beloved country was so injuriously treated." Is there no smile, however slight, in that? The smile may be wry, but that is to be expected. The wry smile is the visible sign of irony.

Huxley's Fifth Earl has learned how to live indefinitely by eating carp extract. "With advancing centuries of existence," says Mr. Johnson, "he gradually degenerates into a hideous Struldbrug-like anthropoid monster inhabiting a foul den filled with an intolerable stench." Mr. Johnson then quotes a passage in which the Earl's appearance and conduct are described, and comments: "The reader who is impelled to laugh at this passage has a strong stomach and a strange sense of humor." Certainly one is not impelled to laugh, but here also, as in Swift, he feels his lips twisting. He does so, at least, if he reads thoughtfully, as Huxley expects him to read, considering the Earl as we see him now in contrast to the splendor and vanity of his background. And Huxley is careful to give the reader his cue. "Knotted diagonally across his powerful chest was a broad silk ribbon that had been the blue Order of the Garter." How grotesque this reminder of feudal pomp and pious idealism (*Honi soit qui mal y pense*), injected into this foul scene!

Among this author's satirical novels *After Many a Summer Dies the Swan* is not his best, but it is full of Huxleian irony, biting and ludicrous, like the picture he draws of the monstrous musical Hollywood cemetery where death is "glamorized." The Fifth Earl, by contrast, is immortality made horrible,—and at the same time absurd. When Mr. Johnson calls one who feels such absurdity a person with "a strange sense of humor" he falls into *argumentum ad hominem*. He also gives his case away by admitting the existence of a comic effect in the act of condemning it. As for the condemnation, we need not plead *de gustibus* ... ; surely a person with mature intellectual detachment sufficient to follow and find interest in Huxley's underlying moral argument may be permitted also the amusement which Huxley's ironical method affords—such as it is—without having to bear the suspicion of harboring perverse inclinations!

CHAPTER II

Emotions That Clash

IN IRONY, emotions clash. Suggestively, a sixteenth-century
writer called it the "dry mocke."[1] According to a recent
theorist inclined to literary metaphor, "it hesitates between Dionysus and Apollo."[2] Both gods at least inspire it,
for it is both emotional and intellectual—in its literary mani-
festations, at any rate. To perceive it one must be detached
and cool; to feel it one must be pained for a person or ideal
gone amiss. Laughter rises but is withered on the lips. Someone or something we cherish is cruelly made game of; we
see the joke but are hurt by it.

It follows from this view that contrasts which conform
exactly to the objective definitions of irony are not ironical
at all when they do not rouse these conflicting feelings.
They will then be purely comic, purely pathetic, purely
horrible, or purely tragic. We shall consider some examples.
But first it may be instructive to examine what happens
when the purely comic effect and the ironic effect can both
be observed in a single situation, both present and yet distinct. As the effects cannot be felt from short extracts, I
must quote in full. It is the opening scene of Henry Becque's
play, *La Parisienne.*[3]

CLOTILDE *enters hurriedly in outdoor costume. She takes a
closed letter in her hand, goes to the table, lifts the cloth, and*

---

hides the letter underneath. She goes to the desk, drawing a keyring from her bag. Enter LAFONT. *He sees her there. She makes a pretense of locking the desk.* LAFONT *puts down his hat and approaches her, much agitated, but holding himself in with difficulty.*

LAFONT. Open that desk and give me that letter.

CLOTILDE. No.

(A pause.)

LAFONT. Open that desk and give me that letter.

CLOTILDE. I won't.

(A longer pause.)

LAFONT. Where have you been?

CLOTILDE. Oh, *now* it's something else.

LAFONT. Yes, it's something else. I ask you where you've been.

CLOTILDE. I'll tell you.... But I wish you could see yourself as you are looking now. You aren't a pretty sight, my dear. You please me better in your ordinary state. My heavens, how are things going to end if you lose your head over a stupid note that maybe anybody might have sent me?

LAFONT. Open that desk and give me that letter.

CLOTILDE. Very well, you can see it.... But you'd better consider. If you keep on making scenes like this, you'll soon lose me. I warn you, I won't submit to cross-questioning every time I step outdoors.

LAFONT. Where have you been?

CLOTILDE. Try at least to be logical, my dear. If I had just left some man, it isn't likely I'd find a letter from him the instant I got back.

LAFONT. Open that desk and give me that letter.

CLOTILDE. You're joking, aren't you?

LAFONT. Do I look like it?

CLOTILDE. You are suspicious of me, then?

LAFONT. That's more like it.

(He points to the desk.)

CLOTILDE. You wish it? You require it? You demand it? Very well. (*She searches slowly and with affectation in her bag for the keys. First she pulls out a handkerchief, then a note-book, then the keys. She puts back the notebook and handkerchief, and tosses the keys on the table.*) Open it yourself. (*She walks away; he stands undecided, biting his lip.*) Well, pick it up and open the desk. Once a person starts something, he ought to finish it. That shows he's a man. (*He makes up his mind, goes to the keys and lowers his hand. She goes to him.*) But be very careful what you do. If you touch those keys with the tips of your fingers ... with the tips of your fingers ... *I'll* not be the one to regret it. You will.

(LAFONT, *hesitating, picks up the keys and gives them to her.*)

LAFONT. Take your keys.

(*Pause, during which* CLOTILDE *takes off her hat and gloves and adjusts her hair.*)

CLOTILDE. You know, it's getting worse.

LAFONT. What is?

CLOTILDE. I warn you, the disease is getting worse.

LAFONT. What disease?

CLOTILDE. I've noticed before how you have been watching me, and I've laughed at all the trouble you've been giving yourself ... so uselessly. But till now I didn't have to say anything. It was jealousy, to be sure, but an amiable jealousy that flatters a woman's vanity and amuses her. Now you are succumbing to the other sort of jealousy, stupid, gross, brutal, the kind that wounds deeply, and that a woman can't pardon twice. Are you going to start it again?

LAFONT. Clotilde?

CLOTILDE. Are you going to start it again?

LAFONT. No.

CLOTILDE. Well, that's something.

LAFONT. Clotilde?

CLOTILDE. What, my dear?

LAFONT. Do you love me?

CLOTILDE. Less today than yesterday.

LAFONT. Don't you want me to be happy?

CLOTILDE. I think I've shown you that often enough.

LAFONT. I'm afraid of all those young men who meet you everywhere and flock around you.

CLOTILDE. You shouldn't be. I chat with them now and then, but once I've turned my back I don't even remember who I've been talking with.

LAFONT. You don't remember anybody you might have encouraged unintentionally, who would think himself authorized to write you?

CLOTILDE. Nobody.

LAFONT (*piteously*). Open that desk and give me that letter.

CLOTILDE. At it again! ... That letter was from my friend Mrs. Bernard (LAFONT *makes a movement*), the most virtuous of ladies ... underneath her giddy airs. I know what Pauline has written me and I'd be the first to tell you if you stopped demanding me.

LAFONT. Clotilde?

CLOTILDE. Well?

LAFONT. You'll be reasonable?

CLOTILDE. More than ever.

LAFONT. You won't get excited?

CLOTILDE. No, nor jealous either.

LAFONT. Think of me, Clotilde, and of yourself. Consider how an imprudence is easily committed and never undone. Don't you acquire this taste for adventures that nowadays causes so much trouble. Resist it, Clotilde, resist it! Faithful to me you are a worthy and honorable woman, but the day you deceive me—

(*She stops him, takes a few steps toward the rear, and returns.*)

CLOTILDE. Be careful. Here comes my husband.

Having often read this scene aloud to classes in modern drama, I can testify to its normal effect. On that final "punch line" there is first a gasp of shocked surprise, then, after a momentary silence, gradually increasing laughter. The mechanism of comedy which we discussed above is obvious: the whole scene leads us to assume the jealous husband and the coquettish wife, then suddenly requires us to make a complete readjustment.

But the laughter that results is never wholehearted. An audience recognizes the cleverness and completeness with which it has been taken in, but there is also something unpleasant that reduces mirth. This is the discomfort that causes the ironic discord. It is felt later than the purely comic effect because it is not anticipated; and it grows on a mature reader the more he thinks about the scene. He recollects how all through the nineteenth century, from the time of Hugo and Dumas, Parisian drama had been romanticizing adultery and making the jealous husband ridiculous. He realizes how trenchantly Becque satirizes this tradition. And with what disillusioned truth! It is merely Romantic convention which leads us to assume that unmarried lovers do not act and feel toward each other like married ones— even to preaching fidelity! And we who have accepted that convention are made fools of. In this scene the comic joke is on the surface, the ironic one underneath—waiting to catch us in a sentimental attitude and show us up.

Pure comedy, then, is the effect of a sudden contrast which does not hurt our feelings, but gratifies them instead. Irony results from a comic situation when we are also pained.

But this generalization requires some qualification. First of all, there are three different points of view toward an irony: that of the person using it for attack, that of its victim, and that of the onlooker. If our view is that of the attacker we shall probably feel no sympathy but rather rejoice at the discomfiture we cause. Contrariwise, if we are the victim we shall hardly be amused at all. The action be-

comes ironical in its full sense only when we have the onlooker's view. We may take sides: in comic irony, as we shall
see in a later chapter, on the side of the attack; in tragic and
sentimental irony, on that of the victim. But we must feel
both sides to feel the irony.

Are all comic situations when pain is felt ironical? Are
painful practical jokes, for example, a form of irony?

Let us consider Saki's "Sredni Vashtar," cited in the preceding chapter to illustrate irony of character. Conradin
murders his guardian and then contentedly munches but-
tered toast. To us this is not funny; it is horrible. Yet there
is a joke in the situation, and the joke creates its gruesome
irony. "Whoever will break it to the poor child?" We can
see the smirk on the "poor child's" lips. If they only knew.

Saki's stories are generally funnier and kindlier than this
one (kindlier at least by comparison), but they have a fundamental kinship with it: their usual formula is the painful
practical joke. Their author, according to his sister, never
outgrew his hatred of the maiden aunts who brought him
up. An English critic, Mr. S. P. B. Mais, she writes, showed
an "uncanny insight" into her brother's character when he
remarked in a review: "Munro's understanding of children
can only be explained by the fact that he was in many ways
a child himself: his sketches betray a harshness, a love of
practical jokes, a craze for animals of the most exotic breeds,
a lack of mellow geniality that hint very strongly at the
child in the man. Manhood has but placed in his hands a
perfect sense of irony and withheld all other adult traits."
Irony, like other appeals to emotion, has various levels. On
the level of mature and humane spectators it involves a conflict in the moral sense: what is *versus* what ought to be. But

on the level of schoolboy humor it may, as with ten-year-old Conradin, be primitive and savage.

We now proceed to test our theory at greater length.

1. IRONY OF SPEECH. A sarcastic tone needs no words, but words make it more explicit. "Oh, yeah?" might be paraphrased in the vernacular as, "You poor sap, do you think me fool enough to believe that?" An expression that says so much in so few words is a witty one, or was when invented. Doubtless that is one reason for its popularity. But the main appeal of sarcastic mockery is that it neatly combines ridicule of another with self-glorification. It also has the advantage of seldom permitting a wholly adequate retort. It amuses and gratifies the speaker with little or no danger and it hurts the hearer and leaves him frustrated. Such attractions give sarcasm universal usage. We *will* mock, even though by the age of twenty we should have learned from unhappy experience that our victims, frustrated at the moment, will take it out on us later if they can; and that using sarcasm is one of the surest ways of losing friends and antagonizing people. But its appeal to the savage ego in us is too great to be resisted.

Its crudity, however, barring occasional exceptions, limits its use in literature to dramatic speech which reflects the vocal interchanges of life. An excellent example from the Bible is Elijah's jibes at the priests of Baal when for all their prayers their god does not send down fire from heaven to kindle their sacrifices. "And it came to pass at noon, that Elijah mocked them, and said, Cry aloud: for he is a god; either he is talking, or he is pursuing, or he is in a journey, or peradventure he sleepeth, and must be awaked."[5] Is the spirit of this very different from that of a "Bronx cheer"?

Yet to an anonymous English author, writing under the title "Is Irony a Form of the Ludicrous?" this, along with the "higher irony" of Carlyle, Swift, Sophocles, and Isaiah, is not ludicrous at all, but purely pathetic or sublime.[6] Clearly the circumstances of a sarcasm affect our attitude toward it. If one is a pious gentleman brought up to feel such reverence toward the Bible that it embraces even the fiercest of the Old Testament prophets, one may find the adjective "sublime" suitable to this passage. Otherwise one can hardly feel as this author does that "the effect is not ludicrous at all" but "profoundly and overpoweringly solemn." The critic certainly takes it solemnly, but did Elijah's partisans? One can almost hear their loud jeers and scornful laughter.

Sarcasm is partisan, though it is not fully ironical unless in some degree we feel both with the giver and the receiver. But most literary uses of irony appeal to us as more or less impartial onlookers. We are detached, at an "esthetic distance" from what we read or see; and even when we identify ourselves imaginatively with a character, as we so often do at a play, our sympathetic emotion never remotely approaches in intensity that of an actual participant.[7] Thus the bitterest words and most horrible events may excite us pleasurably because they do not excite our emotions to a degree painfully discomfiting. They give us rather a heightened and more vivid sense of life, and this may easily be more satisfying artistically than the milder "pleasant" effects.

The pleasure in mild physical pain is a normal experience. We enjoy a sore tooth, or tickling, or amorous violence, until, as we say, "it hurts"; and our enjoyment is keenest just before that point is reached. Thus there should be no difficulty about accepting the paradox of pleasant pain in art, where all pain is imaginative.

Indeed, given the hint conveyed in such words as "amorous violence," one might easily understand the paradox too well. Esthetic pleasure in pain need involve no eroticism—unless of course one equates eroticism with the whole of life. But there certainly is an element of cruelty in it, as Émile Faguet argued when he wrote that it is the residual savage in us which sends us to the theater: "at comedy as at tragedy we come to see suffering."[8]

Cruelty is an element of our enjoyment, but not the whole of it. Human motives are numerous, mixed, and often contradictory. I have discussed Faguet's general theory elsewhere.[9] We are here concerned only with the effects of irony. Cruel people undoubtedly enjoy a cruel pleasure in observing ironies, and kindly people may, also, in slighter measure. What seems more significant about such experiences when we gain them from art is that they give us what I described as a heightened and more vivid sense of life.

The distinction between the spectator who observes an irony and an actor who inflicts it is often ignored by students of literature, who inevitably take the view of the onlooker and identify the ironic spirit with his. He is, they say, objective, above the battle, even—as Friedrich Schlegel put it—godlike in his superiority. But the man who uses irony for offense is certainly an ironist, and in the sense that he makes irony he is more justly so called than the passive observer. And this active ironist can be said to feel for his victim, generally, only in the sense that he must imagine the pain he inflicts in order to enjoy his act. Swift was such a person, and Voltaire. They were objective, so to speak, in the first degree: they saw and were amused by the irony they created. But they, unlike us who read them, were not objective in the second degree, for they were impelled to irony by hate or indignation and therefore could feel no pity for their victims.

The full force of irony, then, is felt by the spectator, and since we are concerned with dramatic effects, we shall be dealing chiefly with him and his feelings. If we need to refer to him, it would be awkward to call him an appreciator of irony, or something of the sort, instead of simply an ironist, but it would be well to keep the distinction in mind. The parallel is exact with poet and poetry-lover, but there the distinction is always clear.

2. IRONY OF CHARACTER. We saw that the feigning of ignorance is the type of irony which the Greek word originally designated. In *The Clouds* Aristophanes has Strepsiades say, "... if indeed I can escape my debts and appear to be bold, ready-tongued, daring, impudent, disgusting, a fabricator of lies, a word-monger, tricky with legalities, a shyster, a chatterer, a fox, a knave, a sly fellow, a dissembler [εἴρων], oily, an impostor [ἀλαζών]..."[10] Both the *eiron* and the *alazon,* then, were rogues; and in this context they seem much alike. The theory, however, is that in Old Comedy the former, the seeming simpleton, comes into conflict with the latter, the boaster, and gets the better of him.

The theory of the development of Old Comedy from Dionysiac ritual, as elaborated by F. M. Cornford,[11] requires that impostors (*alazones*) appear especially in the latter part of the play, following the parabasis, when a feast is begun, to claim shares in it and be driven off with mockery by the *eiron.* But few of these characters, as Cornford lists them, fit the role of boastful impostor or play important parts in the comedies as antagonists to the heroes. Some of them, in fact, fit the scheme of *eiron* versus *alazon* only with difficulty.[12]

Cornford is trying to prove that a ritual underlies Old Comedy; he is not interested in the *eiron-alazon* relationship from any other point of view. Hence in *The Acharnians* he lists as *alazones* the envoys from Persia and Thrace, Euripides (even though in this scene it is the *eiron* who is begging for something), two informers, Lamachus' servant, a farmer, and a groomsman; but he does not list Lamachus himself except as he appears in part of the *agon*. Yet to the disinterested reader Lamachus is the one character in the play who best fits the role of boastful impostor. He is indeed the prototypical *miles gloriosus,* the character who plays so frequent a role down through Latin comedy and *commedia dell'arte.*

This theory of *eiron* versus *alazon* as simpleton worsting boaster is developed in J. A. K. Thomson's study of the origin of irony; and since that study is concerned wholly with our subject it should be more helpful. Yet Thomson discusses only two *eirons* from Aristophanes. The first is Dicaeopolis in *The Acharnians,* who is "not such a fool as he looks."[13] Unfortunately he does not fit Mr. Thomson's theory very well. The one scene cited is that in which he begs Euripides for some rags and other "tragical" equipment that will be useful to him in pleading with the Acharnians, who want to stone him for making a private peace with Sparta. The most obvious thing about this scene is the satirical attack against Euripides for lowering the dignity of tragedy by sentimental appeals. But in this scene it is, as we have said, the *eiron* who begs for something. And the scene is merely a preliminary to the *agon* or contest with the Acharnians. It seems strange that Thomson does not mention the later scene in which General Lamachus and Dicaeopolis engage in a sort of antiphonal duet, the one bemoaning the discomforts of war, the other glorying in the pleasures of peace. This scene, with its ironic contrast, is central to the author's aim of showing the desirability of peace. And he develops Dicaeopolis' character with this aim in mind, making him little concerned to fox boastful soldiers but much concerned to enjoy the fleshly delights that his private peace makes possible. This single-minded lust for eating, drinking, and wenching is not the duplicity of an *eiron*. The irony which we see occasionally in the play is a dramatic irony arising from the contrast between peace and war, not an irony of character arising from the seeming simplicity of a dissembler.

Strepsiades, in *The Clouds,* Mr. Thomson's second example, seems even less the *eiron* of his theory. He thinks this character, like Dicaeopolis, shrewd underneath his "rustic simplicity."[14] It is difficult to discover the shrewdness. He goes to Socrates hoping to learn sophistical tricks that will fool his creditors, but he is too stupid to be taught and is forced to send his son instead. The first use the latter makes of his new skill is to beat his father. Strepsiades now sees the error of his ways and repents. His adventure is a comic parody of a tragic plot in which the hero shows *hybris,* suffers *nemesis* in a sudden *peripeteia* or turn of fortune, and comes to a final *anagnorisis* or realization of his fault. But *hybris,* or sinful insolence, is the attitude of an *alazon,* according to the theory; and according to the theory the *eiron* is supposed to win, not lose, his contest. There is dramatic irony when the biter is bit; and in *The Clouds* there is for a modern reader a strange irony that the immortal *eiron,* Socrates, should be represented as a boaster and, in several other ways, the exact opposite of what he really was. But of the *eiron-alazon* formula I see little.

Mr. Thomson's theory is attractive, and one may regret to find it poorly supported by his own evidence. At all events, it has a general value for our study in emphasizing an irony of character which occurs frequently in life and is often employed in comedy. We shall note examples in later dramatists.

Mr. Thomson also finds the comic poet's general attitude ironic. "There is in Aristophanes a conscious intellectual superiority to his puppets.... He never identifies himself with any of his characters."[15] But this could be said with equal justice of any successful writer of farce or burlesque. One cannot write that sort of play otherwise. Freedom from identification is necessary for the comic spirit in general, not merely for irony.[16] And it is this general comic spirit that Aristophanes maintains throughout his plays, even in handling matter the nastiness, the brutality, or the wickedness of which is sometimes appalling to our less robust sensibilities. How he could view such things with so unwavering a spirit of amusement is difficult for us to understand. If not more civilized than his original audience, we are most of us more squeamish; and intellectually we are habituated to qualified judgments, for we have been trained to realize that there is seldom a simple explanation of anything or anybody. Not so Aristophanes. He has in this respect a small boy's or a primitive man's undivided attitude, and no two ways about it. (Irony is exactly taking "two ways.") Euripides, as Aristophanes presents him, is simply absurd. So is even Socrates, who to us is a saint and a sage. Aristophanes was a genius, but his genius was manifested in straight comedy—or farce, if you will,—not in irony.

These observations do not alter the fact that to the ancient Greeks *eironeia* meant dissimulation. The word gained its modern meaning chiefly as a result of Plato's portrayal of Socrates, who in his conversations with cocky young friends played the mock-modest questioner, conscious both of his own comparative wisdom and their folly. Since *eiron* was a term of abuse, it was natural for his enemies to call him by the name. But he was also essentially a humble, heroic seeker after truth and virtue. His character as Plato has pictured it is one of the noblest literary portraits in the world; and on the basis of it there are many who rank him not far below Jesus in their catalogues of saints. Hence the word irony became ennobled by association with him.[17]

Nonetheless, as we view his dissimulations in the dialogues our feelings are mixed. We hardly sympathize with his victims, especially those whose boastfulness predisposes us to enjoy their undoing. But since we are seriously concerned with the ethical issues involved, we are uneasy about such methods, which usually cause more antagonism than conviction. Though Socrates used irony for high ends, it is nevertheless a method of ridicule, and all the more intolerable because indirect and unanswerable. Indeed, since it is bound to make enemies, if Socrates really used it as freely as Plato represents him as doing, the hostility which led to his condemnation may have been due to it quite as much as to his doctrines.

When even in the dialogues of Plato we feel this discomfort, it is clear that the irony of dissimulation arouses the emotional discord which we have postulated.

3. IRONY OF EVENTS. Before we proceed to examples here, some clarification of common terms is needed. Mr. Worcester hardly assists it when he writes: "It is best to regard dramatic irony, tragic irony, and Sophoclean irony as interchangeable terms."[18] In thus casually lumping them together Mr. Worcester follows current usage. "Such double-edged speech [as in a scene from *The Bacchae*]," says Professor Sedgewick, "is usually called by the names—all three are still used with complete impartiality—Sophoclean, tragic, dramatic irony."[19] But the usage is nonetheless confusing. We limit what we call "Sophoclean irony" (in quotation marks) to the verbal device that gives the audience the wink and thus calls sharp attention to a discrepancy in the situation of the speaker. The discrepancy, however, may be ironical itself in a different sense, without specific verbal emphasis. By itself it constitutes an irony of events, or what is usually called dramatic irony. To extend the adjective dramatic to irony in a novel, or in life, is unobjectionable in ordinary usage, but may well be confusing in a special study like the present one. We shall limit "dramatic irony," then, to irony of events as exhibited in a play. Bishop Thirlwall called the general type "practical irony." This use of *practical* in its etymological sense has its merits, but it is not generally understood. "Irony of events" avoids possible ambiguity in meaning.

Again, we shall not equate "tragic irony" with "dramatic irony," however current the confusion may be. Dramatic irony includes comic irony also. And the term "Sophoclean irony" is open to the objection that Euripides was even fonder of it than Sophocles, if we can judge by their extant plays, and used it with really terrific effect in such plays as *The Bacchae,* as I shall argue in detail in a later chapter. The term is of course firmly established and will remain so, but we shall avoid using it when possible.

Thirlwall seems to be responsible not only for originating "Sophoclean irony" but also the rather melodramatic "irony of fate," which he employs in reference to Hercules in *The Trachinian Maidens.*[20] Of this very popular expression Mr. Worcester well observes that "it is frequently used but more frequently abused, as in the sentence: 'By the singular irony of fate, the shipment arrived two minutes before the embargo went into effect.' "[21]

Dramatic irony, then, is our term for irony of events when we see them on the stage. It may be tragic, but it may be comic, or horrible, or sentimental, or of some other intermediate type. The adjective we use depends on the predominating emotion, aside from amusement, that it excites.

Since dramatic irony is most noticeable when a character's fate proves the opposite of his expectation or desert, it has a basic likeness to the reversal of a tragic plot. Cornford points out the resemblance of *alazoneia* in a comedy to *hybris* in a tragedy. Thomson expands this comparison in relation to irony: "We watch the hero challenge Destiny and fall, and we feel that this is tragic. We observe the fool running his head against the force of circumstances, and that (if the consequences are not serious) we feel to be comic. In either case ... the feeling is mixed with Irony."[22]

It is easy to go further. In his next paragraph Mr. Thomson not merely finds tragic feeling "mixed with Irony"; he finds it wholly ironical. "There are scholars who write as if, in mentioning this verbal form of Irony ['Sophoclean'], they had exhausted the subject. Why, a Greek tragedy is all Ironical; it is Ironical in its very nature." This is because the spectator at a Greek tragedy generally knew the outcome from the beginning.

But why stop at Greek tragedy? Professor Sedgewick does not. Irony, he says, "in some form is a practically inevitable result, almost a corollary, of the working of dramatic principle."[23] This is because the spectator at any play experiences a "fusion ... of superior knowledge and detached sympathy."[24] This fusion he calls "general dramatic irony," and what most writers on the subject call dramatic irony is to him only a sharp emergence into consciousness of this "pervasive sense of Reality controlling Appearance."[25] As a consequence of thus equating "general dramatic irony" with spectatorship he is able, not surprisingly, to see it where others do not.

Thus his interesting and often enlightening study of irony in *Othello* has to my mind the weakness of a *parti pris,* though he admits that "the precise ironic point of view is not common."[26] Shakespeare, he says, induces an ironic attitude in us by letting us know at the outset Iago's villainous intentions. This attitude is an expectation of calamity which colors our observation of all subsequent scenes. "We see things tending inevitably—as it seems to us—in one direction, though that direction is hidden from the Moor and the gentle Desdemona."[27]

We can agree with much of his analysis. Iago, considered separately as a personality, is an "arch-ironist" of a sort. But that fact has no necessary bearing on the question of dra-

matic irony in the play as a whole. His irony would become
ours only if we shared his attitude, despising mankind and
watching the progress of his villainy with his own cruel
amusement. Again, we can admit that Shakespeare pointed
up the wording of many speeches with ironic intent: the
phrase "honest Iago," uttered or paraphrased repeatedly by
Othello, by Desdemona, even by Emilia—who ought to
know him better,—brings an ironic twitch to our lips. There
is, as Mr. Sedgewick says, a dreadful irony of Sophoclean
kind in Othello's line: "My life upon her faith! Honest
Iago—" And there is a comic irony not mentioned by Mr.
Sedgewick which Shakespeare is very bold to use in the
circumstances, when Cassio has been wounded by Iago (Act
V, Scene 1) and, not knowing that Iago was his assailant,
turns to him as a friend.

> Iago. . . . What villains have done this?
> Cassio. I think that one of them is hereabout . . .

This line Professor Kittredge (according to my lecture
notes) considered most dangerous for the stage because the
audience is likely to laugh. I am not as sure as he that the
audience should not laugh; but the point in this connection
is that Shakespeare obviously wrote it with ironic intent.

All this, and more, we may admit. But the fact remains
that the total tragic effect of *Othello* is not to most of us
ironic. Mr. Sedgewick sees as irony what most of us would
call merely dramatic anticipation or tragic suspense. This
is the whole point at issue. We may, if we wish, so define
irony as to make it identical with tragic suspense, but if we
do we must call all tragedies ironical, for in watching all of
them we know that the protagonist will come to misfortune.

If he utters a hopeful word, that is irony. Even if he says nothing, his situation is ironic. Indeed, all drama is ironic, as Mr. Sedgewick says. If things happen as we expect, there is irony in our superior knowledge; if they happen differently from what we expect, the joke is on us and there is irony in it still. And all life is nothing but irony, at that rate. . . .

Such a view is perfectly logical, but we prefer a definition of irony which distinguishes it from other sorts of contrast or discrepancy, and in particular from tragic peripeteia. The latter does not necessarily involve a clash between amusement and pain. I for one feel no amusement at Othello's ruin, still less at Desdemona's death. They are among the most painful scenes in all dramatic literature both to read and to watch, and the pain they cause is unmitigated except, in some measure, by the magnificence of Othello's rhetoric. The total impact of the play is not such as to make us intellectually detached, so as to enjoy the irony of it, but on the contrary to make us identify ourselves almost too cruelly with the sufferers. Shakespeare as an artist kept himself above his characters so far as was necessary to perfect their inherent dramatic logic, but his genius lay chiefly in his unrivaled imaginative identification with them, particularly with his sympathetic characters, and in his ability as a consequence to attach us to them and make us feel with them. We are not ironical when we are doing that.

The ironical state of mind involves some degree of detachment, for it is in part a comic point of view. If we are not detached from painful things we cannot be amused by them; and we are not detached from Othello and Desdemona—not, at least, if we are normal spectators. Dramatic critics and scholars, unfortunately, are seldom normal spectators, especially when they watch a work as familiar as *Othello,* for their original emotions toward it have been overlaid by all manner of intellectual considerations and speculative interests. If they happen to be pursuing a particular speculation at the time, they are likely to see everything in its light. They can return to their original "normal" emotions only by an effort of memory, and they may well refuse to make the effort, being pridefully conscious of how much more they now know and apprehend than they did then. This is a handicap that all of us should keep in mind when we discuss a play's emotional effects: we are not representative spectators any longer. We cannot see the play as the author intended it to be seen. Shakespeare did not write *Othello* for us.

So far as I have been able to ascertain, intelligent spectators who have no critical axes to grind and who are therefore more representative than I am, do not feel irony in the catastrophe of *Othello*. And indeed Mr. Sedgewick admits as much. Shakespeare, in other words, was not making game of the Moor. And in making game of somebody or something lies the distinctive quality of irony as normally recognized. In a limited sense Sophocles was making game of Oedipus by letting Fate make game of him; and therefore we think of the Greek play as ironical, but not Shakespeare's.

This view has been stated with more vigor than sobriety by Mr. Eastman. "At times," he writes, the Greek dramatists "exchange with the audience a gruesome wink at the expense of their doomed hero.... You might almost describe these typical Greek tragedies, if you did not care

much about incest nor feel disturbed when people chop up
their close friends and relatives, as practical jokes played
by the author and enjoyed by the audience upon some
haughty character who needs 'taking down.' "[28] Of course
we do care and are disturbed: hence the irony. Mr. Eastman may seem offensively flippant, but he correctly recognizes the comic element, subordinate but present, in tragic
irony. A tragic reversal is ironical if it has for us who watch
it some quality of the practical joke.

A plague has fallen upon Thebes because, as an oracle
explains, the murderer of King Laius remains unpunished.
Before the suppliant citizens Oedipus makes a speech in
which he pronounces a solemn curse upon the criminal.
Neither he nor his hearers know that he himself has done
the deed;—nay, murdered his own father and married his
own mother. But the audience knows.

> Now on the man of blood, whether he lurk
> In lonely guilt, or with a numerous band,
> I here pronounce this curse:—Let his crushed life
> Wither forlorn in hopeless misery.
> Next, I pray Heaven, should he or they be housed
> With mine own knowledge in my home, that *I*
> *May suffer all I imprecate on them.*
>   ... But now
> I, to whom fortune hath transferred his crown,
> And given his queen in marriage,—*yea, moreover,*
> *His seed and mine had been one family ...*[29]

I have heard a distinguished Greek scholar confess that
he shrank from teaching this play, so painful did he find
such passages as this. Fully to enter into the significance of
the last line is to experience a shudder hardly paralleled by
anything in literature.

Yet at the same time the duplicity of the meaning has an appeal to our sense for cleverness, for wit, even—I think I may say—for punning.

κοινῶν τε παίδων κοινὰ ἦν ἄν ἐκπεφυκότα

(Common things [κοινά] of common [κοινῶν] children would have been generated.)

"The language of this passage is carefully framed so as to bear a second meaning of which the speaker is unconscious, but which the spectators can feel: Iocasta has actually borne children to her son Oedipus: thus in κοινῶν παίδων κοινά ... ἐκπεφυκότα, the obvious sense of κοινά, 'common to Laius and Oedipus,' has behind it a second sense, in which it hints at a brood who are *brothers and sisters of their own sire* ..."[80]

Our sense of the joke being played on Oedipus and of the author's wit in framing such language to point it up is suppressed in consciousness because of the ghastliness of the situation, but it remains there nevertheless.

Perhaps the highest point of tragic horror in the play occurs when Jocasta realizes the truth about her relation to Oedipus, while he remains in the dark.

> Wretched one,
> Never may'st thou discover who thou art!

Oedipus misunderstands these words as scorn of him because of his plebeian birth, which the Corinthian shepherd has just revealed.

> OEDIPUS
> ... Leave her to revel in her lordly line!
> JOCASTA
> O horrible! O lost one! This alone
> I speak to thee, and no word more for ever.
> [*Exit*]

We know that she goes within to hang herself, but Oedipus
does not know it.

OEDIPUS

Leave her to raise what storm she will. But I
Will persevere to know mine origin,
Though from an humble seed. Her woman's pride
Is shamed, it may be, by my lowliness.
But I, *whilst I account myself the son
Of prospering Fortune,* ne'er will be disgraced
For SHE *is my true mother....*[31]

If we could consider the word-play here on the double
significance of "mother" without taking into account the
total impact of the dramatic action in which it is a tiny part,
we might feel it to be too trivially punlike for the heights
of tragic poetry. It is a trick, and it is a trick that calls attention to itself.

This verbal irony, according to the writer of a recent essay
on the subject, is used "to emphasize for the audience . . . the
irony of the situation."[32] On the modern stage a wink would
suffice, he says, but "no winks were possible where all actors
were masked. Consequently the . . . words were made to
wink." Exactly. There can be no doubt that the Athenian
audience got the point and felt its comic effect *at the same
time* that they felt its tragic horror.

That this interpretation of Sophocles will not be universally accepted is clear from remarks made long ago by
Lewis Campbell. As a lifelong student, translator, and lover
of the poet he protested against applying the term "tragic
irony" to him. "It detracts from the simplicity and tenderness which are amongst the chief merits of the Sophoclean
drama. It injures the profound pathos of Greek tragedy by
suggesting the suspicion of an *arrière-pensée,* of the poet's

face behind the mask, surveying his own creations with a
sardonic smile."[33] Apparently Professor Campbell had in
mind the more primitive connotations of the word irony—
the connotations derived from sarcasm. He does not object
to irony in a high philosophic sense. "For Sophocles, behind
and above the sadness which he portrays ... stands the
vision of the moral law which is the same from everlasting.
In this conception both horror and pathos are ultimately
resolved, but they are not the less keenly felt, although poet
and spectator alike know that there is a fixed centre amidst
the moving scene. Hence results what has been called the
'irony of Sophocles,' which is nothing else than the contrast
between fleeting appearances and abiding realities, which
pervades the whole dramatic action and is subtly indicated
by many turns of language."[34]

"Is subtly indicated by many turns of language." It is
clear from this that Professor Campbell did not deny the
equivocal language that we have called verbal irony; and
by the use of the word subtle he shows that he did not consider Sophocles "simple" in a technical sense. Greek art
gives a direct and uncomplicated first impression, generally
speaking; and it is this perhaps that he meant by the word
simple. But it gained this impression by extraordinarily
subtle and artful devices. This he clearly admits. What he
objects to is an interpretation of Sophocles as in any way
"sardonic" toward his creations. If sardonic means "disdain-
fully or sneeringly derisive," as the dictionary says it does,
we can agree. But irony is not necessarily sardonic in this
sense, and a writer may possibly be "tender" and ironical
at the same time. He can pity his characters and still perceive
that fate, or the gods, have played a sorry jest at their ex-

pense. He can pity them and even find esthetic gratification in artfully emphasizing the jest. Such a point of view will not be "simple," but surely we must assume it from the evidence of designed two-edged language in Sophocles.

There is no difficulty in thus viewing the great dramatist if we approach him not with an attitude of pious reverence, like a worshiper in church, but with open minds and the assumption that he was a man like us. The dangers of the pious attitude toward Shakespeare have been thoroughly exposed by recent attacks on Romantic criticism of him. Perhaps the tradition of awe has unduly lingered among students of the Greeks. I say this with full realization of the eminent scholarship of men like Professor Campbell. Indeed, the very depth of their scholarship may tend to make them lose sight of matters obvious to the Athenians for whom Sophocles wrote. They saw his plays performed at the same festivals with the burlesque satyr plays and the scurrilous comedies. Their sense of comedy must have been alive and quick.

In any case, to many readers if not all, passages in *Oedipus* become sharply and poignantly ironical because mingled with the horror and pity there is also a comic effect, subordinate but nonetheless distinctly felt.

Next let us consider the reverse of this effect. When we have a contrast between expectation and event, pointed up by verbal ambiguities of the "Sophoclean" type, but for a purely comic effect, does it remain irony?

Here we must search for examples, as none comes to mind as preëminent; and in so doing we run the risk of choosing those that may prove our case best. But we can guard ourselves by applying the definition quoted earlier

for "Sophoclean irony": "A speaker is made to use words
bearing to the audience, in addition to his own meaning, a
further and ominous sense, hidden from himself, and, usually, from the other persons on the stage." "Ominous" is
perhaps too strong a word for the effects of comedy, but if
we understand it as merely foreboding of ills suited to a
mirthful play the definition should serve.

One naturally thinks of Maugham's plays when studying
irony, for they are saturated with it. His masterpiece is *The
Circle,* which is indeed one of the great high comedies of
recent times. Its final scene fits Bradley's conditions just
quoted inasmuch as Champion-Cheney uses words bearing
to us, the audience, a meaning hidden from himself, and
one which involves a reversal of his expectations. The joke
is distinctly on him. That his hearers on the stage share our
knowledge and our glee alters the situation slightly from
that in *Oedipus,* but not essentially.

Champion-Cheney is a clever old *bon viveur* whose vanity
and selfishness preclude our sympathy. He has been working to prevent his son's wife from eloping with another
man, and he is filled with glee at the cleverness with which
he thinks he has succeeded. His method was to make his
son, Arnold, pretend to be generous and offer Elizabeth
freedom to choose. Perhaps Maugham had in mind the
similar situation which marks the turning point in *The
Lady from the Sea.* There the wife is won from her infatuation and returns to her husband. But in Ibsen's play the
situation was essentially different. Dr. Wangel really wins
Ellida not when he gives her this choice but when he explains that he is able to do so "because of my great love for
you." He speaks from his heart, and she responds. Arnold

Champion-Cheney is no Dr. Wangel; his chief interest in life is period furniture. Elizabeth elopes.

The other members of the house party know that the car heard starting outside contains Elizabeth and Teddie, but Champion-Cheney does not. He enters "rubbing his hands. He is as pleased as Punch."

CHAMPION-CHENEY. Well, I think I've settled the hash of that young man.

LADY KITTY. Oh!

CHAMPION-CHENEY. You have to get up very early in the morning to get the better of your humble servant.

[*There is the sound of a car starting.*]

LADY KITTY. What is that?

CHAMPION-CHENEY. It sounds like a car. I expect it's your chauffeur taking one of the maids for a joy-ride.

PORTEOUS. Whose hash are you talking about?

CHAMPION-CHENEY. Mr. Edward Luton's, my dear Hughie. I told Arnold exactly what to do and he's done it. What makes a prison? Why, bars and bolts. Remove them and a prisoner won't want to escape. Clever, I flatter myself.

PORTEOUS. You were always that, Clive, but at the moment you're obscure.

CHAMPION-CHENEY. I told Arnold to go to Elizabeth and tell her she could have her freedom. I told him to sacrifice himself all along the line. I know what women are. The moment every obstacle was removed to her marriage with Teddie Luton, half the allurement was gone.

LADY KITTY. Arnold did that?

CHAMPION-CHENEY. He followed my instructions to the letter. I've just seen him. She's shaken. I'm willing to bet five hundred pounds to a penny that she won't bolt. A downy old bird, eh? Downy's the word. Downy.

[*He begins to laugh. They laugh, too. Presently they are all three in fits of laughter.*]

[*Curtain*]

Our attitude toward a character who suffers an irony of this sort determines its emotional effect on us. The delight we feel here at the cleverness of the author and the coming discomfiture of Champion-Cheney is fully comic because we feel no sympathy for him or for the abandoned husband. The effect is ironic to us only as we put ourselves in Champion-Cheney's place.

I speak of the scene as isolated from the rest of the play. But actually it comes as the ending of a work the theme of which is one of bitter philosophic irony. No generation, it says in effect, can profit by the mistakes of its elders, even when those mistakes are presented in the most concrete and horrifying fashion, if the effect of the object lesson conflicts with passion. We are fond of Elizabeth, so vital and honest, and of Teddie, so gallant and boyish. Yet Lady Kitty and Lord Porteous were not less charming, not less promising, when *they* eloped—and now look at them! This second elopement is not a really happy ending; far from it. Hence the final scene is colored by the feelings arising from the underlying situation, and those are painful as well as amusing. The particular dramatic irony of the single incident fits into the mood of the pervading irony of the entire comedy.

If we do judge the scene by itself, our attitude is that of the active ironist toward his victim. From the latter's point of view the situation is painful enough. Arnold has not only lost his wife; worse, he has become ridiculous, and even his position as an M.P. is endangered. The old man has to see his son treated as he himself had once been treated, and—what is intolerable to a man of his character—he must suffer that most painful of injuries, a wound in the vanity.

How much ironic effect we feel depends on our point of view toward them. With little sympathy we feel little irony.

With no sympathy we feel none. This is the situation in farce. Let us consider *Arsenic and Old Lace*.[35]

In particular, let us consider the two situations which bring down the curtains of the second and third acts—and bring down the house also. Prior to the end of Act II, Jonathan, the sadistic maniac (played originally by Boris Karloff), has been preparing to murder his brother Mortimer by having his accomplice, Dr. Einstein, practice his surgery on the victim. These prospective horrors are of course purely comic to us. We can take nothing in the play seriously after our initial shock of discovering that Mortimer's sweet maiden aunts make a practice of poisoning lonely old men with elderberry wine and, after appropriate religious services, burying them in the cellar. Jonathan has learned that in the tally of murders his aunts are, so to speak, one up on him with thirteen victims to his twelve. Naturally his vanity is piqued. He argues that actually he also has done thirteen people in; but Dr. Einstein is a stickler for accuracy: one died of pneumonia; "he don't count." Jonathan grudgingly agrees. However—

JONATHAN. That's easily taken care of! All I need is one more! —that's all—just one more!

[*Mortimer enters hastily, closing the door behind him, and turns to them with a nervous smile.*]

MORTIMER. *Well,—here I am!*

Words with an "ominous sense" hidden from the victim?

At the end of Act III the two aunts, Abby and Martha, have signed papers which commit them to an insane asylum. (They have done this voluntarily because they cannot bear to be parted from a nephew whose hornblowing at unseemly hours—under the delusion that he is Teddy Roosevelt—has forced official action.) Mr. Witherspoon, the superintendent of the institution, has come to take the nephew away and agrees to take the aunts along also. At the end of the act he is alone with the latter.

ABBY. ... If Mr. Witherspoon won't have breakfast with us, I think at least we should offer him a glass of elderberry wine.
WITHERSPOON. Elderberry wine?
[*Martha takes out a wine bottle ...*]
MARTHA. We make it ourselves.
[*She uncorks the ... bottle*]
WITHERSPOON. Why, yes! ... You don't see much elderberry wine nowadays. *I thought I'd had my last glass of it.*
ABBY. Oh, no ...
MARTHA. (*handing it to him*). Here it is!

"A further and ominous sense, hidden from himself ... " If the italicized words in these two passages do not fit this definition, what does?

But there is no feeling of irony here; only laughter. The inadequacy of this definition is clearly due to its being purely objective, concerned with the dramatic device as a device and not with its effect. When, as in *Arsenic and Old Lace,* everything is a huge joke, there is no pain and no conscious irony.

The prehistoric Greek division of drama into tragedy and comedy rests on a sound psychological basis, but rather strangely this basis is even now too seldom fully recognized. Yet an understanding of it is fundamental to dramatic theory and, incidentally, to a psychological understanding of irony. Without an awareness of it, studies such as those

we have reviewed are likely to run into confusions or overlook essential distinctions. It is therefore advisable to end
this chapter with a brief analysis of it.[36]

Tragedy is the most distinguished form of a general class
of plays (for want of a better term I call them drames)
which depend for their intended success upon casting a
spell of illusion over the spectator which makes him feel,
for the time being, that the actions he watches are real, and
makes him identify himself with the protagonist. Modern
"serious" plays of all sorts, including social dramas and
naturalistic studies and problem plays and propaganda
plays, and even many so-called comedies (when their emphasis is on realistic character portrayal and social criticism)
are thus drames. So also are old-fashioned melodramas. Indeed, when an audience takes an *Uncle Tom's Cabin* or a
Two Orphans or a *Dracula* "seriously," in the spirit in
which it was written, such thrillers are, psychologically
speaking, the purest representatives of the class because
they rouse the fullest identification. Real tears were shed
for Little Eva, real curses hurled at Simon Legree; and
when the vampire bat flew out from the stage (on an in-
visible wire) real shrieks of terror rent the air. Such full
imaginative participation is seldom observed nowadays
when tragedy is performed! Shakespeare's original audiences, however, must have enjoyed it when they watched
Hamlet or *Macbeth*. And the ancient Athenians are reported as having been terrified at the sight of Aeschylus'
furies with snakes in their hair.

A melodrama is the purest type of drame—when it is
taken seriously. But a striking transformation occurs when
the play fails to cast its spell. Then the tricks designed to

jerk tears and raise the hair become, one and all, ridiculous.
The melodrama turns into a farce. It is a special kind of
farce—an unintended burlesque. Sometimes it is very successful. *The Drunkard* in revival has been enjoying runs
that have lasted years at a stretch.

Yet the play is the same play, and when it is properly
performed even the acting is as close as possible to the
original style and carefully avoids clowning. What happens
to a spectator when he laughs at things that his grand-
mother wept over?

He stops taking them seriously and instead takes them,
as Mr. Eastman would say, in fun. He does not identify
himself with a character any longer; he detaches himself
completely from the action. And "the reason for this lies
in the nature of laughter," as I have written elsewhere.[37]
"The sense of the ridiculous is mainly a sudden perception
of incongruities that are not painful to us who laugh though
they are often painful to the objects of our mirth, and . . . its
essence is an awareness of difference or contrast, especially a
difference from the customary or habitual. . . . Laughter, or
the impulse toward it, comes only when the observer is insulated for the moment from sympathy for the object of his
laughter. Children think it funny when an old gentleman
falls on an icy pavement; adults put themselves in the old
gentleman's place and feel alarm or sympathy. Detachment
is essential to laughter, and hence comic plays must keep the
spectator in a comparatively unidentifying state of mind."
The distinction between drames and comedies, then, is
psychologically a difference in the spectator's point of view.

When I wrote the sentences quoted in the last paragraph
I was seeking to define the sense of the ridiculous and had

no thought of irony in mind. Rather I was mindful of Aristotle's observation that comedy arises from "some defect or ugliness that is not painful or destructive."[33] Comedy becomes ironic when there is pain. Irony is mockery in tragedy; it is a taste of wormwood in comedy. It tears our emotions between conflicting and incongruous attitudes. In irony the defect or ugliness *is* painful or destructive, yet it retains enough of the grotesque or the ridiculous to make us want to laugh.

The result of marked irony in a play is to diminish our identification. It is like allegory in that it makes us intellectually conscious of double meanings;[39] and the more we are made to think of these the less we can lose ourselves in the illusion. Thus theoretically it is better suited to a comedy than to a drame. Yet we are more aware of it and find it much more memorable when it occurs in a serious play; above all, when it occurs in a tragedy. The reason for this, I think, is that while we like to be amused, we remember longest what hurts us, and the irony of serious drama often hurts us a good deal. In a comedy the pain is reduced; in a farce like *Arsenic and Old Lace* it is reduced to zero and what would otherwise be irony becomes mere fooling. In a tragedy the pain is increased; and if comedy also remains in our consciousness, it becomes a violent irritant—it shocks us like sacrilege. We are not likely to forget such an experience quickly.

"We," of course, are understood to be normal spectators. It is possible to cultivate so detached an attitude that everything becomes spectacle and painful objects mere stimulants to amusement. A person who has acquired this insulated view can laugh at anything and so feel himself superior to everything. This Olympian position will enable a person to find comic aspects in the sufferings of Hecuba. Such a person avoids pain by removing himself from humanity. And often he calls his attitude ironical.

This point of view has especially attracted writers in times of spiritual frustration like the present, but at the end of the eighteenth century it had a peculiar development which gave rise to what is called Romantic irony. The meaning of this term, as used by the German Romantics and their critics, is so confused and obscure that we cannot treat it briefly. And though the form of "Romantic irony" practiced by Tieck was a mere fad, the underlying point of view which the term designates has serious importance, and remains widespread in art and life. Hence we are justified in giving a separate division of our study to a discussion of it.

Part Two

SELF-MOCKERY:
"ROMANTIC IRONY"

Besagter Paul habe ferner oft Lesern ins Dampfbad der Rührung geführt und sogleich ins Kühlbad der frostigen Satire hinausgetrieben...

JEAN PAUL RICHTER

Nella concezione umoristica, la riflessione è, si, come uno specchio, ma d'acqua diaccia, in cui la fiamma del sentimento non si rimira soltanto, ma si tuffa e si smorza: il friggere dell'acqua è il riso che suscita l'umorista; il vapore che n'esala è la fantasia spesso un po' fumosa dell'opera umoristica.

PIRANDELLO

CHAPTER III

The German Sources

R OMANTIC IRONY, in its simplest meaning, is the name
given the willful destruction of illusion in works of
fiction and drama, as practiced by certain members
of the Romantic School in Germany at the turn of the
nineteenth century. As other meanings are far from simple,
it will be well to postpone considering them for the moment.

To call the destruction of illusion irony is to the student
of the drama almost a misnomer. It is essential to the emotional force of genuine dramatic irony that we feel the
illusion of the character's reality within the fictive world of
the dramatic action. To put the matter in another way,
there must be no distraction of the mind from his situation
to such irrelevances as that he is a fiction in a play. We all
know that he is one, but we go to the theater exactly because we hope at least momentarily to forget such uninter-
esting facts in imaginative illusion. A "willing suspension
of disbelief for the moment" constitutes not only poetic
faith but the necessary condition of dramatic effect. Even
comic irony of the classical tradition depends on this single-
ness of mind toward the characters. At a comedy of this
type, to be sure, we do not identify ourselves seriously with
a character; we maintain considerable detachment from

him. If we did not, sentiment might prevent us from being amused. But we are never for a moment forced to consider him as a fiction. In other words, the irony we feel is an irony of contradictions that lie wholly within the fiction, never one of contradiction between the fiction and factual reality.

Nevertheless, "Romantic irony" was the name given this trick of mocking illusion, and Ludwig Tieck was chiefly responsible. In the drama his most notable use of the trick is in plays written in his youth, in the last decade of the eighteenth century. The best known of these is *Puss in Boots* (*Der gestiefelte Kater,* written in 1797). *Prince Zerbino* (1798), a sequel of sorts, is in some ways even more ironical, in the Tieckian sense. So also is a work published in 1799 with the appropriate title, *The World Turned Topsy-turvy* (*Die verkehrte Welt*). Although the last two pieces were not written for production, they offer such astonishing examples of Romantic topsy-turvydom that I shall cite them briefly. *Puss in Boots* was produced within Tieck's lifetime, and is reported as having achieved some success under Jürgen Fehling's direction at the Berlin Volksbühne, even so recently as 1921.[1] Such a success at first surprises us when fresh from a reading of the work; but we recall that the early 'twenties in Germany were the heyday of Expressionism, and after its fantastic extravagances Tieck's skit may well have seemed quaintly charming and simple in an old-fashioned way.

The plot of *Puss in Boots,* about which the author troubles himself little, is that of the fairy tale, with a talking tomcat, Hinze by name, as hero. The real interest is literary satire, directed principally against stodgy eighteenth-century Ra-

---

[1] For notes to chapter iii see pp. 263–264.

tionalism. In the Prologue, members of the "audience" express fears that the play they have come to see will lack "good taste." What is "good taste" to them is very bad taste to Tieck, the Romantic rebel: a taste for the moralizing sentimentalities of Iffland or Kotzebue, the popular playwrights of the time. The "author" of the play then appears before the curtain to reassure the "audience." His play, he tells them, will at least contain a few jokes, which is more than can be said for most of the German dramas of the time. After this interchange the curtain is allowed to rise on Act I, Scene I, which shows Gottlieb, the farmer's son, alone with his sole inheritance, his cat. When the latter begins to talk, the "audience" object. A talking cat, they say, destroys illusion!

Throughout the play, members of this make-believe "audience" interrupt the action from time to time with stupid criticisms. In so doing they themselves destroy the illusion and thus serve as a means of Romantic irony. At the same time, it is irony of a normal sort that they express opinions the exact opposite of Tieck's own, the true nature of which the real audience must infer. And it is easy to see how this satirical irony must have diverted Tieck's Romantic fellows—young men who, like Friedrich Schlegel, were burning to overthrow the old intellectual regime of "good sense" and dogmatic criticism. A modern reader is less fortunate, since to share the fun he needs a whole apparatus of explanatory notes.[2] The satire is like that of Aristophanes in its wealth of local references, but it has little of Aristophanes' universal applicability.

The play abounds in minor contrasts, most of which can hardly be called ironies because little or no pain can be felt in them. Taken together they make an effect of mildly humorous satire and fantastic whimsicality. Thus Hinze will at one moment talk with a burlesque grandiloquence which causes his master Gottlieb to apostrophize him as "sublime friend," and in another moment he will climb the roof to hunt pigeons. The king, who appears in Scene 2, is a silly old man who confesses that his deceased wife henpecked him almost beyond bearing, yet weeps over her memory. He often wished for death, he says, he was "so bebrawled, scolded, vexed, snarled upon, sulked at, roared at, pouted at, upbraided, bitten, grumbled at, growled at, and buzzed at ...["3] In such pious fashion he warns his daughter, who is much pursued by princely suitors, of the dangers of matrimony. This mock-sentimental domestic scene wins the approval of the "audience."

The palace tutor next looks over the princess's exercise in composition and finds a grammatical error. The exercise is called "Night Thoughts," and was appropriately written the day before, just after lunch. It expresses emotions with "tenderness and finesse." "All the poplars and weeping willows, and the golden moonshine weeping in, and the murmuring murmur of the murmuring cascade ..."[4]

The king, who returns with a newly arrived suitor, is surprised that the latter, Prince Nathanael, speaks German. Sh! says the prince, the audience down there will notice it too and find it very unnatural. If I didn't talk your language, nobody could understand the play. The make-believe audience object to such unnatural talk. The characters are inconsistent, they say; why shouldn't the prince speak a foreign language, and why doesn't the princess talk ungrammatically, since she writes so badly?

The third and last scene of the act shows a deserting soldier escaping across the border of the kingdom, pursued by two huzzars, and drinking a beer amicably with them in the territory of Prince "Bugbear" (the monster of the fairy tale who can transform himself into animals). During the entr'acte discussion which follows, the make-believe audience observe that it gets crazier and crazier, and ask, reasonably, what the point of the last scene was. They get no answer.

To supply the sentimental scene demanded by the audience, Tieck next drags in two lovers, whose highfalutin conversation is loudly applauded. This is an outdoor scene. Hinze catches a rabbit and delivers a moral tirade on the duty of noble souls to restrain selfish desires (such as the longing to devour the rabbit) for the sake of others. This speech also is loudly applauded. Hinze gives the rabbit to the king, who rejoices. (He loves rabbit, and nobody ever gives him any.) Among those present at the following state dinner is Hanswurst, the traditional clown, recently banished from the stage because it is dominated by polite French influence. Hanswurst complains to Hinze that Germans banished laughter with him. (Elsewhere Tieck remarks that his countrymen are very backward at understanding jokes.)[5]

This banquet scene is long and full of buffoonery. Among other matters, Leander, the tutor, delivers at the king's order a discourse on astronomy. The king then turns to things minute and, calling for a microscope, examines one of Hinze's hairs through it. With Hanswurst he puzzles over what makes that organ-like rumbling inside Hinze when he is pleased. The cook brings in the rabbit and the king

starts greedily to eat it. But it is not as he expected it. He
starts up in wrath.

> The rabbit is burnt!
> 'O all you host of heaven! O earth! What else?
> And shall I couple hell?'[6]

He continues to rage in blank verse until appeased by the
music of chimes; then he weeps. The play-audience stamp
and hiss. Hinze climbs a pillar. The author rushes in to
beg for quiet. To appease the audience he has apes and bears
brought in to dance. An eagle perches on Hinze's head, to
his great anguish. Two elephants and two lions also dance:
a real ballet and no mistake. The audience are not only appeased; they are delighted. Curtain, to great applause.

Act III, Scene 1, is set in the farmhouse and discovers the
author arguing with the machinist. They go off leaving the
stage empty. The king, backstage, is heard refusing to
enter. Hanswurst comes on. The foregoing scene, he explains, was not part of the play; the curtain rose too soon.
In his opinion it really makes no difference, for the whole
play (to employ the modern vulgarism) stinks. Enter the
author in indignant protest. And so on . . . Finally, Gottlieb
and Hinze proceed with the plot. Gottlieb extemporizes his
lines and blames the prompter for not speaking clearly.
Hinze promises Gottlieb the throne. Some of the spectators
gag one of their number who insists on admiring Hinze's
acting. Hinze continues to hunt rabbits for the king and is
interrupted again by the lovers, who are now quarreling.
The king in full court hears a formal debate between the
tutor and Hanswurst on the question whether *Puss in Boots*
is a good play, the prize of victory being a hat stuck on a

pole. Hinze climbs the pole and gives the hat to Hanswurst.
The king decides to visit the Marquis of Carabas in grati-
tude for Hinze's gifts. Hinze, alone on the stage, soliloquizes
in melancholy vein on the thought that he helped a fool to
the prize for condemning the play in which he himself is
the hero. "Ah, fate, fate, into what confusions dost thou
lead us mortals!"

Need one continue? We are tempted to mention at least
the bit when, to admire Beautiful Nature, the king climbs a
tree and finds it full of caterpillars, giving the princess occasion to observe that nature needs to be ennobled by imagination. Let us skip to the finale.

In accord with the fairy tale, Hinze induces Prince Bugbear to turn himself into a mouse, then eats him and exclaims: "The Law is devoured. Now the *Tiers état* Gottlieb
will come into power."[7] Uproar from the play-audience,
who interpret the allusion as revolutionary (this being
1797). They are appeased this time by a bit of spectacle from
The Magic Flute, which Tieck seems to have disliked. In
this unexpected fire-and-water setting the principals of the
play manage to complete the last scene, and the curtain falls.
There follows an epilogue in which the author again comes
on to argue with the play-audience, who throw rotten pears
and wads of paper at him.

In *Prince Zerbino, or the Journey to Good Taste* the old
king has abdicated in favor of his son-in-law Gottlieb, and
occupies his time, in a fashion reminiscent of Uncle Toby,
playing with lead soldiers. "This game," he says, "is really
a child's game, and what indeed do we do seriously?" He
enjoys true happiness with his lead soldiers, free from the
tribulations of actual rule. (Not otherwise will Pirandello

argue, more than a hundred years later.) He decides that
every fifteenth soldier must die. *He* is Fate, or whim ...

Prince Zerbino, the nominal hero of the piece, is shown
deathly sick as a result of reading too many sentimental
best-sellers. To be cured he goes in search of "good taste."
The journey permits much burlesque satire of popular literature in allegorical form. Zerbino fails to find good taste,
and in despair decides to search for it in the play itself.
(Here indeed is Romantic irony!) He decides to run the
scenes backward so as either to reach his goal or destroy the
play and himself with it. The preceding scenes begin to
unfold. Author, in desperation, calls to his aid Compositor,
Reader, and Critic. These stage a burlesque battle with
Zerbino and knock him down. The play once more goes
forward. Zerbino returns from his journey unsuccessful and
is judged insane when he says that the wise man of the
court is none other than his old watch dog. He is released
only when he declares "that poetry is folly and the Enlightenment admirable."[8]

The World Turned Topsy-turvy, "an historical Spectacle
in five Acts," is another allegorical burlesque. It lives up to
its title. "Epilogus opens the play, Prologus closes it. Instru-
ments talk in pauses. Why shouldn't one think in tones and
make music in thoughts? asks Violino primo solo. Pierrot
[one of the actors] sits down in the parquet; Mr. Grünhelm
[a spectator] goes to join the actors without having to stop
being a spectator. 'The theater represents a theater.' And
indeed in such a way that this stage represents progressively
the auditorium of a further stage—till Scaevola [a spectator]
revolts: 'This is too crazy! See, friends, we sit here as spectators and see a play; in that play spectators are also sitting

and seeing a play, and in that third play another play is going to be played by those third actors. . . . People often dream that sort of thing, and it is terrible; also many thoughts spin and spin like that further and further into the inwardness. From both one will go crazy.' [End of Act III.] 'Anyway,' comforts Menuetto con Variazioni in the last entr'acte 'music,' 'a good confusion is better than a bad order.' "⁹

Perhaps we have put forward more than enough examples of Tieckian irony. For all its tricky variations it is fundamentally a simple and trivial thing: the hand of the manipulator, as Tieck expressed it, thrust into the puppet stage.¹⁰

Difficulties arise about the meaning of Romantic irony only when, as we shall see presently, it becomes involved with high matters of metaphysical speculation on the Objective and the Subjective, Imagination and Reality, and the like. In practice it can be confusing when it is not distinguished clearly from other features of plays like *Puss in Boots* with which it is associated. I am thinking particularly of literary satire, which here as usual takes the form of the dramatized parody traditionally called burlesque. This satire was Tieck's chief interest and that of the Schlegels, whose encouragement led the author to use it more extensively in *Zerbino*.¹¹ And the dramatists whom he himself acknowledges¹² as influences are much more notable for satire than for tricks with illusion. They are Aristophanes, Fletcher, Jonson, Holberg, and Gozzi.

Aristophanes may be said to break illusion in his parabases, during which the chorus harangues the audience directly on behalf of the author. But when we consider that

the parabasis was a convention as well recognized then as
was a prologue (directly addressed to the audience) in the
seventeenth century, it becomes doubtful whether the one
was any more disillusioning than the other. It comes in the
middle of the play, but it serves there as a sort of entr'acte
diversion. (According to one scholar's suggestion, the address to the audience was actually in origin a prologue to an
agon or contest between the two halves of the chorus.)[13]
Nearer to Romantic irony in the Tieckian sense are Aristophanes' jibes at the audience. "The dramatic illusion ...
is greatly abused. Old Comedy laughs at everything, including itself and its audience. Trygaeus in the *Peace* is flying
to heaven on his winged beetle when he suddenly addresses
the audience and warns them not to attract his beetle by
indulging in certain natural processes for the next three
days; and he has soared aloft only a few more feet when he
calls down to the stagehand to be careful with the flying
contraption!"[14] But illusion is never important in Aristophanes, and still less important are these occasional violations
of it. What is important, of course, is the political and social
satire, because of which the plays, taken as wholes, become
moral allegories.

Jonson, whose chief debt in comedy was to the Roman
comedists, might have violated illusion by their authority.
In *Casina,* for example, Plautus has an old man, Lysidamus,
address the audience when desperate for help. ("... Is there
anyone here to perform this task in my place?") Similarly,
in *Aulularia* the miser Euclio, on the loss of his pot of gold,
cries Stop thief! and calls on the audience to aid him;
whence Molière's use of the same device in his *Miser*
(*L'Avare*), though it is contrary to all French usage. But

Jonson, I believe, nowhere uses such tricks. Tieck no doubt mentioned him because of his use, in plays like *The Poetaster,* of a burlesque satire rough enough to encourage bold experiment. The reference to Fletcher probably means *The Knight of the Burning Pestle* (now generally ascribed to Beaumont), in which actors play spectators and interrupt the plot with naïve comments. This feature of the play, however, is less important than its burlesque of chivalric melodramas, in which the influence of *Don Quixote* is clearly visible.

Holberg's burlesques occasionally break illusion by farcical anachronisms and direct references to the audience. Helen of Troy: "Listen, what a lovely song the sweet nightingale sings!" Marcolfus (Paris's servant), aside: "Anybody who hears that is a rascal, and I'd tell him so to his face. All I hear is people in the gallery cracking nuts."[15] But Holberg was having fun at the expense of the *Staatsactionen* and *Zauberstücken* then popular on the German stages, and these jests with illusion were, as in Aristophanes, merely in passing.

The influence of Gozzi on Tieck was so great that *The Love of the Three Oranges* is almost a prototype of *Zerbino*.[16] But this influence, again, is that of literary satire rather than Romantic irony. Thus Gozzi's Tartaglia, Prince of Spades (symbolizing Venetian audiences), is ill from boredom caused by the plays of Chiari and Goldoni, and can be cured only when made to laugh. The cure is accomplished by a clown of the *commedia dell'arte,* a member of the troupe whom Gozzi was championing. Gozzi's method of satirical allegory has little serious illusion to break, but does not intentionally break what illusion there is.

We have, then, a dramatic tradition as old as Aristophanes in which a free extravaganza is the medium for satire, principally by means of parody, and in which what has come to be called Romantic irony was used occasionally, but merely as an incidental jest.

Irony of the conventional sort is also used for satirical ends, not only in the plays mentioned, but also in many other burlesques such as *The Rehearsal, Tom Thumb the Great,* and *The Critic.* But conventional irony is not essential to burlesque, and still less is Romantic irony. Parody, which is the essential, is not irony. Parody is a verbal equivalent of caricature. It stresses not contradictions, but exaggerations. It must keep a recognizable resemblance to its original and at the same time accentuate features of the original into absurdity. We are delighted at the skill with which this literary game is played, and if the original work has betrayed us into solemn emotions which we feel ashamed of, we find a pleasing retaliation in seeing its weaknesses exposed. The essence of the game is a constant comparison between the butt of the satire and its caricature, and its high moments are those at which some particular feature of the original is pointedly ridiculed. The contrast is between an object and its exaggeration, not its opposite.

Tieck and his fellows were also influenced by undramatic sources, some of which we should briefly touch upon. Chief of these, according to our scholarly authorities,[17] are Cervantes, Swift, Fielding, Sterne, and Goethe. The German Romantics worshiped Shakespeare but could not claim his support for tricks with illusion. (Friedrich Schlegel, as we shall see later, managed to attach Shakespeare to a larger theory of Romantic irony.) It was *Don Quixote* that set the

example for the last three romancers of addressing the
reader directly and of "kidding" his own work as well as
his hero in a mock-solemn manner. A little of this sort of
thing goes a long way with most of us, and Cervantes does
not overdo it. Neither does Fielding, nor Goethe, whose
Wilhelm Meister was a powerful influence on his younger
contemporaries. But Sterne is of tricksiness and japery all
compact, and it is easy to see how his eccentric genius might
easily demoralize a young Romantic like Jean Paul Richter
or Tieck, impatient of rationalistic rules and formal restraints. We can see much less of Swift's bitter classical irony
in these men than we do of Sterne's irresponsible whimsicality.[18] And the personal tone of Sterne's style had a particular appeal to their Romantic subjectivity.

Subjectivity is indeed the distinguishing quality of the
Romantic temperament in any period, and in no period has
it been more notable than in that of the *Romantische Schule,*
whose members were introverts not merely by temperament but on principle. It would be surprising if the Romantic irony which they developed were not a highly
subjective thing; and we might suspect without evidence
that it is more than the mere trick of destroying illusion.
Friedrich Schlegel, who gave the term currency, certainly
had a far more grandiose meaning for it. According to the
Fichtean metaphysics which influenced him, every man
creates the world in his own mind, and hence is sovereign
over it, though restricted by it. The more objective he can
be toward it, the greater his spiritual freedom. In objectivity toward his special artistic creations Schlegel found
Goethe notable but Shakespeare preëminent. At the same
time even the most objective artist is also within his work.

To combine extreme objectivity and immanence, as Shakespeare did, is to resemble God Himself. And this state of godlike self-division and self-consciousness is Romantic irony.

Moreover, according to one recent scholar, Professor Lussky,[19] Schlegel found Tieck lacking in this true Romantic irony because lacking in this high objectivity. It is probable, according to Professor Lussky, that Tieck drew his theory of Romantic irony from conversations with Schlegel, and both emphasized the artist's freedom over his creations. According to Professor Lussky's thesis, the vital distinction in the views of the two men is that Schlegel was opposed to mere caprice.

His opposition can hardly have been consistent, however. We find him arguing in one place, for example, that the condition of perfection is joy in unrestrained freedom. This joy acts "in glad enjoyment of itself out of pure caprice and whim alone, intentionally without reason or contrary to reason."[20] Compulsion destroys it. But the true nature of Schlegel's thought is a question I shall gladly leave to specialists who are at ease with Romantic concepts of *Objektivität* and *Subjektivität*. It does not greatly concern us in a study of dramatic irony. The historical fact is that Schlegel's transcendental theory was hard even for his contemporaries to grasp, whereas Tieck's practice was easy. Hence Tieckian tricks with illusion came to be considered the essence of Romantic irony.

CHAPTER IV

The Pirandellian Universe

Mere illusion-breaking is too trivial a device, considered merely by itself, to justify so long a discussion as occupied the last chapter. Its importance lies in its causes. It is but one manifestation of the Romantic temperament; viewed medically, as it were, it is merely a striking symptom, not the disease. To understand the latter so that we may, as good diagnosticians, recognize it when we encounter it elsewhere, is of real critical value. It is therefore desirable to enlarge the meaning of Romantic irony to include its psychological causes. This enlarged meaning will not be Friedrich Schlegel's, but will analyze the motives which led Schlegel to formulate his theory and led other Romantics to put Romantic irony into practice.

Such a clinical examination has been performed by Irving Babbitt.[1] His emphasis is moral rather than psychological, and implicit throughout his discussion is his condemnation of the whole Romantic Movement; but even those who would defend Romanticism against him will hardly deny the incisiveness and penetration of his analysis or the clarity with which he exposes a very confused subject. Basic in his analysis is the thesis that classical irony, such as that of Socrates, is a drawing of contrasts between an ethical faith

---

[1] For notes to chapter iv see pp. 264–265.

or philosophy central to human nature, because founded on
the normal experience of mankind, and centrifugal extravagances. In other words, it is the irony of wisdom toward
folly. But Romantic irony is, "as Friedrich Schlegel says,
identical with paradox"; it is "gypsy laughter from the
bushes." "The universe of Tieck ... is a truly romantic universe: it has no centre, or what amounts to the same thing,
it has at its centre that symbol of spiritual stagnation, the
philistine, and his inability to rise above a dull didacticism."

The Romantics were the original bohemians. They believed that genius is God-given, unique, a law to itself.
Naturally each one flattered himself as much as he could
with the assumption that he possessed it, and acted accord-
ingly. His extravagances became evidence if not proof of
his genius. Genius, being a law to itself, denied any control.
"In the absence of central control," says Babbitt, "the parts
of the self tend to pull each in a different way." But experience is always defeating romantic dreams, and disillusion
follows illusion. The swift transition from the mood of sentiment to the mood of self-mockery is a natural consequence. It is evidence of the Romantic's centerlessness and
the essence of his peculiar irony.

The Romantic ego in its introspectiveness tends to split
like that of the hysteric with multiple personality. "In my
consciousness," says Jean Paul, "it is always as if I were
doubled; as if there were two I's in me. Within I hear myself talking."[2] Hence, though Jean Paul maintains a traditional definition of irony in his esthetic theorizing,[3] his
definition of what he calls "humor," in which, as he says,
his exemplar Sterne excelled,[4] is in effect a definition of
Romantic irony under another name. "... I divide my

ego into two factors, the finite and the infinite, and I make
the latter confront the former. People laugh at that, for they
say, 'Impossible! That is much too absurd!' To be sure!
Hence in the humorist the ego plays the lead; wherever possible he brings upon his comic stage his personal conditions,
but only to annihilate them poetically. For he is himself his
own fool and the comic quartet of Italian masks, himself
the manager and the director ...''[5]

Tieck expressed himself similarly. In an anthology of
several of his early works which he published in the second
decade of the nineteenth century he supplies conversational
links, after the style of the *Decameron,* which permit him
to comment indirectly on his own writings. In the link
which follows *Puss in Boots,* one of the characters questions
the artistic propriety of making the theater parody the theater, and another character rises to the author's defense.
"With the origin of the theater the jest over the theater
originated also, as we see in Aristophanes; it can hardly
prevent from being ironical over itself that which lies beyond unnecessary poetry and even more beyond artifice
because its basis rests on the division and duplicity of the
human spirit, on the wonderful contradiction in us.''[6]

Romanticism did not end with the *Romantische Schule,*
nor Romantic irony with Tieck. But the similarity of
Tieck's devices to certain familiar effects in recent plays
must not blind us to essential distinctions. In some modern
melodramas, for example, actors are stationed among the
spectators to yell, shriek, rush down aisles, or otherwise stir
the audience up. In such plays, however, the effect sought—
if not always achieved—is not destruction of illusion, but
heightening of illusion, and gooseflesh. Again, to turn to a

play of vastly higher quality than these, Thornton Wilder's
Our Town uses actors in the audience, a bare stage, no literal properties, and a stage manager who comments on the
action; but the effect is not that of Romantic irony. On the
contrary, the illusion which this play produces is, considering the technique, extraordinarily vivid. Its aim is not
mockery or satire, but poetic realization of the eternal values
residing in the ordinary experiences of ordinary people.

Wilder, however, has shown himself to be a highly eclec-
tic writer, and he may well have had Tieck in mind as well
as the conventions of the Chinese stage and Greek tragedy
when he wrote *Our Town*. The influence of Tieck as well
as of James Joyce is certainly plausible in *The Skin of Our
Teeth*. The world of this philosophical extravaganza is a
topsy-turvy world. The Ice Age is mixed up with twentieth-
century New Jersey, the Flood with Atlantic City; eras
from the age of the dinosaurs to World War II are fused
and confused. The Antrobuses are an ordinary American
family; they are also *Anthropos* and *Gynê;* they are also
Adam, Eve, and Cain. (There is no Abel, for some reason,
but there is an unbiblical daughter named Gladys.) Sabina
is a servant girl, a boardwalk siren, and perhaps Lilith.
Every so often the confusions of the play are too much for
Miss Somerset, the actress who plays Sabina, and she steps
out of character to tell the audience how she hates the part.
Then the Stage Manager comes in to persuade her to act
once more. At the end of Act I, the audience are asked to
help break up their theater chairs for firewood against the
advancing ice. At the end of Act II, Mr. Antrobus, now
Noah, is escorting his family and the animals into the ark,
which is also a boat at the end of a pier at Atlantic City. At

the beginnings of the first two acts, there is a loud-speaker
with "news events" illustrated by stereopticon views. Pieces
of the walls of the Antrobus house sag and fall or ascend
into the loft on occasion. A dinosaur and a mammoth are
house pets. Moses and Homer appear as a New York rabbi
and a blind beggar. And so on.

This bare account sounds a good deal like Tieck; but unlike Tieck's plays *The Skin of Our Teeth* lets us glimpse
meanings in its madness that are not satirical or mocking.
It turns out to be, underneath, an earnest morality that in
a time of peril to all civilization celebrates the nobility of
man's endurance and bravery and unending search for
knowledge. The tricks with time help to emphasize the
endlessness of the human struggle. The tricks with illusion
hardly have a like justification. Possibly they amuse some
spectators more than they confuse them. For other spectators they quickly become a distraction and a bore.

We may conclude that tricks with illusion are not truly
Romantic irony unless they express the author's mockery
of his own emotion and indicate his spiritual self-division.
"The effect is often that of a sudden breaking of the spell of
poetry by an intrusion of the poet's ego. Some of the best
examples are found in that masterpiece of romantic irony,
Don Juan." Thus with fervent words Byron celebrates
Juan's and Haidee's amour:

> Their intense souls, into each other pour'd,
> If souls could die, had perish'd in that passion ...

Then a little later he feels the reaction and apostrophizes
Love as follows:

> Thou mak'st the chaste connubial state precarious
> And jestest with the brows of mightiest men ...[8]

Arcadian dreams cannot endure the harsh daylight of actuality; hence the Romantics were constantly suffering from disillusionment. The idealized maiden, won and married, turns out to be just an ordinary woman (Shelley). Or (Heine) she marries someone else for money and position. It is the night before and the morning after. Byron amplifies the thought:

> Let us have wine and women, mirth and laughter,
> Sermons and soda-water the day after.[9]

The German Romantics began as "knights of 'agile chaos' " and of " 'transcendental buffoonery.' "[10] But as they grew older, unable to endure the strain of this self-division, they tended to cling to the stiff spiritual integrity of Mother Church, after the fashion, as Babbitt used rather unkindly to say, of the jellyfish on the rock.

The difficulties of maintaining Romantic attitudes became greater and greater as the nineteenth century wore on. Nature could seem genuinely Arcadian and benevolent to Wordsworth. After it had been put through the scientific laboratory, to hold seriously such views as his became impossible. As a consequence, the disillusionment expressed by Romantics in the 'nineties was more than the expression of personal disappointments; it was rather dismay at a mechanical cosmos empty of spirit. As Anatole France put it, "Drowned in the ocean of time and space, we have realized that we are nothing, and this has depressed us."[11] Again: "... as for man himself, what has science made of him? It has deprived him of all the virtues that constituted his pride and his beauty. It has taught him that all within him, as all around him, is determined by inevitable laws;

that the will is an illusion and that he is a machine ignorant
of his own mechanism. It has suppressed even the sense of
his identity, on which he founded such proud hopes."[12]

The irony in which this cosmic dismay finds expression
has a gravity and significance which the personal frustra-
tions of an individual like Byron or Musset could not yield;
and with Hardy it takes on a tone that critics have called
Sophoclean. We do not find Hardy's excessive reliance on
chance and coincidence Sophoclean; even less, his personi-
fying of the blind forces of nature as malevolent deities; but
his tone is solemn and his method classically impersonal.
Thus natural objects wonder why they exist:

> Has some Vast Imbecility,
>   Mighty to build and blend,
>   But impotent to tend,
> Framed us in jest, and left us now to hazardry?[13]

Thus the poet reflects:

> Crass Casualty obstructs the sun and rain,
> And dicing Time for gladness casts a moan. . . .
> These purblind Doomsters had as readily strown
> Blisses about my pilgrimage as pain.[14]

But in another mood Hardy wishes he were "freed from
the fret of thinking":

> Loosed from wrings of reason
> We should laud the Powers![15]

It only needs a spice of flippancy to get the Romantic irony
of A. E. Housman:

> Malt does more than Milton can
> To justify God's ways to man.[16]

Thus the poet of the end of the century faced a radical
dilemma and was torn between his need of faith and his

inability to believe. Hardy expressed his sense of this dilemma with tragic gravity. Housman hurled imprecations
at an empty heaven and then turned against his own passion with ridicule:

> Terence, this is stupid stuff:
> You eat your victuals fast enough.[17]

The field of modern irony as expression of the cosmic
dismay of the late nineteenth and early twentieth centuries
is a vast one and full of fascination. There is the detached
mockery of Anatole France: "The sciences are beneficient:
they prevent men from thinking."[18] There is Conrad's
brooding sense of the mysterious ironies in man's fate.[19]
There is the romantic alternation of sentiment with satire
in the once-popular books of James Branch Cabell. There
is the intellectual irony, of almost Swiftean savagery, in
Aldous Huxley's novels. Early in *Brave New World*, for
example, "two Alphas are described as flying toward the
great crematorium where the dead [in that scientific Utopia
of the distant future] are scientifically disposed of. Henry
explains how the phosphorus thus liberated is carefully re-
covered for industrial purposes. They pass over a chimney,
and the column of hot air shoots the helicopter upward.
' "What a marvellous switchback!" Lenina laughed de-
lightedly. But Henry's tone was almost, for a moment,
melancholy. "Do you know what that switchback was?" he
said. "It was some human being finally and definitely dis-
appearing. Going up in a squirt of hot gas." ' And with it
go up, by implication, the Christian belief in the soul of
man ascending to heaven, all human longing for immortality, and even the dignity with which we try to invest
death."[20]

We must consider also T. S. Eliot's juxtaposing of incongruities for ironical effect:

> The nymphs are departed
> Sweet Thames, run softly, till I end my song,
> The river bears no empty bottles, sandwich papers ...
> Or other testimony of summer nights ...[21]

Is this mingling of Spenser and twentieth-century garbage, psychologically, anything but Romantic irony? When Mr. Eliot, in a later period, found spiritual integration in the Church, he wrote *Murder in the Cathedral*.

But we have set out to study dramatic irony. We shall conclude this chapter with a more detailed consideration of a modern dramatist in whom the Tieckish self-division is once more put on the stage, but with a modern difference. This dramatist is Pirandello.

When Pirandello's plays appeared before the Western world shortly after the First World War, people thought he must have his tongue in his cheek. After all, *Six Characters in Search of an Author* must be merely a clever spoof. Here we see a director on a bare stage rehearsing one of Pirandello's own plays, and we hear him and the actors joke complainingly about its absurdities. Then, without warning, the six "characters" enter. They are parts from a play the author found himself unable to complete, or so they say; and they demand that the director bring their incomplete drama to a conclusion. After some argument he agrees, and assigns the roles of the "characters" to his regular actors. The actors try to "play" the parts which the "characters" "live," thus deftly illustrating the difference between theatricality and reality. By mistake, the curtain is lowered on the rehearsal; this gives us actually an intermission. Between the "characters" and the actors the melodramatic plot for which the former were created is enacted in fragments interspersed by comments from all and sundry. The satirical strokes in this extravaganza are obvious, and there are even, now and then, a few good laughs. Surely Pirandello was no more serious about it than Shaw was about *Fanny's First Play*.

Six Characters is Pirandello's best-known play but not his most obviously serious one. If his early critics had considered some others, they would not have been so ready to think him joking. *Naked* is the title of a play about a girl who is brought to the rooms of a novelist after attempting suicide. Why did she seek to kill herself? She is eager to accept the novelist's flattering explanation, but gradually it is revealed that she is lying. She is finally confronted with the unlovely truth which she has tried to evade by fictions. In other words, the clothing is stripped from her soul and she is left naked. A second time she takes poison, and this time dies. *"Henry IV"* is outwardly the fantastic drama of a madman who for years has been allowed to play the role of the Emperor Henry, and who, when he becomes sane, decides that the life of "normal" folk is intolerable, and by a deed of violence condemns himself to live forever in his insane world of make-believe. No one could call these plays merely fantastic comedy. The author calls *"Henry IV"* a tragedy.

We gradually realize that Pirandello was deadly serious about his paradoxes. We might indeed have known it from the beginning, since long before he became known as a playwright he had published a book that states his views directly. It is a work of philosophical and psychological despair called *Humor*.[22]

Never was there a more somber treatment of that subject! And we do not wonder when we realize that the author was there founding the philosophical basis on which he was to build all his later literary and dramatic expositions of man's desperate estate in a universe of flux and mystery.

The reader will already have inferred that "humor" has a special meaning to Pirandello. He offers as an illustration to show the difference between the humorous and the comic an old lady with dyed hair done like a girl's. At first glance her appearance makes one laugh: she is the contrary of what a respectable old lady should be. Comedy is exactly an awareness of contraries.[23] But if reflection suggests that she knows how ridiculous she is, but deceives herself into thinking that thus she may retain the love of a much younger husband—then one cannot laugh as at first. "From that awareness of a contrary [reflection] has made me pass to the *sentiment of the contrary*. And there is the whole difference between the comic and the humorous."[24] Thus, again, we at first laugh at Don Quixote, but gradually we also grow fond of him, even grow to admire him as a hero.

In one sense, humor is a contrast between the ideal and the real.[25] Human beings cannot bear merely to accept the universe like other animals or to "grope in the vault"[26] of creation. They construct ideal fictions to give life meaning and stability. Then humor, like a little demon, comes to destroy these fictions and reveal them as the Vanity Fair of the world. "Life is a flux we try to stop, to fix in stable and determined forms. . . . [These are] the ideals to which we would like to attach ourselves, all the deceptions which we create, the conditions, the state in which we tend to fix ourselves."[27] In times of stress these fictions sometimes break down and we see as in a flash the flux of life, strange and terrible. In fear we try to return to our familiar fiction, but now we see it as "a deception for living."[28] (Ibsen called such fictions "life-lies"; Pirandello may have been consciously quoting him.) In general we learn not to perceive our own defects, though we see others' and others laugh at ours. Masks, masks! "Each of us constructs his mask as he can— the external mask."[29] Truth is discoverable about rocks and trees, but not about man, whose soul is complex and mysterious, unknowable by himself or others. He tries to apply logic to his mystery, but logic is an infernal machine that nature in its benevolence has given men to deceive themselves with. It is a pump and filter to transfer from heart to head such nostrums of rationalization as are wanted, to give "an absolute value to what is relative."[30] Thus we project our personal illusions as universal truths.

We do this in particular through the medium of art, which is one of our devices for *fixing* life by abstracting and concentrating it. Humor finds such art too simple to be true; it objects to artistic "order" and "coherence." The soul is not simple. "Suppose we have in ourselves four, five souls in conflict with each other: the instinctive, the moral, the affective, the social?" Hence humor is opposed to the simplifications of the epic or dramatic poet who constructs a hero of a few elements. Humor decomposes such a "character" to show its incongruities. "The humorist does not recognize heroes."[31] He sees the world naked, or at least clothed only in its shirt.

In short, Pirandello gives the name of "humor" to what would generally be called the irony of a skeptic and a pessimist. (To him "irony" means merely the rhetorical device that creates "a fictitious contradiction between what one says and what one wants to be understood," whereas the contradiction in humor is essential.)[32] Pirandello's "humor," like Jean Paul's, is really Romantic irony. The German Romanticists were optimistic, Pirandello pessimistic, about the universe. Is there any other essential difference between them? Pirandello's theory of knowledge was Hegelian if not Fichtean; he studied in Germany and apparently sucked from the same metaphysical teats. Romantic irony, he says, comes from the belief that the ego can dominate and annihilate the universe by turning it into a "transcendental farce." It thus "has or can have, at least in a certain sense, some relation to true humor."[33]

In the same discussion he makes an acute observation regarding the relation between rhetorical and Romantic irony. In the former one need not take seriously what is *said;* in the latter one need not take seriously what is *done.* Rhetorical irony is to Romantic irony like the frog in the fable who succeeded in swelling himself up to the size of a bull. Rhetorical dissimulation is blown up to the vain appearance of the universe. If humor were merely the pin that pricks that swollen frog, irony and humor would be the same thing. But humor is more than that.[34]

To Pirandello, humor is, alas, no laughing matter. Life is too painful for simple merriment. His audiences may laugh at the contrasts he discloses between men's pretenses and their actuality, or at the paradoxical way in which they cling to fiction and avoid truth, as does his "Henry IV" in preferring to live as a madman rather than return to the world of sane people. But Pirandello does not laugh. He is in deadly earnest.

We have noted how romantically inclined writers grew
more and more pessimistic during the century that elapsed
between Friedrich Schlegel and Pirandello, and it is clear
that the latter is fully influenced by such forces as made pes-
simists of Hardy and Housman. But, unlike them—indeed,
unlike almost every other writer of importance in our
time,—he decided that the real world is unknowable, that
if it were knowable it would be intolerable, and that man's
only resource is the resource of desperation: making up a
fictitious world nearer to the heart's desire. His characters
all do this, and their misery lies in their constant but un-
admitted knowledge that their made-up worlds are false.

This sort of thing has been called "autistic thinking" and
noted as a first step on the road to madness. Did Pirandello
know about Freud? There is no mention of Freud in his
essay, though he refers once to Binet.[35] Probably he came by
his peculiar insights through his metaphysical studies in
Germany and his private introspection. He had also intimate acquaintance of insanity in his madly jealous wife.
"As his wife accused him of duplicity and of unfaithfulness,
he saw near himself the shadow of another man, of the one
that his wife had created, hateful and low, the one who
made her shout and go into hysterics. Pirandello must have
often wondered which of the two was the real one."[36]

Certainly this man was not a happy Romantic. He has
been called a realist, even a naturalist;[37] but realistic as his
notations of the surface of life certainly are, the core of his
work is a fantastic, paradoxical reversal of normal views.
If he was not Romantic in the early nineteenth-century
sense of the word, he was at least remarkably like Friedrich
Schlegel in his irony. Schlegel thought that the poet cre-

ates the world in his imagination. So also did Pirandello. To Schlegel the consciousness that he has created a world, and hence has the power to destroy it, was irony. So also it was to Pirandello, calling the attitude "humor." Schlegel was optimistic, Pirandello pessimistic; but on these fundamental matters they agree. They both deny centrality and stability: Pirandello insists that we cannot know the truth outside our subjective dreams, and that indeed all things change and flow from moment to moment. Πάντα ρεῖ.

Socrates, who believed that we can know the truth, found irony in contrasting that truth with ignorance and folly. Pirandello believed that we cannot know the truth, and his irony lay in contrasting the inexplicable flux of life with the foolish—and pitiful—efforts of those who try to impose some sort of pattern upon it. Romantic irony becomes in its ultimate development the exact reverse of classical. Psychologically, it is a way of avoiding spiritual self-destruction by laughing at the sources of one's despair.

Part Three

PAINFUL LAUGHTER:
COMIC IRONY

Ce qui me paroît assez plaisant, c'est qu'un homme qui a de l'esprit, et qui est averti de tout par une innocente qui est sa maîtresse, et par un étourdi qui est son rival, ne puisse avec cela éviter ce qui lui arrive.

URANIE, in La Critique de l'École des femmes

MOLIÈRE [in the role of a marquis]. "Ma foi, chevalier, mon ami, il faudra que ton Molière se cache."
BRÉCOURT. "Qui, lui? Je te promets, marquis, qu'il fait dessein d'aller sur le théâtre, rire avec les autres du portrait qu'on a fait de lui."
MOLIÈRE. "Parbleu! ce sera donc du bout des dents qu'il rira."
BRÉCOURT. "Va, va, peut-être qu'il y trouvera plus de sujets de rire que tu ne penses. On m'a montré la pièce; et, comme tout ce qu'il y a d'agréable sont effectivement les idées qui ont été prises de Molière, la joie que cela pourra donner n'aura pas lieu de lui déplaire."

L'Impromptu de Versailles

My way of joking is to tell the truth. It's the funniest joke in the world.

KEEGAN, in John Bull's Other Island

I came not to call sinners, but the righteous, to repentance.

Inscription on the monument to St. Henrik Ibsen, as reported by the Archbishop in Back to Methuselah, Pt. III

CHAPTER V

Molière

ROMANTIC IRONY is rare in first-rate comedies. Of all artists the dramatist, and of all dramatists the comedist, needs most to treat life objectively and to interest himself (and his audience) in what other people do rather than in what he himself is thinking and feeling. He is thus generally opposed in temperament to the Romantic whose preoccupation is listening to the discords in his own soul. If he makes capital out of his spiritual self-division, it is by way of a thoroughgoing objectification into independent characters. Strindberg, the rare exception among dramatists who won fame by dramatizing his own paranoid personality and his marital difficulties, did so in plays of intense seriousness. Comedy and introversion are contradictory terms.

The supreme comedists—Aristophanes, Shakespeare, Molière—were notably objective. Aristophanes parades his political prejudices and personal antipathies; indeed, he makes capital of them; but once they are expressed by devices for public laughter, they cease to be subjective. And all they tell us of the poet concerns his public opinions, not his private life, still less his states of soul. They would be no less personal, in this sense, if he had been the spokesman for an organized political party, speaking from an official platform, or an editorialist writing for a partisan journal. We know a man's real self better by what he is serious over than by what he laughs at. To joke is an excellent means of concealing oneself.

Of Shakespeare's objectivity one might merely repeat Arnold: "Others abide our question. Thou art free." Unfortunately one feels uneasy about this assertion. The frequency with which it is quoted does not make it true; it sounds rather too much like something Friedrich Schlegel might have said in his youth; and when we think of what we know of Shakespeare from his works, we are inclined, perhaps mistakenly, to believe we know a good deal. However, even if we cannot accept the dictum literally, we shall all agree that Shakespeare did not wear his heart on his sleeve—least of all in his comedies. We know how much information the most avid analyses of his sonnets give of Shakespeare the man—how much, and how little. If in these verses, which are designedly self-confessional, we can never be sure that the poet is not playing a literary role rather than telling his love affairs, how much less can we rely on anything he makes the characters say in a comedy!

Molière, the master of high comedy, is perhaps also the most objective of all dramatists. No wise biographer draws on his plays for data about his private life—though unwise biographers have tried to. Was he unhappy with his wife? Probably; but his plays are no evidence one way or the other. Alceste is certainly not Molière. Even less is Arnolphe! Was he fearful of his coming death by tuberculosis? His last work, at a performance of which he suffered his mortal collapse, was called *The Imaginary Invalid*. "Molière, sick unto death, writes the comedy of the man sick

only in imagination, an act of courage and detachment unequalled in the history of genius."[1]

If we shall not expect much irony of a subjective sort in
the great comic poets, we shall also not expect much irony
over the ultimate dilemmas of mortality. Their work will
be penetrating in its insight into human nature, and even
at times profound in its implications; but their concern is
in the problems of social living, not of suffering and death.

Since I have already considered Aristophanes in some
detail, he need not detain us here. We found him a blunt
partisan, not an ironist above the battle; we found that his
favorite weapon was not irony, but burlesque—when it was
not direct abuse.

Of Shakespeare I shall speak but briefly. His comedies,
except for his three farces, are what we call romantic rather
than "pure" or "high" comedies. That is to say, their appeal
is chiefly through romantic incident, poetic expression, and
above all, attractive characterization, not through farce and
satire. Psychologically, he leads us to identify ourselves
with his protagonists, not to detach ourselves from them.
We feel sympathy, not ridicule, toward them. Even the
butts of the jokes in his farcical scenes are treated with
kindliness in the spirit of good fun, not of social criticism.
He need only be compared with Ben Jonson for his kindliness to be obvious. In a work called *Shakespeare's Satire,*[2]
Oscar James Campbell makes the best case he can for the
poet as satirist. "Though not an innovator in the designing
of satiric patterns, he richly filled the forms invented by
his contemporaries, vivifying them with his own genial
sense for the absurd and later with a deepening scorn of

---

[1] For notes to chapter v see p. 265.

vice and folly. As the spirit of ridicule came more and more to dominate him, he found it increasingly natural to cast his plays in familiar satiric forms. Because this fact has not been recognized, *Troilus and Cressida, Measure for Measure, Timon of Athens,* and *Coriolanus* have all confused the critics."[3] This seems a reasonable summing up, but we are here dealing with comedy, and unless one wants to make a case for that gloomy melodrama, *Measure for Measure,* none of the plays Mr. Campbell mentions is a comedy at all.

Aristophanes' comedy appeals to collective prejudice and to "the collective belly"; Shakespeare's, to the poetical imagination. (The former's lyrical passages are not essential to his comic effects.) Molière's comedy is preëminent in rousing what George Meredith called "thoughtful laughter." It was he who, almost alone, created high comedy—the comedy that criticizes society through vital characterizations that represent opposing faults and the Golden Mean, and does so by laughter of the mind, without descending to brutality, as does Jonson, or grossness, as does Wycherley, or mere wit for wit's sake, as does Congreve. There must have been something of this comic perfection in Menander, whom Terence adapted, if we can judge by such a play as *The Brothers.* Certainly Molière profited by his knowledge of Terence. But the remains of the ancient comedists are scanty, and at best the Roman is far below the Frenchman in *vis comica.* High comedy scarcely existed before the latter lifted his work from the crude level of Italian farces to such plays as *The School for Wives,* and finally to the unequalled height of *The Misanthrope.*

Molière was not interested, like Congreve or Wilde, in verbal wit for its own sake. He was always dramatic in his

dialogue, which as a consequence is seldom quotable in isolated sentences, for his wit takes its point from the situation
or the character it reveals. (Such oft-quoted lines as "Mais
nous avons changé tout cela" or "Que diable alloit-il faire
dans cette galère?" have meaning only as we recall the circumstances in which they were spoken.)

He sometimes uses verbal irony of a "Sophoclean" type,
but since his spirit was not combative or bitter, he seldom
gives it the mingled sense of the ridiculous and the painful
that we recognize as irony rather than merely comedy. For
example, in *Les Fourberies de Scapin,* Act III, Zerbinette
comes out into the street (stage front) chuckling over the
story she has just heard, of how miserly old Géronte has
been tricked into paying 500 écus to rescue his son from a
nonexistent Turkish galley. ("What the devil was he doing
in that galley?") She does not know Géronte by sight, and
when she sees an old fellow in the street (Géronte himself,
of course) she cannot resist sharing the joke with this
stranger. In order to tell the story, she tries to recall the
name of its victim, and appeals to the stranger for aid. "Help
me a little. Can't you name that fellow here in town who is
known as the biggest miser around?" Géronte says, "No."
The monosyllable is ironically expressive, but the audience,
feeling no sympathetic pain for him, is purely gleeful. Like
most of Molière's characters, Géronte is wholly an object
of fun, not a rounded personality with whom we are expected to sympathize; and his discomfiture then, as earlier
in the play when he is hidden in a sack and beaten with a
club, is merely a source of innocent merriment like that
which a Punch and Judy show excites. At least, that is what
he is intended to be, and certainly was for seventeenth-

century audiences. Those audiences lacked the tenderheart-
edness (or shall we call it the sentimentality?) some of us
suffer from.

Molière could use the weapons of satire, to be sure. When
his enemies baited him into writing a dramatic defense of
his work, he turned upon them in the *Critique de l'École
des femmes* and the *Impromptu de Versailles,* but even then
he was reluctant to descend to their level in personal abuse.
His burlesque of the hostile actors, and his irony at their
expense, are witty rather than vindictive. (Of the tragic
manner of a Mademoiselle de Beauchâteau: "Admire that
laughing expression she maintains amid the greatest afflic-
tions.") His purpose in his comedies, as he explains, was to
represent general faults, not to satirize individuals.

His dramatic irony, as distinguished from verbal, is
chiefly found in his use of such traditional farcical devices
as having a character accomplish in ignorance the exact
opposite of his wishes, and in his reversals, when the audience rejoices to see a biter bit. But his reversals are not necessarily ironical. For example, the peripety in which the
triumphant villain Tartuffe is suddenly brought low is not
even comic; rather, it is crudely melodramatic. This ending
was, of course, forced on Molière by circumstances, not his
own taste: to get permission to perform the play at all he
had to provide a "moral" ending that would satisfy the civil
authorities if not his clerical enemies. But a really ironical
reversal precedes Tartuffe's fall (Act V, Scene 3). Orgon
is finally convinced of Tartuffe's villany, and enlarges
upon it to his mother, while Dorine listens in. He had
thought Tartuffe a holy man; he had lodged him, fed him,
treated him like a brother, even offered him his daughter

in marriage and his property in trust. All the while, the villain has been trying to seduce his wife, has stolen his property, and has denounced him to the police! Dorine cannot resist taunting her master at this point by quoting his own words back at him: "The poor man!" As for Orgon's mother, Madame Pernelle, these revelations do not affect in the least her besotted faith in Tartuffe. She replies primly that she cannot believe a word. Orgon is flabbergasted. Nothing he can say makes any impression on her. The tables are neatly turned; she treats him now exactly as earlier in the play he had treated his wife and son. The more he argues, the more frustrated and angry he gets, the more she lectures him (in his own former style) on Tartuffe's saintly character. "Quelle progression d'effets comiques!" exclaims a French commentator. What masterly comic irony! we might add.

In *The Misanthrope* there are two principal characters, Alceste and Célimène. Alceste suffers a series of rebuffs rather than a reversal. To those who take the "atrabilious lover" humorously, these rebuffs are purely comic. To those who, like Rousseau, take him sentimentally, they are painful. (Rousseau inveighed bitterly against Philinte as representative of a corrupt society, and elevated Alceste to the heroic moral level of Bunyan's Faithful in Vanity Fair.)⁴ According to either interpretation, irony is hardly the term we should normally think of in connection with the young misanthrope's misadventures, for there are no sharp contrasts between expectation and event, but rather the natural consequences of his conduct. As for Célimène, she is punished by a public exposure of her duplicities in having played the coquette with her suitors and satirized them all behind their backs. They all, even Alceste, thereupon abandon her. But we do not think of the scene as ironical. It could be made so. If Célimène were more the object of our aversion; if she had been shown as willfully ignoring fate, full of conceit, and the like; if she had expected success and were then suddenly confronted with a defeat which directly resulted from her own deeds:—then we would have a familiar ironic situation which, as we shall see, Molière uses often and with masterly skill. But Célimène is thoughtless and giddy rather than fundamentally false; she is a charming belle of twenty, and consequently not the natural object for ironical laughter. Our feelings toward her and toward Alceste are mixed and somewhat troubled (hence the perennial difficulties of critics and actors in interpreting this masterpiece), but the mixed feelings are not the result of situations contrived for ironic effect.

Irony in Molière occurs incidentally as heightening to purely farcical or comic situations. As such, it is a device of which he was thoroughly conscious, and in the use of which ancient comedy had instructed him. The "New Comedy" of the Greeks, through its adaptations by Plautus and Terence, had a wide influence on the drama of the Renaissance, and on Molière in particular. (His *Amphitryon,* for example, is adapted from Plautus; his *School for Husbands,* from Terence's *Brothers.*) Its influence may indirectly have affected him also through Italian comedy, since it is possible that the tradition of Roman comedy survived through the centuries in Italy to emerge during the Renaissance as the *commedia dell'arte.* Hence a brief examination of irony in these ancient plays is appropriate here before we consider how Molière uses the devices that they developed.

New Comedy, indeed, affords the simplest and clearest illustrations of the comic type of irony. It does so because at the beginning it nearly always informs the spectators of the secret hid from the characters. This early revelation is clearly derived from the practice of the tragic poets, especially Euripides, whose *Ion,* in particular, needs but an alteration of tone from that of melodrama to that of domestic comedy to become a play that Menander might have written. The usual means of revelation is the Euripidean device of an "omniscient prologue" in which a character frankly explains the situation to the audience. This device is of course awkward, and the dramatist, by revealing the secret at the outset, gave up both a principal source of suspense in the excitation of curiosity, and the advantage of surprise when the revelation of the secret to the characters brings about the resolution of his plot. But an effective exploitation of ironic effects sometimes compensates for these disadvantages. This irony is the comic version of what in tragedy is commonly called Sophoclean, and is clearly derived from it.

"The omniscient prologue was almost indispensable in plays which exploited dramatic irony based on hidden identities."[5] Yet to any persistent playgoer either in fourth-century Athens or in second-century Rome there could hardly have been much mystery about the secrets on which the plots were made to turn, since they were all the same secret repeated, with minor variations, from play to play in a fashion that can only be described as doggedly pertinacious. Let but a baby or a young girl be mentioned whose father is unknown, and the secret is already half out of the bag. If it is a baby whose parentage is in question, the father is sure to be the very young man who wants to marry the

baby's mother, or who has already married her and has—
quite naturally—been upset by the baby's unexpected arrival. (In case the reader is unfamiliar with the plays in
question, it may be advisable to explain how so unusual a
situation could be imagined to have come about. Nine or
ten months prior to the opening of the comedy, we are asked
to believe, this young man had had a drunken amorous encounter with a strange girl at a festival, and as it was dark,
never saw her face, but gave her a ring or other token which
turns up at exactly the right moment to untangle the situation.) If the mystery involves a grown girl, her father in-
variably turns out to be an old gentleman of position, a
citizen of Athens and a friend of the youth's father. Thus
the girl becomes also a free citizen with a desirable dowry,
and all obstacles to the wedding are removed.

Whether or not the explanatory prologue was needed, it
was generally provided; and from then on the audience was
prepared to enjoy the misunderstandings and cross purposes
and incongruities of mistaken identity which were developed from the situation. Consider *The Girl from Samos,*
which is one of the three comedies of Menander that we
possess in fragments sufficient to let us make out their main
action. Demeas, a good-natured Athenian, has taken as con-
cubine Chrysis, a girl who has fled from Samos during a
war. As she cannot prove her Athenian citizenship, he cannot marry her. During an absence of his she bears him a
child, which dies. Meanwhile, his son by a former wife has
had an affair with a neighbor's daughter, the fruit of which
is another baby. The young people want to get married,
but the girl's father, a stingy fellow, will not consent. They
hope that Demeas, on his return, will do so. While they

await his arrival, the baby must be concealed and cared for. Chrysis agrees to be wet nurse. Demeas arrives and thinks the baby his own. He is delighted. He agrees to sponsor the marriage of his son and the neighbor's daughter. Then, alas, he overhears a conversation which makes him think that during his absence his son has seduced Chrysis and that the baby is theirs!

"Misunderstandings soon come thick and fast until it looks as if there would be no wedding at all; and it is hard to get the misunderstandings explained because the truth itself involves some difficulties and because the misunderstandings are so terrible that they quite deprive the victims of the ability to listen to reason. One character after another loses his balance and contributes to the confusion. The discovery that calms one sets another going until the dance is ended. Chrysis and the baby come flying first from one house, then from the other. Comic irony is everywhere. It is always just the attempt to clear things up, to make the best of them, that introduces new complications."[6]

Of Menander's *Arbitration*, the most fully preserved of the extant plays, Professor Harsh says, "The play's elaborate exploitation of dramatic irony...closely approaches Euripidean technique as displayed in a drama like the *Ion*."[7] The father of the mysterious baby in this play is an upright youth who is so much horrified at his wife's apparent premarital misconduct that he turns to drink and dissipation, much to the concern of his frugal father-in-law. When the time comes for revelation, and he finds out that he himself fathered the infant (at one of those festivals), he has a very proper fit of remorse in which he condemns the double standard of sexual morality.

This situation is repeated in Terence's *Mother-in-Law,*
which was indirectly based on Menander's play. Here the
irony is delightfully developed through the inability of the
baby's two grandfathers to understand why the young husband is unwilling to live with his wife.

We shall close this digression with the play of Terence's
that partly influenced Molière in the comedies we wish to
consider next. This is *The Brothers (Adelphi).*

There is no omniscient prologue here, but the secret is
revealed early. Demea has brought up one of his two sons
severely and thinks the boy a model youth. Because of his
poverty he has let his other son be adopted by his brother
Micio. Micio is indulgent and acts on the principle that a
child should behave well from desire, not compulsion. Before the opening of the play, however, Aeschinus, the
adopted son, has apparently belied his guardian's kindly
theory, for he has abducted a slave girl from her owner by
force. This outrage fills Demea, the young man's real father,
with mixed emotions: concern for his son and triumph that
his brother's indulgent philosophy is proved wrong. What
he does not know is that Aeschinus abducted the girl for
his brother Ctesipho—the supposed model youth,—who is
her lover. But the audience knows this and can enjoy the
irony of hearing Demea praise his model son and condemn
his brother's educational methods.

Demea is inveighing against Micio, with his slave Syrus as
audience. The latter is too circumspect not to agree. Syrus:
"Would you have let your son do this?" Demea: "Would
I have let him? Wouldn't I have smelt a rat six months before he set about doing anything?" Syrus then amuses himself by pretending that young Ctesipho is indignant with

his brother for the latter's supposed misconduct. Demea rises to the bait: "Long may he live; he, I hope, is a chip off the old block."[8]

Further and worse outrages on the part of Aeschinus next come to Demea's ears. The youth has seduced a free Athenian girl with a promise of marriage and then abandoned her—and on the eve of her lying-in, too!—in order to live with the abducted slave girl. And not only that: Brother Micio has actually taken the girl into his house!

We expect that with the revelation of the true state of things the laugh will be on Demea, but, unlike Molière, Terence was not inclined to look on indulgence such as Micio's with unmixed approval. He makes Demea experience a comic if not psychologically convincing conversion. The erstwhile stingy parent suddenly decides to use his brother's generous methods, and he succeeds so well that he not only pulls down the party wall between his house and his brother's and unites the two families, but also insists that Micio, the happy bachelor, marry the mother of his son's bride. The irony of this unexpected reversal is accentuated when the son himself joins Demea in urging this act of generosity. In addition, they insist, Micio should support the woman's next of kin, destitute old Hegio. Says Demea, "I am now myself putting into practice the maxim which you, Micio, enunciated so wisely and so well a short time ago: 'A vice common to all mankind is that of being too keen after money when we are old.'" And while Micio is about these good deeds, adds Demea, generous at his brother's expense, the latter might as well free the slave who engineered the whole thing . . . and also his wife . . . and also provide him with a sum of ready cash . . .

In this one play of Terence's we have an element not elsewhere marked in New Comedy—the satirical commentary
on social customs and attitudes. The play even builds upon
what Meredith called a "comic idea"—a moral question of
general significance, treated humorously. It is this quality
of social criticism through laughter that Molière perfected,
and along with it he developed, when they were suitable,
incidental ironies, as we see in *The School for Husbands*.

Sganarelle (played by the author) is a grotesque from
the masks of Italian comedy—tyrannical, egotistical, jealous.
Guardian of a young girl, he keeps her immured in his
house and plans to marry her. Naturally, when Valère
makes eyes at her from below, she casts about to circumvent
her jailor. Please, she begs Sganarelle, go tell that presump-
tuous young man to stop annoying me with his attentions!
Her guardian is delighted to obey her. His vanity is tremendously flattered, and his malicious glee at the thought
of the youth's discomfiture can hardly be expressed.

> Dans quelle ravissement est-ce que mon cœur nage,
> Lorsque je vois en elle une fille si sage!

What a good girl indeed! She is making Sganarelle serve
unknowingly as her go-between, to let her lover know that
she has observed his ogling and is interested.

Once again she gets Sganarelle to call on Valère, this time
(as Sganarelle understands it) to return with scorn an un-
opened letter which (Isabelle tells him) the bold creature
sent her. After delivering it to Valère, Sganarelle goes away
and the much surprised young man reads the missive,
which proves, of course, to be one from Isabelle to him. He
is naturally transported with delight, and at that moment

Sganarelle returns, being unable to resist the pleasure of gloating over what he supposes must be his young rival's woe. Valère hastily assumes a downcast look. Ha! jeers Sganarelle, you see she's not for you. Look elsewhere; get out! Yes, yes, agrees Valère; your merit is indeed too great an obstacle for me. I should be crazy to pretend to Isabelle.— You would indeed! Whereupon Valère humbly begs for just one last favor: Tell her I loved her truly and would have sought her for wife had you not won her.—That's proper talk, says Sganarelle, feeling generous; I'll tell her that; *she won't be shocked.* . . .

This is a delightful handling of the *eiron-alazon* situation such as would be hard to match in Aristophanes. The rest of the intrigue is one ironic situation after another. A third visit to Valère: Isabelle wants him to know that he is not to think he can deceive Sganarelle by pretended submission when he has really been planning all along to carry her off! Valère is naturally astonished at such a message and doubts that Isabelle can really have sent it. Come! says Sganarelle, bursting with vanity; I'll let you hear it from her own lips. In the next scene the ambiguous language with which she confirms the message lets Valère come to an understanding with her and at the same time lifts Sganarelle to such a height of delight that he can feel sorry for Valère:

> Pauvre garçon! sa douleur est extrême.
> Venez, embrassez-moi . . .

"That," says John Palmer, "is the *coup de génie*—a supreme touch. The drunken egoist embraces in his rival an embodiment of his own triumph."[9] And what comic irony that the triumph is false!

This is full irony, however, only if we think of it from Sganarelle's point of view. As it is, the comedy of the situation is all that much affects us, and further than that we feel only one-half of the ironic complex: triumphant amusement at the expense of the *alazon*.

Thus also in *The School for Wives,* in which the basic situation of *The School for Husbands* is preserved but with the difference that here the jealous guardian is confided in throughout by both lover and ward and yet cannot prevent their union. This is a situation which, as Molière has one of his characters in the *Critique* remark, is "assez plaisant"!

Arnolphe, the guardian of Agnès, is peculiarly fitted by his excess of vanity and egotism to be the butt of ironic ridicule. Though a more rounded characterization, less a stock figure from Italian comedy, than Sganarelle, he makes us eager from the very beginning to see him also come to grief. He chuckles with malicious pleasure at observing how other men are deceived by women, and he brags that *he* is no such fool: *he* knows all their little tricks! He has, he thinks, circumvented cuckoldom by bringing up his future wife in such ignorance that she won't know how to deceive him. Here is *hybris* with a vengeance—a vengeance to come!

Immediately after the introductory scene in which this character is exhibited the ironic reversals commence. Arnolphe has been out of town for some days. As he goes on his way to his house he meets Horace, the son of an old friend. A letter from the friend flatters him so much that he expansively offers to assist the youth in any way he can. Horace promptly takes him at his word: "I need a hundred pistoles right away!" In the chat which follows, Arnolphe recurs to his favorite theme of deceived husbands. You are

a likely youth to help deceive them, he says jocularly, looking Horace over. The ingenuous young man admits having
had an amorous adventure already, since he arrived in town.
Arnolphe (aside): "Good! Here's another spicy story to
put in my notebook!" Horace says it's a girl who lives *there*
—and indicates Arnolphe's house.

The reversal is sharp enough as it stands, but Molière has
pointed it still finer. Horace does not know that the house
belongs to Arnolphe, and the reason for his ignorance is
that out of vanity Arnolphe has adopted the would-be
aristocratic name of Monsieur de la Souche. (*Souche* means
stump or blockhead.) His own weakness has brought about
his discomfiture. Horace: "As for the man [the girl's guard-
ian], they call him, I believe, de la Zousse, or Source. I didn't
pay much attention to the name. Rich, they tell me, but not
very smart. I've heard he's something of an ass. Do you
know him? —Hey, you don't answer . . . " Arnolphe: "Ugh,
yes, I know him." Horace: "He's a fool, isn't he?" Arnolphe:
"Mm . . . " The youth runs on, happily oblivious. Ridiculously jealous, too; a crazy old guy! What a shame that
sweet Agnès is under his control. I'm doing my best to get
her away from him. You know, *that money I just borrowed
from you is to help do that.*

In the next scene, the immortal scene between Agnès and
Arnolphe, we discover that it is the very ignorance in which
he has kept her that makes Horace's advances easy. She tells
her guardian all about it, and he advises her to throw a rock
at her admirer next time he appears, then preaches to her
a while, and reads some thoughts he has written down
under the title, "The Maxims of Marriage, or the Duties of
the Married Woman." Alone, he exults: "She's like wax in

my fingers!" Once more triumphing, he meets Horace and can hardly hide a grin when the latter says that the door was shut in his face. Yes, and Agnès threw a rock at him! Only ... at last it comes out: there was a letter tied to the rock. "Don't you find it funny, the role my jealous friend has played in all this business? Tell me." Arnolphe: "Yes, very funny."

It is a pleasure to recount a masterpiece, but we have indulged ourselves more than enough to make our point. So far as irony is a matter of device to bring about results exactly the reverse of a character's intentions, this is masterly irony. But we, as spectators, are not involved emotionally except to be amused. For us there is no sting, and unless we are looking for irony we may not recognize its presence.

Molière had few illusions about mankind, but he was not embittered. Not his the *saeva indignatio* of Swift or even the pessimism of Mark Twain. Of human nature Philinte advises, "Voyons ses défauts avec quelque douceur." At the same time Molière's eye was unclouded: he might not grow indignant, but he saw men as they were. His realism is indeed too penetrating at times for conventionally minded people to follow him. Consider how audiences have traditionally been taken in by the candor of Alceste (of which, as he admits, he is vain)—taken in so far that they overlook his inconsistency, his pettishness, and even his profound egotism. When he learns of Célimène's duplicity, he pours out his complaints to Éliante and Philinte, working himself up to a passion. Éliante: "You ought to moderate your transports; and the outrage—" Alceste (interrupting her): "Madam, that task is for you. My heart has recourse to you today, to free me from this torture. Avenge me on a per-

fidious ingrate who has basely betrayed my constant ardor!
Avenge me . . . " How? she asks. By marrying me! ("Constant ardor," indeed). Is this the conduct of a man of honor?
And he makes his caddish proposal in front of his friend
Philinte, who is in love with Éliante, as Alceste would have
known if he had ever paid attention to other people's feelings. And after gratuitously insulting the lady, Alceste remains wholly unconscious of what he has done, since he is
wholly wrapped up in himself.

It is understandable that Rousseau should have approved
of this self-righteous egoist, because Rousseau was a self-
righteous egoist himself, at odds with society. But why
should generations of actors and playgoers have senti-
mentalized him into a sensitive and high-minded idealist,
wronged by the world? It would seem that, great as *The
Misanthrope* is, Molière should have provided more carefully against such a misinterpretation. To be sure, he did
give the play a subtitle, "The Atrabilious Lover," which
ought to have indicated his intentions. But the subtitle is
usually omitted; and of course ambitious actors naturally
want to play the part in such a way as to gain the greatest
sympathy from the audience.

Molière's irony of clear-sightedness is perhaps best illustrated by the seduction scene in *Tartuffe*. Orgon has been
hidden under the table where he can hear for himself how
his supposed friend makes love to his wife. The stipulation
is that he can stay under the table until he wants to stop the
lovemaking. "Don't expose me," Elmire begs, "to more than
is needed to disabuse you." Well!—the lovemaking goes on
and on, and she coughs and coughs, but in vain: her husband stays hid. Nothing Tartuffe says to her moves him,

no matter how scandalous, until his own vanity is pricked. Elmire has grown desperate, and to create a diversion asks Tartuffe to see whether her husband is in the next room. Tartuffe: "Why should you worry about him? He's an easy man to lead by the nose..." At *this*, out comes Orgon, raging.

For the thoughtful, such turns as these involve a full irony in which amusement and pain are combined. But they are easily overlooked, especially in the bustle of the stage; and Molière's fame rests primarily on his purely comic genius.

CHAPTER VI

Shaw

GREAT COMEDISTS see in the world around them far more sources of laughter than other men do. This comic perception is an armor against bitterness; and even if this armor fails them at times, the playful mood which comedy demands in the theater is chilled by irony. Bernard Shaw, the preëminent comedist since Molière, is not only extraordinarily detached, as Molière was; unlike Molière he is a man of unquenchable gayety and optimism. We might assume at once that Shaw is not primarily an ironist.

But we cannot settle the matter so simply on *a priori* grounds. We have, for one thing, Shaw's own statements to the contrary. Thus, he describes himself as dealing "in the tragicomic irony of the conflict between real life and the romantic imagination."[1] And elsewhere he says, with characteristic immodesty, "I am a master of comic irony."[2] Also, as we shall see, his plays abound in situations latently if not overtly ironical. It is difficult to draw a line between ironies that we can discover and ironies that the author forces on our attention, especially in dealing with an author who, whether a master of irony or not, is certainly a master of anticlimax and paradox. His delight is to trick expecta-

[1] For notes to chapter vi see pp. 265–266.

tion and confound accepted ideas. This is making game of
us, and its effect may well be sometimes painful. It cannot
be far removed from irony.

Before attempting an analysis, we need to assemble the
evidence. First of all, some knowledge of Shaw the man is
certainly needed. How did he come by his idiosyncrasies?

To begin at the beginning, he had a very unconventional
childhood. His father was a witty talker who, whenever he
had blown up a balloon of solemn admonition or reverent
religious disquisition, was forced by some inner compulsion
immediately to stick a pin in it. Bernard takes after him.
Shaw Senior, however, very unlike his son, was a failure as
a businessman and husband; perhaps as a consequence, he
was also addicted to liquor. Mrs. Shaw seems to have been
a woman of no very strong wifely or motherly instincts, but
with a strong love of music. She retired into a private world
of music, not merely from her husband, but from her
children, too. Bernard might almost have been a boarder
in the household so far as tender emotions were concerned.
"Though I was not ill-treated—my parents being quite incapable of any sort of inhumanity—the fact that nobody
cared for me particularly gave me a frightful self-sufficiency,
or rather a power of starving on imaginary feasts that ...
leaves me to this hour a treacherous brute in matters of pure
affection."[3] Since he cared little for games, he read enor-
mously of adult books, being, he says, "saturated with the
Bible and with Shakespeare" before he was ten.

No wonder his characters lack normal family feeling,
either for love or hate. It is normal for people to be emotional about their near kindred, and usual, as a consequence,
for their domestic relationships to be irrational and mud-

dled. This muddle is often painful, but the normal person would rather suffer the pain than be lonely. His emotional needs would starve without a constant pulling and hauling on his heartstrings. Shaw is—in this sense—the rare abnormality, a man with no heartstrings to be pulled. Hence the adult characters in his plays are one and all abnormal in the same way. They are not perverted: their emotions are not twisted or distorted. They are thoroughly mature intellectually, with a Shavian vocabulary to prove it. But emotionally they are all about twelve years old. Perhaps some of the women are a bit older, but not the men. A boy of that age is not interested in other people; he is interested solely in—let us say—building model airplanes. The Shavian character is not interested in other people, either, except intellectually; he is interested solely in building a utopia. Naturally, the Shavian hero runs away from an amorous woman; he does not want to be interrupted. John Tanner is the type for them all. It is significant that his author should have thought him a modern version of Don Juan! And it is obvious that John Tanner is, even more than usual among Shaw's more talkative heroes, largely Shaw himself.

The detachment fostered by Shaw's upbringing was further fostered by his experiences as a young man. His parents had separated, his mother going to London to teach music. When almost twenty, Bernard followed her; and for the rest of his life he has remained cheerfully away from his homeland. A man without a country, he never felt the sentimental need of exclaiming, "This is my own, my native land!" Brought up a Protestant, of English ancestry, in southern Ireland, he never felt the ordinary Irishman's pleasure in hating England. Long before he left Ireland he

had lost all belief in Protestant Christianity, though psychologically he has remained a Protestant throughout his life,
in his attitude of protest and in his extreme individualism.
He could never take seriously the enormous family pride
that some of the Shaws felt. He left Dublin with no attach-
ments of any consequence.

In London his chief interests were, and have remained,
large and impersonal. He read Samuel Butler, Ibsen, and
Karl Marx; he became an active Socialist, a leader of the
Fabian Society (with the Webbs), a pamphleteer and jour-
nalist, a soapbox orator and debater; he was even for a time
a hardworking member of the council that administered
one of the London boroughs. His male friendships were
intellectual; with young women, he flirted but did not give
himself emotionally. (Could any dramatist but Shaw have
written *The Philanderer?*) He was already wrapped up in
the building of his utopia, and had no emotion to waste elsewhere.

Thus, sometime before he started writing plays he had
come to view the whole of Western civilization with critical
disapproval. But since he was so detached emotionally, he
could be amused by it. Unlike most thoughtful men of his
time—Hardy and Ibsen are notable examples,—he had not
suffered disillusionment, and felt none of the bitterness that
the loss of cherished illusions entails. Mrs. Webb called him
a sprite. He could see the shortcomings of the world with a
clarity excelled by few and yet be spritely about them. He
is still spritely about them, after two world wars!

The source of his optimism is, of course, not merely negative detachment. Ordinary passions do not affect him, because his vision of an ideal society in the future absorbs all

his deeper emotion. Hence the comparison with a twelve-year-old is superficial: the child's dream is not a religion, but Shaw's is. It is fortified by all manner of arguments, but it is not primarily a matter of reason. On the contrary, one more than suspects that his multitudinous reasons for his doctrines are motivated by his desires: that they are, in short, rationalizations. To say this is not to condemn them as arguments. Shaw is a brilliant debater. And for the matter of that, he has been as consistent with his principles as anyone should expect so voluminous a writer to be. If he is not above taking a forensic advantage, he is certainly well-informed, free from the slightest meanness or malice, and on most matters notably sensible and sane. Naturally, we must allow for the exaggerations of the social satirist, who seems to maintain a position more extreme than he really holds so as to shock us out of complacency. And I do not defend his antivivisectionism, his vegetarianism, and his skepticism about the existence of germs, which are fairly harmless crotchets, or his antebellum admiration for Mussolini, which was not. But his demands for social justice, his analysis of present economic and political evils, and his hope for reform through man's intelligence and will, are all fundamental matters, and matters which we can respect intellectually. The point is, however, that his vision is more than a mere philosophy; it is a genuine religion; and on the all too rare occasions when he writes like a poet he is inspired by love of it.

This vision is of an earthly paradise to be attained only by our remote descendants, and then only if men will to attain it. Life is a process of evolution; and even now, for all its present imperfections, it is good because it offers us opportunity to serve the Life Force. We do so by exercising our wills to improve. Thus we help to evolve higher beings. This is possible because evolution is not determined, as the neo-Darwinians believe, but creative, as Lamarck taught. Sometime, men may outlive Methuselah—if they will to. Then they can finally put away such childish things as sex and art and war, and turn themselves into vortices of pure thought. Meanwhile, wars and revolutions are not unmixed evils, for they make possible a more rapid evolution. So Shaw might sing with a poet in many ways very unlike him, "Rejoice that we are hurled / From change to change unceasingly, / The soul's wings never furled." There is certainly something very Browningesque about Shaw's optimism.

We have indicated that Shaw had matured his views before he turned to drama. He was born in 1856 and his first play was written in 1892. At thirty-six he had already engaged in most of the activities mentioned earlier, and in addition he had written several novels, and had been a book reviewer, an art critic, a music critic, and a champion of Ibsen. Archibald Henderson's exhaustive biography[4] of him contains 832 pages exclusive of its index; it does not get to Shaw as a playwright till page 353. This is an anomaly in the history of the drama—a great dramatist who never served an apprenticeship in the theater; who had no vocation to write plays; who was primarily a religious prophet, secondarily a critic of the arts; who turned to playwriting solely and expressly to forward his cause, not for art's sake or even for money's sake. "I am a specialist in immoral and heretical plays," he wrote. "My reputation has been gained by my persistent struggle to force the public to reconsider its morals.... I write plays with the deliberate object of converting the nation to my opinions in these matters.... If I were prevented from producing immoral and heretical plays, I should cease to write for the theatre, and propagate my views from the platform and through books."⁵ His attitude toward his art is that of the preacher; the drama is an instrument of propaganda. In short, his dramatic purpose is, as he puts it, "to stick pins into pigs."⁶

His method of forcing his ideas on the public has been, like Ibsen's, to shock and startle it, but unlike Ibsen's, also to make it laugh. I doubt, however, whether he deliberately chose to play clown as well as preacher. His clowning has set a vast number of people unalterably against taking him seriously—an effect which he could hardly have intended. Yet his defenses for his practice are singularly question-begging: "All genuinely intellectual work is humorous";— "Why does the imaginative man always end by writing comedy if only he has also a sense of reality?" Like many other arguments of his, these defenses sound like rationalizations, only less able than most. Actually, he seems to be carried away by an extravagant imagination and a puckish humor which—in spite of his serious purposes, not because of them—he cannot resist. "Shaw never plotted a play in advance," declares a biographer. "Having got the main idea, he sat down and trusted confidently to inspiration, never seeing a page ahead while writing and never knowing what was going to happen."⁷ It is hard to believe this statement literally, since most of his best plays give as much evidence of design as Paley's watch. Even if the biographer got the assertion straight from Shaw himself, as presumably he did, we can believe it no more literally than we can believe Poe's

contrary explanation of how he wrote "The Raven." But
the frequent looseness and whimsicality of his dramaturgy
certainly need accounting for; and the picture the biographer suggests—of the "giant intellect" lulling itself to slum-
ber in order to permit a subliminal uprush of inspiration,
even as Romantic poets are supposed to do—is an amusingly
ironic one. Is Shaw the avowed enemy of Romanticism because he feels Romantic weaknesses in himself?

Another irony not intended by the dramatist is that these
antiromantic works of his, which preach such disturbing
doctrines as communism of property, benevolent dictator-
ships, the "liquidation" of the unfit, and the evolution of
men into vortices of pure thought, are really popular—those
of them that are popular—as romances. Shaw's plays are the
escape literature of the intellectual. From messy personal
relationships and a painfully chaotic society set free, he
dwells temporarily in a Never-Never Land where nobody
loses his temper, but, instead, everybody makes the perfect
retort; where everybody says right out what in real life he
would not dare to say, and gets away with it; where people
never become passionate and consequently never suffer;
where even the good folk are amusing and the bad ones are
never villains; where the pains of living are always subli-
mated into witty disquisition.

A playwright who will not inflict pain on his audiences
cannot write tragedy. Most readers who notice that *The
Doctor's Dilemma* is called "a tragedy" probably take the
designation as just another Shavian paradox. On the contrary, Shaw wrote: "I was perfectly unconscious of anything
funny about it. I was as serious as Galileo when he said that
a five-pound weight would fall as fast as a ten-pound,

though no doubt that struck the Pisans as a screaming joke." And again, *"The Doctor's Dilemma* was called a tragedy partly for the absurd reason that Archer challenged me to write a tragedy, and partly for the much better reason that its theme: that of 'a man of genius who is not also a man of honor,' is the most tragic of all themes to people who can understand its importance."[8] Maybe the theme is all of this, but the effect of the play is comic. Dubedat dies, with rhetorical flourishes, a cheerfully unrepentant blackguard to the end. If there is any great pathos in the scene, it is overlaid by quite contrary effects. Besides, it is not Dubedat but Dubedat's wife who is the central character, and she ends the last act by triumphing over her doctor-lover with the announcement of her second marriage. And the unsuccessful suitor takes his defeat with the graceful wit of high comedy: "Then I have committed a purely disinterested murder!" This ending might have been at least bitingly ironical, if not tragic, but one scarcely notices that it is ironical at all, for it is really a happy ending. Though we are not actually told that Jennifer will live happy ever after, at least we know that she is much better off married to anybody else than Dubedat; and as for Dr. Ridgeon, his massive ego will easily adjust itself to his disappointment.

Only one of Shaw's plays moves us with genuinely tragic emotion—*Saint Joan.* There are moments in the others when, as we have said, his characters are poetically inspired by a vision of a better world. Keegan, in *John Bull's Other Island,* is one who comes to mind, and Lavinia in *Androcles and the Lion,* and Lilith in *Back to Methuselah.* At those moments Shaw's deepest emotions express themselves. In *Saint Joan* the historical facts forced him to subdue his un-

ruly whimsicality, and its central figure embodied exactly
the qualities that to him are genuinely saintly. For once he
restrained his lust for anticlimax and sustained serious emotion. Yet, even so, he would not harrow us with too direct
an account of the burning; and after it is over he brought
Joan back to life in the Epilogue—if only as a figment of a
dream—with all her wonted bounce and forthrightness. (I
shall have more to say of this Epilogue when I come to deal
with Shaw's irony in detail.) *Saint Joan* is in my opinion
a tragedy, and a great one; but it is a tragedy subject to the
limitations of its author's peculiar genius.

But these limitations help make him supreme in comedy.
His emotional uninvolvement enables him to tackle matter
of the deadliest seriousness and show it in an amusing light.
His extraordinarily bold and whimsical imagination enables him to range further and to achieve a greater variety
and unexpectedness in theme, setting, and incident than
any other great dramatist, even Shakespeare. His religion
gives him a doctrinaire position from which to pass judgment on all he observes and records. And since his Articles
of Faith generally contradict those of his conventional contemporaries, the effect of his judgments is highly paradoxical—hence generally funny. He may be wholly in earnest;
it does not matter so far as the effect on an average spectator
is concerned; his paradoxes are taken as startling jokes.

Thus we come to the central technical device of Shaw's
comedy: paradox dramatized. A received moral opinion or
social doctrine is embodied in a character who at first seems
to the audience perfectly sensible, honorable, right-minded.
To this person is opposed a character who embodies the
Shavian contradiction of this conventional attitude. Their

conflict—mostly verbal—is the central action of the play. The outcome may be victory for the Shavian character, but it is just as likely to be an enigmatic stalemate that leaves the audience puzzled and disturbed. Shaw's resolutions upset us: they seem either perverse or no resolutions at all. Actually, they are logical enough from his point of view; and when audiences come round to his point of view the startling force of his paradoxes is lost. That has already happened to some of them, notably that of *Arms and the Man*. This play asserts that the good soldier is not the rash romantic hero, but the cool, efficient realist who avoids unnecessary risks (by running away if need be) and in an emergency stuffs his cartridge cases with concentrated food (chocolate) in preference to bullets. That proposition was shocking in 1894. The play is still amusing, but the electricity has gone out of it; the world has caught up with Shaw.

Nevertheless, the range and shock power of the Shavian paradoxes is extraordinary, as can best be shown by citation. Let us consider the major plays chronologically.

1. *Widowers' Houses*. The income of the respectable may be derived from the exploitation of the poor.

2. *Mrs. Warren's Profession*. Prostitution is due less to depravity in woman than to poverty, for which the respectable are largely responsible.

3. *Candida*. The manly man proud of his spiritual strength may really be weaker than the craven Romanticist whom he scorns.

4. *You Never Can Tell*. Children brought up without restraints and inhibitions turn out to be charming and admirable. (This play was written in 1896, long before the First

World War and "progressive" education; it presented a
flapper a quarter of a century before she appeared commonly in real life.)

5. The "devil's disciple" in the play of that name is "genuinely religious,"[9] whereas the "religious" Puritan, his mother,
against whose cruelty he rebels, is devilish.

6. The great ruler of men (*Caesar and Cleopatra*) is, like
the professional soldier in *Arms and the Man,* a sensible
realist, not a Shakespearean hero-villain.

7. *Captain Brassbound's Conversion.* The revenge motive
of Romantico-melodramatic tradition as embodied in a
hardened brigand is actually unconscious childishness, best
exorcised by a gentle lady who treats the brigand as a
mother treats a wayward child. (Lady Cicely: "*All* men are
children in the nursery.")

8. *Man and Superman.* Woman is the real "pursuer and
contriver," for it is she, not man, whose first biological duty
is thus to serve the Life Force.

9. *John Bull's Other Island.* The "practical" Englishman
of conventional opinion is really an arrant sentimentalist,
while the "romantic" Irishman of conventional opinion is
really an utter realist. ("The real Irishman . . . is the Englishman of tradition, whilst the real Englishman is the traditional theatrical foreigner.")[10]

10. *How He Lied to Her Husband.* In real life, contrary
to theatrical convention, husbands may well be offended
when lovers do *not* pursue their wives.

11. *Major Barbara.* Poverty is the real crime; it is better to
distribute wealth even by manufacturing whiskey or arms
than confirm the poor in their poverty by the methods of
the Salvation Army.

12. *The Doctor's Dilemma*. Is it better to save the life of a good nonentity or of a bad genius? (We leave this a dilemma, since Shaw does.)

13. *Getting Married*. Marriage laws are all wrong, but it is better to get married just the same.

14. *The Shewing-Up of Blanco Posnet*. To do God's will one may have to flout conventional Christianity.

15. *Fanny's First Play*. Prison and hard labor for kicking a policeman (note the symbolism) may be preferable to middle-class home life! ("Our respectable middle class people are all as dead as mutton.")[11]

16. *Androcles and the Lion*. "A Christian martyr was thrown to the lions not because he was a Christian, but because he was a crank."[12]

17. *Pygmalion*. The classes are distinguished not by character, but by speech. (The gentleman-scholar is a boor; the flower girl turns out to be a real lady.)

18. *Heartbreak House* is an exception among Shaw's plays, for it is too much the "fantasia" he calls it to be reduced to a formula. Yet in main outline it is an allegory of the English ship of state driving on the rocks, its captain drunk in his bunk. It was written in 1913, and ends prophetically with unexpected bombs dropping from the sky on the peaceful countryside. Paradoxes arise constantly from the interaction of its menagerie of human animals as they strip each other bare of pretense and reveal each other's folly, sentimentality, or incompetence, as also each other's unexpected wisdom and valor. But the Chekhovian method that Shaw had adopted precluded any single unifying paradox, unless it be the paradox, already familiar in *The Cherry Orchard,* that the footling incompetents who bring an old

order to its final ruin often possess very engaging personal qualities.

19. *Saint Joan*. Joan of Arc was "an arch-heretic," fairly tried and condemned, as she would be today. But—true saints are all arch-heretics!

20. *The Apple Cart*. Democracy and capitalism are really allies working against the best interests of the state. It may be necessary for royalty to oppose them in order to preserve those interests. ("The comedic paradox of the situation," says the preface, "is that the king wins, not by exercising his royal authority, but by threatening to resign it and go to the democratic poll.")

21. In *Too True to be Good,* its preface tells us, "the main gist and moral ... is not, as usual, that our social system is unjust to the poor, but that it is cruel to the rich."

22. *On the Rocks*. Better a dictatorship than parliamentary democracy!

23. *The Simpleton of the Unexpected Isles*. Bolshevik methods of "liquidation" are not unlike the Last Judgment. It might be a good thing if they were applied to the parasites in capitalistic society.

24. *In Good King Charles's Golden Days*. Charles II was really "good King Charles" despite his reputation: instead of being lazy and dissolute he was really energetic, wise, foresighted, religious, and even (after his fashion) faithful to his lawful wife! Better such a monarch than parliamentary rule: the only question is how to find him.

Thus paradox is central in Shaw's dramatic output from 1892 to 1939.

A paradox is essentially the serious assertion that we should accept the exact reverse of some one of our conventional beliefs. The sudden contrast between the conventional belief and its reverse, which so often gives the paradox a comic effect, is not essential. So long as the paradox shocks our prejudices it is effective, whether amusing or maddening. That Shaw's paradoxes are usually amusing tends to confuse us with regard to them and him.

His method is to begin with a paradox in the abstract, such as one of those he so lavishly scatters about in his dialogue or collects in the "Maxims for Revolutionists" appended to *Man and Superman.* Thus Ellie in *Heartbreak House:* "A soul is a very expensive thing to keep: much more so than a motor car.... It is just because I want to save my soul that I am marrying for money. All the women who are not fools do." Thus Tanner-Shaw: "Do not do unto others as you would that they should do unto you. Their tastes may not be the same." Or: "Never resist temptation: prove all things: hold fast that which is good." Or (a much more profound one): "Liberty means responsibility. That is why most men dread it." When Shaw writes a play, he takes a paradox of this sort, embodies the contradiction in characters, and lets them fight it out. Their conflict is not necessarily comic; it might easily be tragic, at least painful.

But its painfulness is not ironical. An irony says the expected and means its opposite, whereas a paradox says and means the opposite of the expected. Indeed, since the paradoctor (if we may coin the word) is primarily an advocate, his aim is to win us over, not merely to ridicule our views. The ironist, on the other hand, is a prosecutor: he attacks a folly or an evil, but offers no substitute. His weapon of attack is ridicule: in it there is always comic effect, even when greatly attenuated. And irony is much more painful than paradox because it is purely destructive. The ironist may aim at constructiveness, as did Socrates, but his irony, as irony, merely destroys.

Again, there is a distinction between dramatic paradox and irony in the way in which the characters who embody them are affected by them. The examplars of the paradoxical opposition are not necessarily aware of their roles and do not necessarily suffer or triumph. (The play, as not seldom with Shaw, may end in a draw.) The revolutionary moral of the paradox they illustrate must be drawn by the observer. And it is a serious one but not necessarily a painful one. The victim of an irony, on the other hand, suffers, and in some degree the spectators suffer with him. Generally, he recognizes the irony of his situation. Furthermore, his distress does not necessarily involve a moral. Irony as an instrument is ethically neutral, whereas paradox is always an ethical assertion.

If we feel irony in a dramatized paradox, it must be the result of an ironic conflict in us, the spectators, as a consequence of seeing a demonstration that the very opposite of our accepted belief is true. Thus, for readers of the late 'nineties (very few saw the play) *Mrs. Warren's Profession* contained a stinging irony in the scene in which this wealthy bawd shows herself shocked, like a middle-class Victorian, at the idea of her daughter's being economically and personally an independent person, not a parasite on a man. "It was a masterstroke of irony," says a critic, "to embody the conventional horror of independence in a woman of the character of Mrs. Warren."[13] At the end of the play, Vivie says to her mother: "You're a conventional woman at heart. That is why I am bidding you goodbye now." This curtain line with its characteristic Shavian twist is a paradox rather than irony. There is no painful joke on Mrs. Warren. If the joke is on anyone, it is on the public that dislikes finding itself in a class with her. And it is not even paradoxical to those who consider Mrs. Warren with Shavian detachment and from an economic point of view. As a capitalist entrepreneur whose pocketbook is lined by the system that keeps women in subservience, she naturally upholds the system. If other capitalist entrepreneurs, who consider themselves respectable, dislike her company, that can't be helped: facts are facts.

A recent work[14] which contains much forceful criticism of modern dramatists, Shaw in particular, finds in *Captain Brassbound's Conversion* "dozens of ironies, of which the central irony is the contrast between romance and reality. ...This irony pervades the whole work." Evidently, whether we call the contrasts of a Shaw play irony or not depends on our meaning of the word. This critic does not define his meaning, but we may infer that he does not clearly distinguish ironic from purely comic contrast. Certainly, in *Captain Brassbound's Conversion* the method is, as elsewhere, paradox dramatized. Thus Hallam and Brassbound, "Pillar of Society and piratical hero," are shown to be actually the contrary of the conventional view of them. If these comic contrasts between romantic convention and Shavian realism affect us painfully, they will be ironical. For English audiences at the time the play was written, the shrewd satire of English ways and English prejudices had much sting in it. Today, certainly today in America, the contrasts, though still highly diverting, are painless.

Shaw himself has recognized that the electricity goes out of his twists when audiences grow up to his views. *The Devil's Disciple,* he tells us, has "a genuine novelty in it. Only, that novelty is not any invention of my own, but simply the novelty of the advanced thought of my day. As such it will assuredly lose its gloss with the lapse of time, and leave The Devil's Disciple exposed as the threadbare popular melodrama it technically is."[15]

Incidental ironies, of course, are frequent in the plays. Lady Britomart Undershaft (in *Major Barbara*) is a bossy aristocrat. Of her daughter she remarks, "Ever since they made her a major in the Salvation Army she has developed a propensity to have her own way and order people about which quite cows me sometimes. It's not ladylike: I'm sure I don't know where she picked it up."

When Mrs. Barnes receives for the Salvation Army great sums from the manufacturers of arms and whiskey, she is piously thankful.

Mrs. Barnes (*taking the cheque*). The longer I live the more proof I see that there is an Infinite Goodness that turns everything to the work of salvation sooner or later. Who would have thought that any good could have come out of war and drink?

Cusins (*in a convulsion of irony*). Let us seize this unspeakable moment. Let us march to the great meeting at once ...

And when Undershaft questions his son Stephen about a career, the latter declares himself uninterested in or unable to undertake any of the usual professions.

Undershaft. ... Well, come! is there anything you know or care for?

Stephen (*rising and looking at him steadily*). I know the difference between right and wrong.

UNDERSHAFT (*hugely tickled*). You don't say so! What! no capacity for business, no knowledge of law, no sympathy with art, no pretensions to philosophy; only a simple knowledge of the secret that has puzzled all the philosophers, baffled all the lawyers, muddled all the men of business, and ruined most of the artists: the secret of right and wrong. Why, man, you're a genius, a master of masters, a god! At twenty-four, too!

STEPHEN (*keeping his temper with difficulty*). I pretend to nothing more than any honest English gentleman claims as his birthright.

In *The Apple Cart,* King Magnus has granted an interview to the demagogue Boanerges. The king has been pointing out that his job does not depend on the whim of the electorate, and that hence he is secure in it as long as the monarchy lasts, whereas ministers like Boanerges are not. Suppose the trade unionists don't vote for you? No danger, says Boanerges.

... No king on earth is as safe in his job as a Trade Union official. There is only one thing that can get him sacked; and that is drink. Not even that, as long as he doesn't actually fall down. I talk democracy to these men and women. I tell them that they have the vote, and that theirs is the kingdom and the power and the glory. I say to them, 'You are supreme, exercise your power.' They say, 'That's right: tell us what to do'; and I tell them. I say, 'Exercise your vote intelligently by voting for me.' And they do. That's democracy; and a splendid thing it is too for putting the right man in the right place.

MAGNUS. Magnificent! I have never heard it better described. You certainly have a head on you, Mr. Boanerges. You should write an essay on democracy. But—

BOANERGES. But what?

MAGNUS. Suppose a man with a bigger voice comes along! Some fool! Some windbag! Some upstart with a platform trick of getting the multitude!

Such passages are surely ironical enough, and men like Undershaft and Magnus are typical ironists. But such passages are not important or fundamental parts of the plays. The reason for this has already been suggested: Shaw is not interested in merely making fun of anyone, even though the victim might richly deserve it. It is significant of his attitude that, for example, he is careful to state in the preface to *The Apple Cart* that Boanerges has the makings of a good man in him and is not just the funny caricature that people have taken him for.

The butt of the joke has the makings of a good man in him! That is Shaw's invariable way. The secret of right and wrong is indeed not a simple one. No matter how opposed to his author's convictions a character's views may be, Shaw puts into that character's mouth the ablest and most effective defense that he, with his great forensic skill, can devise. Undershaft, the armament maker, is the wittiest, the wisest, and the most successful person in the play. The Grand Inquisitor is a model of benevolent justice. Mrs. Warren, the bawd, and the unspeakable Sartorius (in *Widowers' Houses*) have things to say on their sides, and say them.

When the issues of right and wrong are really obscure, Shaw revels in the game his antagonists play. Then the situation reminds one of evenly matched tennis players who sweat through rally after rally only to keep the score at love. Thus Marchbanks and Morell score off each other alternately and end their match with a draw. Conventional theatergoers cannot accept any such inconclusive ending. For them somebody has to win. Hence they generally conclude that Morell is a silly fool who gets off well because his wife pities him. (After all, can a stage clergyman be anything but a fool?) But actually Morell is nothing of the kind, and if anybody in the play is silly and gets taught a needed lesson, it is Marchbanks.

There are several explanations for this impartiality of Shaw's. He loves good debate for its own sake. He is unmoved by normal partisan passions. His philosophy is that "every practicable man (and woman) is a potential scoundrel and a potential good citizen.... What he does, and what we think of what he does, depends on his circumstances."[16] Reform is always possible because "there is nothing that can be changed more completely than human nature when the job is taken in hand early enough."[17] He loves no man, he hates no man, because his soul is wedded to his evolutionary utopia. And above all, like his father before him, as soon as he has blown up a balloon of hot air he is seized by a compulsion to stick a pin in it.

The consequence of this quirk of character is that occasionally Shaw kids himself or his own characteristics and beliefs as exemplified by a character, in a fashion that reminds us of Romantic irony. Thus the ending of *Man and Superman*. (To all intents and purposes Tanner is Shaw.)

> VIOLET (*to* TANNER). You *are* a brute, Jack.
> ANN. Never mind her, dear. Go on talking.
> TANNER. Talking!

Thus the comments of the critics on Fanny's play: ".... I've repeatedly proved that Shaw is physiologically incapable of the note of passion." "... At all events, you cannot deny that the characters in this play are quite distinguishable from one another. That proves it's not by Shaw, because all Shaw's characters are himself: mere puppets stuck up to

spout Shaw." "A giant brain if you ask me; but no heart."
And thus Dubedat in *The Doctor's Dilemma.*

> LOUIS. I'm not a criminal. All your moralizings have no value
> for me. I don't believe in morality. I'm a disciple of Bernard
> Shaw.
> SIR PATRICK. Bernard Shaw? I never heard of him. He's a
> Methodist preacher, I suppose?
> LOUIS (*scandalized*). No, no. He's the most advanced man
> now living: he isn't anything.

But the resemblance to Romantic irony is only outward.
Shaw's feelings are not involved, but only his sense of
humor. He is no Byron, shielding a lacerated sensibility
with a show of scornful laughter. On the contrary, he loves
to satirize Byronic attitudinizing. Thus he presents a romantic hero (Sergius in *Arms and the Man*) as ludicrously
torn between his pose and his inclinations. The latter are
victorious, and he embraces the maid in spite of his conviction that he ought to be worshiping the mistress. "Damnation! Oh, damnation!" he exclaims in agony. "Mockery!
mockery everywhere! everything I think is mocked by
everything I do."

One great effect of genuine and profound irony, however, we must record: that of the ending of *Saint Joan.* The
Maid has been canonized. One after another, the people
who had to do with her in the play pay her homage.

> CAUCHON (*kneeling to her*). The girls in the field praise thee;
> for thou hast raised their eyes; and they see that there is nothing
> between them and heaven.
> DUNOIS (*kneeling to her*). The dying soldiers praise thee, be-
> cause thou art a shield of glory between them and the judgment.
> THE ARCHBISHOP (*kneeling to her*). The princes of the Church
> praise thee, because thou hast redeemed the faith their worldli-
> nesses have dragged through the mire.

And in like fashion Warwick, de Stogumber, the Inquisitor, the Soldier, the Executioner, and Charles.

The impressiveness of the ritual, the beauty of the language, the worthiness of the exalted praise, have an overwhelming effect; lumps rise in our throats and tears start in
our eyes. How fitting an end, we think, to that strange but
strangely moving Epilogue! At times, passages that were
almost farcical clashed with the mystic solemnity of the
vision as prophecy and as commentary on the tragedy of
Joan; but here at last Shaw has subdued his impishness and
written like the great poet he could be.

Then Joan speaks: "Woe unto me when all men praise
me! I bid you remember that I am a saint, and that saints
can work miracles. And now tell me: shall I rise from the
dead, and come back to you a living woman?" There is
sudden darkness.

CAUCHON. The heretic is always better dead. And mortal eyes
cannot distinguish the saint from the heretic. Spare them. (*He
goes out as he came.*)
DUNOIS. Forgive us, Joan: we are not yet good enough for
you. I shall go back to my bed. (*He also goes.*)

And so Warwick, the Archbishop, the Inquisitor, de Stogumber ("Oh, do not come back: you must not come back.
I must die in peace. Give us peace in our time, O Lord!"),
the Gentleman, the Executioner, Charles, and even the
humble Soldier. For Joan's curtain line, "O God that madest
this beautiful earth, when will it be ready to receive Thy
saints? How long, O Lord, how long?" she is left ... alone.

After that tremendously moving litany to Joan, what a
reversal! The ironic clash is extraordinary. The painful joke
is a joke at our expense, a joke on us as human beings who

can praise the great dead sonorously but scuttle away at the very thought of having to live with them in the terrible contrast of their greatness to our littleness. Mankind can revere a saint in heaven but not on earth. Could any dramatist but Shaw have conceived this "cold douche of irony" at such a point—in such a play? And yet—how magnificent it is in the way it deflates us to humility and pity and richer understanding! How long, O Lord? ... Shaw's daring in writing the whole Epilogue, with its mingling of the sublime and the farcical, has often been noted. This ending justifies it and lifts us again, in a more complete sense than could otherwise be possible, to the height of tragedy.

Thus once at least Shaw uses irony in a grand fashion; for this once Shaw wrote a whole play with the seriousness of a tragic poet. Then it became possible for him not only to see the joke in human fallibility, but also to feel and communicate the pain of it.

Nevertheless, I am on the whole justified in saying what I said at the beginning—that Shaw is not primarily an ironist. I have come a long way round to my starting point. On the way I reviewed some thirty plays and almost as many prefaces, not to mention books about Shaw. The excursus perhaps was unnecessary to prove my point, but it was highly amusing. Despite the fact that most of the plays were already familiar, they maintained their comic vitality. And the excursus was rewarding in more serious ways. To see Shaw's limitations and peculiarities clearly is to see also his greatness clearly. And that he is a great dramatist there can be no doubt.

Two notable impressions I received during this journey— impressions with which I should like to close. To the rest of us mortals, undowered like him with the detachment of a man from Mars, it is heartening to know that one great man, at least, has been able to live ninety years in the modern world, survive two world wars, and still keep undiminished his optimistic faith in man's potentialities. And we can wholly admire Shaw's freedom from malice. No matter how bitterly a former friend might revile him (as did Henry Arthur Jones), Shaw never returned evil for evil, but always maintained his admirable magnanimity. It may be said that he could do so because he never really cared. This is in a sense true; it is a point I have emphasized. There is a reason for everything, even the rarest of virtues. There is no hatred or bitterness in Shaw. Hence, to conclude, there is nothing to envenom his comic stings into irony, as with Swift and Voltaire and Heine and Aldous Huxley.

Gilbert Norwood has compared Shaw with Euripides.[18] They both challenged accepted beliefs; they both sympathized with and defended women; they both attacked political and moral abuses; they both wrote with extraordinary wit, brilliance, and clarity; they both were at first unpopular. We might add that they both dearly loved debate and paradox. But one fundamental difference between the two great dramatists outweighs all the likenesses. Shaw sees the world as essentially a comedy; Euripides, as a tragedy. As a consequence, the most violent ethical incongruities in Shaw's plays are painless, but Euripides is one of the most powerful ironists in all literature. Our next main topic, and last, is irony in tragedy; and under this heading Euripides will find a leading place.

Part Four

MOCKERY OF IDEALS: TRAGIC IRONY

Il ne faut pas que l'homme croie qu'il est égal aux bêtes, ni aux anges, ni qu'il ignore l'un et l'autre, mais qu'il sache l'un et l'autre. Guerre intestine de l'homme entre la raison et les passions. S'il n'avait que la raison sans passions ... S'il n'avait que les passions sans raison ... Mais ayant l'un et l'autre, il ne peut être sans guerre, ne pouvant avoir la paix avec l'un qu'ayant guerre avec l'autre: ainsi il est toujours divisé, et contraire à lui-même.

PASCAL

Der innere Widerspruch, der in dem Dichter [Euripides] ist, zieht sich auch durch sein Werk.

ULRICH VON WILAMOWITZ-MOELLENDORFF

What is life? a fighting
   In heart and brain with Trolls.
Poetry? That means writing
   Doomsday-accounts of our souls.

IBSEN

CHAPTER VII

Aeschylus and Sophocles

To the observer, irony is recognized as an emotional dissonance. The cause of that dissonance in the ironist himself may be a superficial discord or a profound strife of the spirit against itself and the world. The man of genuinely ironic disposition, as we saw when we examined Romantic irony, is to some extent split-souled, and his irony is both an expression of his inner strife and a defense against it.

A spiritual strife of this kind is not confined to people of romantic disposition. Nor must it be the consequence of personal misfortunes. Anyone with philosophical and religious intelligence is likely to suffer it, for a clash between aspiration and reality is a necessary condition of life.

We are divided creatures from birth. Biologically speaking, it is only recently that our species has evolved from sheer animality by overlaying this animality with the mental activities that we call rational and spiritual. The animal in us remains. Out of shame or fear we usually keep it submerged below consciousness like the bulk of a floating iceberg under the sea. We prefer to look only at the unsubmerged part and call it human. Our very instinct of self-preservation leads us to flatter ourselves. But the facts remain, and sooner or later thoughtful people face them.

Pascal calls this condition of mankind the intestine war between reason and the passions. Physiologically, it has been explained as the conflict in function between the primitive part of the human brain, the thalamus, and the cortex. It has been represented in various descriptive or symbolic ways, some of which have played immensely important parts in religious and moral history. In the more mythical forms, it is projected into the universe as a war between a God of Light and a God of Darkness, Ormuzd and Ahriman, Jehovah and the Devil. To the medieval moralist the clash was between the Body and the Soul. To Freud it was "id" versus "superego." Plato symbolized the human predicament in a much more beautiful and perhaps more accurate myth, that of the charioteer who must drive a team of horses, one handsome and biddable, the other dark, misshapen, and unruly. Other poets have expressed the predicament directly.

> Oh, wearisome condition of humanity!
> Born under one law, to another bound,
> Vainly begot and yet forbidden vanity:
> Created sick, commanded to be sound.
> What meaneth Nature by these diverse laws—
> Passion and reason, self-division's cause.

These verses of Fulke Greville, significantly enough, are the epigraph to one of the most bitterly ironical of modern satires, Aldous Huxley's *Point Counterpoint*. But even the optimistic Emerson described the conflict as a universal one:

> There are two laws discrete,
> Not reconciled,—
> Law for man, and law for thing:

> The last builds town and fleet,
> But it runs wild,
> And doth the man unking.[1]

Emerson, however, stood firm in his conviction that there *is* a "law for man." Unlike Pirandello, he had a positive faith and used no irony in preaching it. The person of ironical temperament is unsure, inclined to hopelessness about mankind in general. At the same time, he is acutely unhappy about man's fate because he is highly idealistic. If he were less so, he might sink into cynical apathy. And he is highly intelligent and perceptive; otherwise, he might ignore the situation and live content on an animal level. His imagination is quick, his sense of relations and incongruities constantly playing upon life. He can laugh, but laughter is not a substitute for a faith; and he is likely to be all the more melancholy because of the clearness of his vision. He is caught in a painful dilemma, and for him irony is a partial relief. The evil thing may seem diminished if one can ridicule it. Thus Heine or Mark Twain.

Well-integrated souls like Socrates or Sophocles may use irony constantly, but with them it is a weapon of offense. The man who suffers inner conflict uses it in defense against himself. And sooner or later he is bound to find it futile, whereupon he will seek salvation in a positive faith. The German Romantics tended to revert to the Roman Church. The bright young cynics of the "lost generation" after the First World War have—many of them—followed a similar trend. T. S. Eliot became an Anglo-Catholic, Evelyn Waugh a Roman Catholic, Aldous Huxley an apostle of a special synthetic religion of his own.

---

[1] For notes to chapter vii see pp. 266–267.

Sometimes, however, no religion serves, the conflict rages unabated, and the brain itself at last gives way. No doubt Swift's madness had immediate physical causes, but certainly the black horror of his view of mankind predisposed him to succumb to them.

Literary folk who suffer such conflicts seldom end like Swift, for they find a relief in their art which, luckily for them, is usually sufficient for mental health if not for happiness. Ibsen used to keep a scorpion in a glass on his desk. When the creature grew sick from too much venom, he used to relieve it by giving it a piece of ripe fruit to sting. "Does not something of the same kind," he asked, "happen with us poets?"[2]

Most artists of the ironic temperament can sting the fruit. By objectifying their conflicts they rid themselves of them. Pirandello obviously did this in ringing the changes on his theme that fiction is to be preferred to reality. He thus preserved his mental balance, and even won international fame, but these successes did not suffice to give him happiness. Anatole France was luckier: he had, in addition to his irony, two other escapes—the escape into estheticism and the escape into sensuality. Or perhaps these are simply aspects of one thing, as a novel like *The Red Lily* suggests. His irony can force the human predicament upon us with extraordinary power, as in the famous ending of "The Procurator of Judaea": "Pontius Pilate contracted his brows, and his hand rose to his forehead in the attitude of one who probes the deeps of memory. Then after a silence of some seconds— "'Jesus?' he murmured, 'Jesus—of Nazareth? I cannot call him to mind.'" But poignant as this is, it is far below the level of Swift or Ibsen. It is the irony of one who is a master at using for esthetic effort any material, including the profoundest issues of human life; it is not the irony of one who is himself desperate to solve those issues.

Such irony as France's is not the stuff of great tragedy. Sincerity and depth of feeling about the profoundest issues, if not philosophical profundity, are surely necessary for a tragic poet. It is not necessary that he be an ironist, of course; but if he be, what sort of tragedy will be write?

We may limit the number of great tragic poets to seven: Aeschylus, Sophocles, Euripides, Shakespeare, Corneille (perhaps), Racine, and Ibsen. How many of these seven were ironists?

Not Aeschylus—not in the sense of suffering an inner conflict. He was essentially a believer, not a doubter. He was, to be sure, troubled by ethical difficulties; it would be strange if any thoughtful man were not; and he dramatized one in the *Oresteia* and another in the *Prometheia*. But he resolved these problems, as a genuine ironist does not. *The Eumenides* tells us in effect that private vengeance must give way to civic justice; and the lost plays of the other trilogy undoubtedly reconciled the wisdom of Prometheus with the power of Zeus. The genuine ironist applies an absolute moral ideal to the world and then, when—as is inevitable—he finds it unachievable, decries the world with bitterness. Aeschylus made no such extreme ethical demands. "Professing no systematic theory of philosophy or theology, the poet must yet let the final issue restore our confidence in the security of a rational and equitable apportionment of things..."[3] Rare genius that he was in poetry, Aeschylus was a typical Greek in practical philosophy, for he believed in compromising and being reasonable.

A poet with no ironic soul strife may of course use irony as a device, and with great effect. Sophocles was such a poet. He was interested in the character who—as Aristotle said, in summing up his method—falls because of some error or frailty in an otherwise noble nature. His tragedy begins with cheerful hopes and ends in misery. And as the audience knows the outcome from the beginning, the contrast between the hero's good cheer and his coming fate is inevitably ironic.

Aeschylean tragedy, however, did not lend itself in this fashion to irony. Aeschylus' heroes "are not men, like Ajax or Oedipus, who deserve a better fate, but men built for ruin from the start." His tragedy begins after their doom is sealed. They are not doomed for "flaws," but for sins which are central to their characters and have already been committed. Aeschylus' plays begin ominously and hence afford no ironical contrast between hopeful opening and calamitous close. "The terrible intensification of foreboding that we have in the *Agamemnon* is as characteristic of Aeschylus as his tragic irony is of Sophocles, and the difference between these effects is intimately connected with the difference between the two types of tragic hero. . . . The tragedy of the Aeschylean hero is virtually complete when the play opens." This hero is "at variance with the moral laws of the universe."⁴ Aeschylus can bring a trilogy to a "happy ending" without lowering artistic standards, because the trilogy presents and resolves a moral problem. But such an ending is not happy for the doomed hero from whose sin the problem has arisen. Agamemnon must die, Clytemnestra must die, Eteocles must die. Prometheus, if not sinful, is in irreconcilable conflict with Zeus and must suffer.

This concept of tragedy does not lead to the Sophoclean plot, with its peripety and recognition, but results in a simple series of climatic "blows, each worse than the last."[15] Hence Aeschylus excels in the episode, which by itself may be extremely sensational in a theatrical sense, like the spectacle of the sleeping furies and their awakening under the tongue lashing of Clytemnestra's ghost, or overwhelmingly powerful in a tragic sense, like the episode of Cassandra outside the palace doors. These episodes are not bound one to another by Aristotle's strict law of probability or necessity, as Sophocles' usually are, but by the Aeschylean law of "increasing tension."[16] Aeschylean tragedy becomes a series of spectacles unified less by our concern for a hero than by our interest in the moral problem which the hero's conduct raises. Hence those of us whose first interest is in dramatic effect find Aeschylean tragedy, as a whole, less powerful than Sophoclean. It approaches allegory, and we are not deeply moved by the abstract. This is not to deny or disparage the splendor of the earlier poet's language or the dramatic power of episodes, which make the *Agamemnon* one of the world's supreme tragedies.

If Aeschylus was primarily concerned with episodes to illustrate a moral idea, we should expect what irony we find in his tragedies to be incidental. After considering it, we are even tempted to call some of it accidental. At least we may say that in the planning of his scenes Aeschylus did not apparently adapt them to conscious ironic effect, as Sophocles did. It would indeed be extraordinary if the former, coming as he did at the very beginning of dramatic art, should have been fully aware of the devices he used. But let us consider the evidence.

In *The Seven before Thebes* Eteocles is told that seven champions of the besieging army propose to assault the seven gates. Each champion is named and described in turn, and to each Eteocles assigns the appropriate opponent from his own army. We are aware, from our familiarity with the saga, that Eteocles and his brother are fated to meet and die by each other's hands at the seventh gate; but for dramatic purposes Eteocles is made seemingly unconscious of the possibility. We wait for the seventh champion to be named, knowing who it will be and knowing that meanwhile Eteocles will find no champion on the other side against whom he must himself stand. The sixth enemy champion turns out to be Amphiaraus, the virtuous seer. Eteocles might escape his fate if he should meet this opponent, but he is obviously unfit to do so. "It is a searing flash of tragic irony," writes a critic, "hardly to be paralleled in Aeschylus, not approached elsewhere."[7] The seventh champion is of course Polynices. Says another critic: "In his tragic economy Aeschylus uses the element of surprise to effect tragic irony. What is evident to the spectator is unexpected to the person of the action."[8]

The irony of this episode-in-little resembles that of *Oedipus the King* in that every wise and kingly action of the hero inevitably brings him unconsciously closer to the doom which only we see ahead of him. But Aeschylus makes no effort to point up the irony with verbal emphasis, as Sophocles does, and the whole episode is constructed in an archaic and unrealistic form which lays stress on lyrical and epic rather than dramatic feeling. To a scholar the irony may be searing, but I cannot help wondering whether to an average Athenian spectator it would have been so impressive.

Professor Sedgewick in his lectures on dramatic irony finds much in the *Agamemnon*. In the *Choephoroe,* on the contrary, there is little; and he thinks the poet avoided it there to avoid paralleling the earlier play of the trilogy and to keep his emphasis on the myth as a whole. In the *Agamemnon,* at any rate, the irony is the familiar irony of anticipation, most fully effective on the triumphal appearance of the doomed hero. The situation is certainly ironical, but we must note that the irony is almost wholly implicit. Clytemnestra's hypocrisy is perfectly straight-faced; we almost forget that she is playing a role. Once indeed she says of the rumors of Agamemnon's death which came to her in the years of separation,

> Had he as many wounds as loose-tongued Fame
> Gave forth, a net had fewer holes than he.

If as she says this we associate it with the method she is about to employ in murdering him, it can have an authentic ironic sting. But we cannot say of her speeches, as we can of many in Sophocles and Euripides, that planning for verbal irony influenced the writing of them.

Earlier in the play, however, there are verbal ironies of considerable power. After the beacon has brought the joyful news of the fall of Troy, Clytemnestra piously hopes that the conquerors will not plunder the holy temples, for if they are sacrilegious there "still remains the home-return." The herald soon informs us that "temples and altars are no more." Again, Clytemnestra asks the herald to send Agamemnon greetings from her.

> Let him come quickly, loved of all the land.
> And may he find the wife he left behind
> Unchanged, still faithful ...

... and holding unprofaned
So long, the pressure of his last embrace.
Of joys with other men, or guilty word,
I know no more than of the blacksmith's art.[9]

These last lines Professor Harsh translates: "I know no joy
of another man or shameful rumor any more than I know
the dipping of the steel." He calls these, "lines of bloodcurdling irony."[10]

I am not averse from crediting Aeschylus with all the
power of irony that these critics find in such passages, but
I cannot help thinking that in the theater, where dramatic
irony must be tested, they might not even be noticed by
many. I am afraid that they are ironies mainly for the study.

This objection, however, hardly holds of one passage
which comes after the murder, when all deceit is over and
Clytemnestra speaks out exultantly. Here the words should
be bloodcurdling to the spectator as well as the scholar. Indeed, I know no passage elsewhere equal to it in jocose
savagery, unless we can find its match in *The Bacchae*. It is
sarcasm in its literal meaning.

Clytemnestra is glorying in her revenge for the death of
their daughter Iphigenia, sacrificed long ago by her own
father's sanction.

Oh, a worthy deed and a worthy doom.
Will he boast in hell of the death he dealt?

Here in the household there will certainly be no tears for
him. But—in Hades:

One—one will receive him in love where he goes, fitly—his
daughter.
By the swift-flowing river of grief she will stand, welcome
to bring him.
She will hold him, enfold him, and kiss him.[11]

This is intentional irony, but it does not seem to have been consciously prepared for; rather, it arose as the natural expression of Clytemnestra's emotions understood imaginatively by the poet. And so we may speak of Aeschylus' irony in general: it was incidental rather than essential, and it was not elaborated with conscious art.

Sophocles' irony was not incidental, but he was no less spiritually whole than Aeschylus. The evidence both of his life, so far as known, and his works, indicates a man of unshaken piety.[12] "Count no man happy..." sing his chorus; but they are moralizing on an unhappy event, not speaking for their creator. "Blessed Sophocles," reads his epitaph, "who lived long and died happy and wise when he had written many beautiful tragedies. He ended well, having suffered no ill."[13] His irony, as we noted earlier, arose from his choice of tragic theme—the fall of a great character with a flaw;—a fall that inevitably entails a contradiction between good fortune and calamity. For this hero we feel, as Aristotle said, pity and fear. These emotions combine with the sense of a malign trickery in the hero's circumstances into what we call tragic irony. And Sophocles exploited this sense of trickery by verbal emphasis.

I say "circumstances," not Fate, because for more than a century altogether too much has been parroted about Sophoclean "fatalism" by writers who have got their ideas from other critics rather than from a study of the plays themselves. There is nothing fatalistic about the Greeks in general; on the contrary they were, above all other great races, believers in the powers of the individual will, initiative, and intelligence. (Odysseus was their chief national hero.) Nor can Sophocles be called a fatalist if one judges by his plays and not according to theories evolved by German metaphysicians. It is not fate, but Oedipus' own nature, that makes him do what he does. If he had not been impetuous and hot-tempered, he would never, for example, have attacked the old man at the crossroads, for he was well aware of the oracle that declared he should slay his own father. The defects of his qualities which in other circumstances made him a wise and a benignant ruler lead him in the particular circumstances of the play to his undoing. That is the irony of his fate; but his fate comes of his own character.[14] Sophocles took a fatalistic legend, but carefully developed it in an unfatalistic fashion.

Sophocles' method of verbal irony was perhaps sufficiently illustrated in Part One. As was there pointed out, this irony is not, strictly speaking, dramatic irony, which is irony of circumstance or event, but a means of emphasizing that irony—the equivalent of a wink. Another feature of Sophocles' technique is the use of the joyful chorus and the presentation of the victim blind and confident, just before disaster. Sometimes a character grieves over a small matter when the audience knows that a greater disaster will befall. Thus Philoctetes is disappointed that Neoptolemus does not know his reputation and is unaware of the woes that Neoptolemus has come to inflict on him. This is called the "irony of confidence." Or irony may anticipate a peripety. Thus Aegisthus thinks that the corpse of Clytemnestra is Orestes' and is gloatingly eager to uncover it. "Take off the covering from the face," he cries, "that *kinship* may receive the tribute of lament from me also."

Thus far S. K. Johnson (in an essay already referred to)[15] analyzes Sophoclean technique. Mr. Johnson makes no reference to the comic effects which I have discussed in chapter i; he notes merely that Sophoclean irony is "closely associated with 'pity and fear.' " I shall not repeat my arguments that it also involves a cruel practical joke.

Bishop Connop Thirlwall's essay, as we have noted, is the source from which the expression "Sophoclean irony" got its currency. Rather than review the tragedies independently, I have thought it preferable, in view of the importance of this essay, to digest it. This digest may have use also as a convenient substitute for the original, since the latter may not be easily available to all readers. My own comments are enclosed in brackets.

ON THE IRONY OF SOPHOCLES

by Connop Thirlwall, 1833

[A digest]

[INTRODUCTION]

[That "irony" was not associated with "tragedy" in 1833 is indicated by the first sentence: "Some readers may be a little surprised to see *irony* attributed to a tragic poet ..."] The chief uses of the word may be defined as follows: 1. *Verbal irony:* "a contrast between ... thought and ... expression." When not merely jocular, this is used mainly in controversy. "... It implies a conviction so deep, as to disdain a direct refutation ..." 2. *Dialectic irony:* pretended admiration of the opponent, best exemplified by Plato's dialogues and by Pascal. 3. *Practical irony:* irony of events, not words. It may be of two kinds: a. malign or wanton, "by which a man humours the folly of another ..." (In this spirit Shakespeare's Timon squanders his gold on Alcibiades and the thieves, and the witches feed Macbeth's hopes.) b. benevolent, when a man of superior understanding finds it necessary to assent to folly, etc. All men of experience have observed the difference between hopes and realization. "When ... we review such instances of the mockery of fate, we can scarcely refrain from a melancholy smile." So also for states and institutions: they often seem at the summit of glory just before their fall. 4. "There is also a slight cast of irony in the grave, calm, respectful attention impartially bestowed by an intelligent judge on two contending parties..." when neither is wholly right. "...Here the irony... is deeply seated in the case itself, which seems to favor each of the litigants, but really eludes them both." This irony is most interesting when there is hostile collision, our sympathy is divided, and there is no earthly reconciliation.

[DISCUSSION]

The dramatist must view his mimic world as he supposes the Creator to view the real world, and the essential character of his poetry will therefore depend on his religious sentiments. Sophocles's work, at any rate, is deeply religious, filled with a sense of "an overruling Power." His religion suppressed the childishness of the Homeric myths, and transferred the concept of destiny from blind force to the justice and intelligence of Zeus. Thus there is not in Sophocles the working of "an iron destiny," "a dark, inflexible fate." Such a concept "affords abundant room for the exhibition of tragic irony; but we conceive that this is not the loftiest kind, and that Sophocles really aimed at something higher." A few examples to illustrate these views are all that will be attempted in this essay.

The Greek dramatist was limited to few and familiar stories of gods and heroes, stamped with the character of a ruder age, and resistent to refinement. Sophocles does not wholly transform his material, but we may admire "the genius which could stamp the ancient legends with a character so foreign to their original import." Irony is "not equally conspicuous in all his extant plays, though we believe the perception of it to be indispensable for the full enjoyment of every one of them."

Let us consider the situation at the opening of *Oedipus the King*. Oedipus, the happy, wise, and kindly ruler, is looked to

for help against the plague; joyful tidings come from Delphi
that the plague will end when the murderer of Laius is punished; Oedipus confidently undertakes to discover this murderer.
The spectator reflects "how different all is from what it seems,"
since Oedipus is himself the murderer. He proceeds to offer the
guilty man immunity if he will voluntarily leave the country.
In case he will not exile himself, the king calls down the vengeance of the gods upon him, and upon even himself, "if he
knowingly harbours the man of blood under his roof." [These
verbal ironies are not quoted.]

In the scene with Tiresias, Oedipus taunts the latter with his
blindness. The "practical irony" of the outcome is that Oedipus
blinds himself. [The intermediate steps of the action are not re-
counted.] The ingenuity of the revelation has been greatly admired, but its real beauty is "infinitely more profound and
heart-stirring than mere ingenuity ..." "... The Poet has so constructed his plot, as always to evolve the successive steps of the
disclosure out of incidents which either exhibit the delusive security of Oedipus in the strongest light, or tend to cherish his
confidence, or allay his fears." After the revelation, "He is cured
of his rash presumption ..." He has not been wholly innocent,
for "all the events of his life have arisen out of his headstrong,
impetuous character."

"Here [in *Oedipus the King*], where the main theme of the
poet's irony is the contrast between the appearance of good and
the reality of evil," Oedipus' subsequent spiritual peace and assurance of divine protection are not emphasized; but in *Oedipus
at Colonus* they are "the groundwork of the play." In this later
drama the contrast is between the appearance of evil and the
reality of good; and Oedipus becomes a blessing to the land
where he dies. [Since this reversal is not painful to us, it is not
ironical in the sense we have adopted. It might be ironical, of
course, to Creon or Polynices.]

The *Electra* is not fundamentally ironic like the foregoing
plays. It seems to be primarily a study of the heroine's character.
But in view of the known outcome there is irony in Electra's

long lamentations and in Clytemnestra's speeches on receiving
news of Orestes' supposed death. Clytemnestra's "sophistical vin-
dication of her own conduct also assumes a tone of self-mockery,
which is deeply tragical, when we remember that, while she is
pleading, her doom is sealed.... It is in the moment of their
highest exultation and confidence, that each of the offenders discovers the inevitable certainty of their impending ruin." [Thirl-
wall might well have noted also the savage irony at Aegisthus'
expense in the final scene.]

   The Trachinian Virgins is considered the least effective of the
plays because its interest is divided between Heracles and Deianira. But the fate of Heracles "is undoubtedly the point on which
the interest of the play was meant to turn." To the Greeks, if not
to us, he was far more important than Deianira, for he was a
national hero who was deified at his death. In the prologue,
Deianira is shown anxious over her husband, who is faced with
a last labor in which "he is destined to fall, or to reap the reward
of his toils in a life unembittered by pain or sorrow." Her joy in
the news of his success is turned to misery when she learns that
he has taken another wife. But "against this evil she has long
had a remedy in store"—[the blood of Nessus, which she thinks
a love potion, but which proves a fatal poison]. "... Now the
irony of fate displays itself in the cruellest manner: all her wishes
shall be granted, but only to verify her worst fears." [Note this
use of the now familiar phrase, "irony of fate": was it the first?]
She need fear no rival, for Heracles will die. "... All this is but
a bitter mockery," and as she cannot save him she can only die
herself. It is proper that her death should come before the end of
the play because Sophocles wishes to show Heracles reconciled
with his fate and receiving immortality from the gods. Deianira's wishes are now granted, but in a higher sense than she
meant. This last scene, tedious to us, may have moved the Athenians. Even Heracles' injunction to Hyllus [to marry his father's
concubine], "the most obscure as well as repulsive passage in the
whole piece, may have had an additional motive, which we cannot fully comprehend."

The *Ajax* shows the hero at the beginning "in the depth of degradation, an object of mockery and pity: this was the effect of his inordinate self-esteem, of his overweening confidence in his own strength." "The irony of Minerva first draws Ajax into a terrible exhibition of his miserable phrenzy." [He boasts of his prowess in killing cattle, under the delusion that they were the Greek chieftains who had denied him Achilles' armor. This madness was Athena's doing—a horribly ironical practical joke at his expense, which she exhibits to Odysseus. But Odysseus is moved not to scornful mirth, but to sober reflection on human mutability.]

[This section of the essay involves a long discussion of Aias' character: Was he selfish and headstrong at the end? Did he consciously use ambiguous language in deceiving his wife and friends when he talked of burying his sword in the ground, really intending to fall upon it? (This ambiguous language is characteristic Sophoclean verbal irony, although Thirlwall does not specifically note the fact.) Was Aias ironical in his submission, or was he sincere? Thirlwall inclines to consider him unselfish and sincere. He next defends the extended scenes that follow the suicide, in which the Atridae and Teucer wrangle over the question of burying Aias as necessary to establish the hero's title to religious honors, which "commenced only from his interment." His conclusion is that this play's irony is similar to that of *Oedipus at Colonus;* Aias "closes his career at peace with the gods . . ." If our view that the latter play was not ironical is correct, this also is not. But it may be that "the end is rather the triumph of Odysseus than the rehabilitation of Aias," as Kitto suggests.[16] If so, we should find elements of irony in its usual sense. Odysseus won the armor that was refused to Aias; Odysseus was the one whom Aias hated above all the Greeks. Yet it is Odysseus and no other who at the end persuades the Atridae to permit the burial:—surely an ironical triumph of *sophrosynē* (a word which epitomizes the ideal of Greek ethics) over pride. This interpretation, indeed, seems most in keeping with Sophocles' methods and spirit.]

In the *Antigone,* the irony is that of "two contending parties," as discussed in the Introduction. "Each party succeeds in the struggle, but perishes through the success itself: while their destruction preserves the sanctity of the principles for which they contend." Contrary to the modern sentimental view, Antigone is in the wrong in disobeying Creon, whose will was the law of the land. Creon, on the other hand, is intemperate and indiscriminate in dealing with Antigone at first, and when he defies Tiresias he becomes impious and justly deserving of punishment.

In *Philoctetes,* it is ironical that the happy issue is not the result of Odysseus' craft and deceit, but of Neoptolemus' honesty. "The end of Ulysses is attained, but not till all his arts have been baffled..." Incidentally, Philoctetes is not wholly sympathetic, Odysseus wholly unsympathetic. "...The poet himself preserves an ironical composure" toward them.

[CONCLUSION]

Although Aristotle did not observe this design, he was not omniscient. As for this view of irony as purely a modern one, "the idea of a humbling and a chastening power, who extracts moral good out of physical evil, does not seem too refined for the age and country of Sophocles."

Thirlwall's analysis of Sophoclean irony was still the basis for scholarly criticism some seventy years later when Sir Richard Jebb in a review of the poet's genius repeated Thirlwall's simile of the ironist as a judge between two litigants.[17] "Irony depends on a contrast; the irony of tragedy depends mainly on a contrast between the beliefs or purposes of men and those issues to which their actions are overruled by higher powers." It is simplest and most direct in the *Trachiniae* and *Electra:* in the former, between Deianira's love for Heracles and the agony she causes him, and between her reading of the oracles and its real meaning; in the latter, in Electra's mourning for Orestes at the moment of his arrival and in the reversal of situation between the opening and the end of the play. The *Aias* and the two Oedipus plays show suffering inflicted by the gods, which nevertheless brings the sufferer "to a higher state." In *Oedipus the King* there is seeming prosperity and real misery; in *Oedipus at Colonus,* the reverse. Irony is "most subtle and most artistic" in *Antigone* and *Philoctetes.* "Antigone buries Polyneices against the law of the land; Creon dooms her to death, and thereby drives his own son to suicide. But the issue is not a simple conflict between state-law and religious duty. It is a conflict between state-law too harshly enforced and natural affection set above the laws. Creon is right in the letter and wrong in the spirit; Antigone is right in the spirit and wrong in the letter. Creon carries his point; but his victory becomes his misery; Antigone incurs death, but dies with her work done." In *Philoctetes* the protagonist "is injured and noble; Odysseus is dishonest and patriotic," and so on. Jebb calls these situations "antitheses" and "contrasts." Is irony, then, the same thing as an issue opposite to expectation? The position here taken is that such an issue becomes ironical only when it is both painful and amusing. Those who prefer Thirlwall's view, uncomplicated as it is by subjective tests, will find Oedipus' final glorification at Colonus ironical. Those who follow what seems to me the normal usage will not.

Sophocles' use of irony is justly celebrated. Nevertheless, it seems rather arbitrary and accidental that the expression "Sophoclean irony" should have acquired its present currency, when examination shows that Euripides not only made frequent use of irony of the "Sophoclean" type, but also had a fundamentally ironical view of the world which was foreign to Sophocles.

Indeed, it seems strange that Thirlwall makes no mention of Euripides' use of irony. Perhaps his application of the term to tragedy was so new and untried that he had not yet begun to generalize it beyond the poet whom he particularly admired and in whose work presumably he had first noted the effect. At any rate, the consequence of his silence was that other critics, rather blindly following him instead of looking at the evidence of the plays, have ever since talked almost exclusively of *Sophoclean* irony. The time is surely overdue for a fair assessment of the facts.

CHAPTER VIII

Euripides

EURIPIDES uses irony in the same way that Sophocles does and in ways that Sophocles does not. It is a device with him, and it is also the expression of his view of the universe. Euripides was a soul divided against itself.

How does one reach that conclusion? The evidence of his contemporaries is meager, and that of his plays is dependent on the subjective judgments of his readers, who now, at a distance of more than twenty-four hundred years, cannot possibly know enough of the conditions under which he wrote, or even of the meaning of the words he used, to understand him as his fellow citizens could. The difficulties of language alone are, for full understanding, insuperable. A modern English-speaking student who reads French fluently and is familiar with French literature finds that there is a barrier to his complete understanding of French verse that he can never hope wholly to surmount. How much greater the barrier that separates us from ancient Greek verse! Further, only eighteen or nineteen out of the ninety-odd plays that Euripides wrote have survived; of Aeschylus' and Sophocles' even more numerous dramas, seven each; of the works of other dramatists of their time (if Euripides wrote the *Rhesus*), none. Since we know that Euripides makes references to the extant plays of the other

great dramatists, we may assume references to others which
would be understood by his audiences but are meaningless
to us. He was fond of theatrical effects; we can merely guess
at how they were achieved. He made innovations in meter
and music; we must often guess at the former, and of the
latter we hardly know enough even to guess. The passages
in *The Frogs* in which Aristophanes parodies his effects are
more tantalizing than enlightening.

These are some of our difficulties, and it would be foolish
to minimize them. But, on the other hand, we have testi-
mony to the effect Euripides' plays had on Aristophanes;
some significant comments by Aristotle; and fragmentary
hints, from other ancient sources, which have been dili-
gently studied by specialists. And of course we have the
extant plays themselves. Granted that we miss much of their
subtler significances, it should be possible for us to draw
conclusions from the general meanings they convey as dramatic actions.

Possible it should be, and conclusions are drawn. Unfortunately, however, almost all the conclusions, as drawn by
the Euripidean scholars, disagree. And for this disagreement we cannot really blame the scholars. The plays abound
in ambiguities; whatever their author intended, we feel
sure that few are just what, on the surface, they seem to be;
and in any case, it is a fact that most of them can be, and
are, interpreted in more than one way. No contemporary
scholar will suggest that it was incompetence that makes
them ambiguous. Naturally, we seek an inclusive explanation which will give the dramatist's whole work logical
coherence; but no such explanation yet offered has won
general acceptance.

But suppose that the ambiguities and incoherences are intentional? that they are part, at least, of what Euripides wanted to say? When we find a dramatist presenting a great hero, for instance, as ridiculous, or driving him mad; when we find him making a murderous witch a torchbearer for women's rights; rewarding a candid youth's chastity by death; whitewashing a notorious wanton as a faithful Penelope; and punishing an earnest monarch anxious for the morals of his womenfolk by having him torn limb from limb: when we find a dramatist writing in this fashion, perhaps we are justified in assuming that such moral contradictions existed first in his mind, and that he meant to express them.

To come to cases, let us first review the opinions of a representative group of competent scholars. These opinions fall roughly into two classes, as indicated.

A. EURIPIDES HAD ONE POINT OF VIEW.

Bates: Euripides was a *practical dramatist,* concerned not with moral but theatrical values. His theophanies were for "startling, theatrical effects." Pitiful children "would go straight to the hearts of the spectators." *Andromache,* "like many other tragedies of Euripides," is "clearly a play to be acted rather than to be read.... It has no hidden motive. The poet's object was to excite the pity of the spectators...." In *The Bacchae* "he had no moral to point." The motive of the *Ion* is "simple—to give a divine ancestor to the Ionian race." The appearance of Athena at the end of *Iphigenia in Tauris,* unnecessary as it is, was made for a "striking effect." And so on.[1]

Grube: His aim was *realism.* His contradictions "are not deliberate, but accidental; they should nowhere be taken to indicate a subtle intention to make nonsense of the story; nor is whatever indirect religious propaganda they may contain a primary concern of the dramatist."[2]

Haigh: Euripides was a *realist,* interested in human psychology. His chief anxiety was "to write a good tragedy."[3]

Kitto: Euripides was primarily an *intellectual* interested in abstract ideas. Except when he wrote mere melodrama he subordinated characterization and plotting to the expression of these ideas.[4]

Appleton: He was an ethical *idealist* concerned in working from polytheism to monotheism, from external to internal morality.[5]

Verrall: He was an ethical *rationalist* propagandizing against the Olympian religion.[6]

So also Sheppard, without accepting the wilder theories of the elder Cantabrigian.[7]

Lucas: Euripides was a disillusioned *skeptic.*

B. Euripides Had More than One Point of View.

Jaeger: The novel qualities in Euripides' plays were "bourgeois *realism, rhetoric,* and *philosophy."* His philosophy was skeptical and pessimistic. He portrayed a "world of doubt and conflict."[9]

Decharme: Euripides was *skeptical, pessimistic, uncertain,* and *restless.* "Ordinarily Euripides reveals his opinion about the popular gods indirectly and in the guise of a doubt." He "seizes every opportunity to give proofs of the deplorable truth" about life.[10]

Norwood: Euripides was both a great *artist* and a great *rationalist.* "Like Renan he was ἀνὴρ δίψυχος, a man of two souls."[11]

Murray: "Euripides was both a *reasoner* and a *poet.* The two sides of his nature sometimes clashed and sometimes blended."[12]

Pohlenz: Euripides was a *poet* and *thinker,* and the two natures conflicted, with a resulting dissonance between old legends and new humanism. He was the first poet of psychological conflict.[13]

Steiger: Euripides, like Ibsen, had two natures in conflict, the *poet* and the *seeker after moral truth*.[14]

On particular issues the differences among the critics might be further illustrated at great length. I shall offer only a few examples.

Euripides' attitude toward women? Decharme, like Aristophanes, says that he was a satirist of them.[15] Steiger considers him to be, like Ibsen, a powerful defender of them.[16] Most other critics think he was simply being realistic!

Ideas versus characterization? Kitto tells us that Euripides put the former above the latter. "Euripides, in his tragedies, has a degree of abstraction reminiscent of those mathematical personages A, B, and C who used to plough fields for us at such convenient rates."[17] Oates and O'Neill assert that Euripides "raised to superior importance the study of character."[18] Stuart, agreeing with Haigh, says that at times Euripides "sacrifices psychology and true depiction of character to theatrical effects."[19]

Was Euripides a great tragic dramatist? August Wilhelm Schlegel and his followers say he was not. "We are forced to censure him severely on many accounts. . . . His constant aim is to please, he cares not by what means." "In Euripides we find the essence of the ancient tragedy no longer pure and unmixed; its characteristical features are already in part defaced." "He takes delight in depicting the defects and moral failings of his characters. . . . The poet has thus at once destroyed the inner essence of tragedy, and sinned against the laws of beauty and proportion in its external structure." He tends to immorality; he takes great license with the fables; he overdoes contrast; his style is too loose; etc.[20] And Swinburne (quoted by Verrall) calls Euripides, *tout court,* a "botcher,"[21] Verrall himself, on the contrary, thinks Euripides a master rationalist who purposely and powerfully satirized the traditional religion. So does Norwood. Steiger exalts him as an unfaltering seeker after moral truth; Appleton, as a noble idealist. And Murray agrees with Aristotle that Euripides was "the most tragic of the poets," because tragedy is achieved by facing evil and horror and showing "that there remains something in man's soul which is forever beyond their grasp and his power in its own right to make life beautiful," and because "Euripides seems to me to have gone further than any other writer in the attempt to combine in one unity these separate poles."[22]

All in all, the conflicting judgments of the critics, from Aristophanes to Murray and Kitto, running the gamut as they do from "botcher" to Master, might not seem very helpful to a student trying to pluck out the key to his mystery. Actually they support very well the point we wish to make—that the central fact about Euripides is a conflict in his own soul. Their conflict in views mirrors the poet's.

The parallel which Steiger draws between Euripides and Ibsen seems to me sound and enlightening. I had not read Steiger until after I had planned this chapter; I was happy to find my unlearned impressions confirmed. We know enough about the Norwegian poet to be sure of *his* soul conflict, and we know how he expressed it in his dramas. If we assume a like character in Euripides, the contradictions which the scholars have proved present in his plays all fall into place as parts of the total truth.

He was interested in stage effects; he was concerned with the soul of man. He was an innovator; he was in some ways the most conservative of the tragedists. He was theatrical; he neglected obvious requirements of good playwriting. He was sensational; he turned from outer effect to inner drama. He was immoral; he was the most moral of dramatists. He was skeptical and disillusioned; he was a mystic. He was a pessimist; he believed in ultimate ideals. He was rhetorical; he was a master lyrist. He was sentimental; he was "the most tragic of the poets." These antitheses, and more, are all facts about him: the scholars have proved them so. The only reasonable thing to do with them is accept them all and conclude that if any poet's soul ever fought a "civil war in the cave," his did.

Irony, then, was fundamental to Euripides as it was not to the pious Aeschylus or the serene Sophocles. Euripides uses verbal and dramatic ironies as the latter does; he uses them for comic, sentimental, and melodramatic effects which the latter—so far as we know—did little to exploit; and finally, he expresses his own conflict through the conduct of events and the delineation of character in an irony so fundamental and so all-pervading that it can be overlooked, even its existence denied. Our next task is to review the evidence for these statements.

To treat the plays chronologically would make any presentation of their ironies confusing, for the effects follow no evident line of progression, and the extent to which Euripides used them varies without evident logic. Thus the earliest plays (*Alcestis, Medea*) and the latest (*The Bacchae, Iphigenia at Aulis*) are full of irony, but some intermediate plays, especially ones written apparently during a fit of patriotic fervor in the early war years (*Heracleidae, The Suppliants*), have little. And the unironic *Suppliants* is believed to have been written not long before the most ironic play of all, the *Ion*.

We shall look for irony in the seventeen recognized "tragedies," not counting the doubtful *Rhesus* and the satyr play *The Cyclops*. To get some sort of order in our findings we shall use the headings Comic, Sentimental, Tragic, Melodramatic, and Philosophical. These categories are of course seldom distinct in fact. One scene may be at once comically, sentimentally, and philosophically ironic; another may be tragically so to some readers, melodramatically so to others. There is no more complex effect than irony. Our classification is mainly for convenience.

And the examples selected under each heading must necessarily be one reader's personal choice. We cannot depend on the authorities, for as we have seen they nearly all differ. Even on so fundamental a question as whether a particular play is to be taken "seriously" or not they sometimes differ diametrically.

Under the circumstances, we might frankly choose a position from among those taken by the authorities. Thus, if we wished simply to make a case as strong as possible for Euripides as ironist, we would be inclined to follow Verrall, to whom everything the poet wrote was compact of duplicity, its surface acceptances of conventional pieties being tongue-in-cheek; its real significance, propaganda against the Olympian religion and ethic; its intended audience, the sophistic intelligensia of Athens. An Athenian Voltaire or Anatole France, in other words—of whom considerations of personal safety required more careful concealment of his real meaning from the unsophisticated multitude than was necessary in the eighteenth or the nineteenth century.

This interpretation would be attractive to a seeker after interesting ironies, and it is possible to read most of the plays in accordance with it. Unfortunately for such an approach, most of Verrall's scholarly critics, much as they tend to disagree in other matters, agree to differ violently from him; and my own impressions are that some of his hypotheses are fantastic. (To rationalize *Alcestis*, for example, he suggests that the heroine did not actually die at all, but fell into a trance from which Heracles rescued her!) He did useful service in counteracting both sentimental and condemnatory views of Euripides prevalent at the end of the last century, and in sharply directing attention to the skeptical and rational aspects of the poet's work. If it had not been for Verrall, our realization of the poet's irony could hardly have been so clear. But I shall not go all the way with him.

One special reason both keeps me from following him very far and gives me courage to offer occasional independent views. In reading the literature of Euripidean criticism, and of criticism of Greek drama generally, I have been struck by a widespread failure to deal with the plays adequately as plays; to judge the author's effects as an audience in the theater would feel and understand them. The plays were written to be produced; and in a day when books were few (Euripides was noted for owning a library!), plays were even more dependent on production than they are now. No one can deny all this, but the scholarly critics too seldom consider it in judging the plays as works of art.

The values of lyric poetry are on the page, and to judge them well a full knowledge of the language in which they are written is indispensable. But dramatic values exist only

potentially on the page; they exist fully only when projected to an audience in the theater. The script, like musical
notation, is a means, not an end; the end is performance;
and the only proper way to read a dramatic script is to
imagine it performed as one reads. Happily, dramatic
values largely survive translation, even from ancient Greek
into the modern English of Murray. Delicate effects may be
blurred, lost, or altered, but the main qualities of a play
emerge. And to the extent that a scholar is immersed in
detailed linguistic and exegetical studies, to the same extent
he is likely to miss a play's dramatic values. These depend
upon the imaginative linking together of all details in sequence during a time approximating performance; but it
is the details themselves, not this total impact, that the
scholar generally concentrates upon.

Most Greek scholars, like the rest of us, must teach classes
a good deal of their time; but while some of the rest of us
can lecture freely about a drama as a whole, the Greek
scholar must for the most part take it up line by line if not
word by word. In a typical hour such topics may be discussed as syntactical difficulties, dialectical forms, textual
emendations, subtle functions of the aorist, variations of
dochmiac rhythm, possible references to Orphic mysteries,
and the opinions of Wilamowitz-Moellendorff on his prede-
cessors in editing a passage. Such matters are often interesting and sometimes important, but they are not dramatic
criticism.

The interest that such matters can excite often leads a
scholar further into making fine-spun interpretations that
no audience would ever have the least notion of. This is a
fascinating occupation, but it involves the fundamental fal-

lacy of regarding a play as existing on the page alone. With respect to Shakespeare, this fallacy was notorious among Romantic critics of the last century, and it has endured even to the present in spite of the vigorous attacks of theater-minded scholars like E. E. Stoll. The students of Greek drama have yet to receive judgment from a Professor Stoll competent in their more exclusive domain.

If the dangers of the fallacy have overcome Shakespear-ean scholars, how much more likely are they to have over-come Greek scholars! After all, Shakespeare is popular in the modern theater. Can we doubt that if the Greek plays were as often performed as Shakespeare's are, so that stu-dents of them could see many of them on the stage at least once, and some often, their criticism would benefit?

In view of these necessary platitudes, our test for irony in Euripides is whether it would be an irony to an intelligent contemporary of the poet on seeing the play in the theater. Since we cannot return to 420 B.C., we shall have to exercise our imaginations toward this point of view. We must take serious account of what the scholars tell us; but when they discover ironies which our ancient Athenian would prob-ably miss in the theater, we shall not claim these as dra-matic ironies. They may well be impressive to thoughtful readers, they may well add beauty or power to the plays when analyzed, but they fall outside our chosen field.

Comic Irony

If we could follow Verrall all the way, we should find comic irony in the prologue of *Alcestis* when Apollo and Death have an altercation over the fate of the heroine. To Verrall, the gods talk merely like clever Athenians in a debate.[23] A hint of burlesque in the acting would certainly set a comic tone; but was that the poet's intention? I do not think so. No skillful dramatist with scenes of exquisite pathos to follow would run such risk of ruining them. He could not afford to be satirical over the reality of the heroine's sacrifice.

He might, however, be satirical at the expense of her husband and father; and I believe he meant their wrangle to strike spectators as ironic. It would be hard to enact that scene, with each egoist blaming the other for Alcestis' sacrifice, without eliciting sarcastic laughter. The critic who found its effect one of "awful seriousness"[24] could hardly have been reading it with a theatrical imagination. Another critic, to whom it was "never far from comedy or satire,"[25] surely realized its theatrical effect correctly, and also harmonized it with the tragicomic tone of the play as a whole. But whether we take it satirically or with awful seriousness, it involves a thoroughly ironical situation.

The foreknowledge of the happy ending which the prologue gives the spectator must not be forgotten when we deal with the more pathetic scenes, for it colors them all, even, as Professor Harsh points out, the farewell scene between husband and wife,[26] with comic irony. This critic is probably indulging in undramatic subtleties, however, when he finds an "irony of fate" in the ending because it is the weakness of Admetus' character that wins him final happiness. According to this view, it is Admetus' "softhearted kindness" to his slaves that gains him Apollo's favor and his "excessive hospitality" that gains him Heracles'. The spectator in the theater would not be likely to think these qualities weaknesses or to feel the painful amusement of irony at Admetus' good fortune.

The spectator would notice, however, the comic and sentimental ironies in the last scene, in which Heracles leads a veiled woman before the king and asks him to keep her for him. The spectator knows who the woman is; Admetus does not. He has sworn to let no woman take the place of his beloved Alcestis. His grief is outraged by the request, but his courtesy to a guest prevents him from a rude refusal. "Must I take her to my dead wife's room?" he asks. And, looking at the woman, he cries, "Ah! By all the Gods, take her from my sight! ... When I look upon her—she seems my wife—" Heracles, smiling inwardly, replies, "Oh, that I might bring your wife back into the light of day from the dwelling of the Under-Gods, as a gift of grace to you!"[27] To extract the full ironic flavor of the situation, Euripides has him play upon Admetus' grief some time more before he unveils Alcestis.

In the *Ion* also, melodramatic and pathetic effects are ironically colored by the spectator's knowledge of the happy ending. Hermes, in the prologue, tells us that Ion is Creusa's son by Apollo and that the god will arrange things to her satisfaction and that of her mortal husband. As we have noted, this play has often been cited as a forerunner of New Comedy, and in the main outline of the plot it is. The audience are prepared by the prologue to enjoy the *double entendres* and the part-comic, part-pathetic, part-melodramatic situations which follow.

When at the beginning of the play mother and son meet without mutual recognition, Ion tells her that he is a foundling. Creusa, thinking of herself, says,

> Alas, another dame
> Like sufferings with your mother hath endured.

She feels bitterness against Apollo (Ion's father), and despite the fact that the lad is a pious attendant at the god's
temple, he sympathizes. His indictment of the god for se-
ducing and abandoning a mortal maiden has been cited as
an example of the dramatist's ethical attack on the Olympians, but surely in the theater, with the happy ending an-
nounced, its effect would be mild.

> No longer is it just to speak of men
> As wicked, if the conduct of the gods
> We imitate; our censures rather ought
> To fall on those who such examples give.

It is an ironic joke on Creusa that she is led to think Ion
not her son but her husband's. After her melodramatic attempt to poison the lad miscarries and she takes refuge at the
altar, Ion declares that not even that sacred place will save
her.

> ... for the compassion
> Thou wouldst excite is rather due to me
> And to my mother; for although, in person,
> She be not here, yet is that much-loved name
> Ne'er absent from my thoughts.

Such elaborate verbal ironies are as consciously designed as
anything in Sophocles and as frequent as those in *Oedipus
the King*. The one play is a romantic comedy, the other a
tragedy. The difference in their effects upon us should not
obscure the similarity of the verbal irony in both.

In *Iphigenia at Aulis* the tone is generally pathetic, but
the characterization of Achilles borders on comedy. He is—
this great hero—obviously more anxious to preserve his
reputation than eager to undertake dangerous exploits for
maidens in distress; and when Iphigenia, by volunteering

to die, frees him from his pledge to her, his relief is ludicrous. This *miles gloriosus,* ironically contrasted to the timid girl who bravely faces death, makes one think of Ibsen's male egoists, and also of Jason in *Medea,* who has some similarities. But the irony is not emphasized in the writing, and might not be apparent to an audience if the actor did not stress it.

Iphigenia in Tauris is another tragicomedy; and since its prologue does not announce a happy outcome, its serious scenes are not affected by the assurance of good fortune. Nevertheless, it has its moments of comic irony. After the recognition scene between Iphigenia and Orestes, they plot how to escape from Tauris with the image of Artemis. When King Thoas appears, Iphigenia, speaking as priestess of the goddess, tells him that the strangers and the image are polluted and that before sacrificing the young men she must cleanse both them and the image in the sea. (Thus they may all escape from him.) "How wisely careful for the city!" exclaims the admiring king. In this scene, says Grube, there is "an undercurrent of satire in the contrast between the simple-minded barbarian and the clever Greek."[28] Iphigenia even warns the king that no Greek is to be trusted! (Query: Does Euripides admire Iphigenia's deceits? The critics, as usual, differ.)

Although there are such comic effects in this play, its tone is serious in a romantically melodramatic way. Not so that of *Helen.* This later play, in fact, seems almost a burlesque of the earlier one. Verrall[20] goes so far as to call it a self-parody. There is no doubt that the Helen here presented— a faithful spouse, repulsing a kingly suitor after seventeen years' separation from her Menelaus—is difficult to take seri-

ously. The explanation to account for her faith, despite the
prevailing belief to the contrary, is that a phantom replaced
her with Paris at Troy. This explanation scarcely adds veri-
similitude to the fable. Theoclymenus, the ardent king who
seeks her hand, is well described by Verrall as a "Gilbertian
tyrant." And Menelaus, when he turns up as a shipwrecked
mariner, is ridiculously disturbed about having to wear an
unkingly ragged costume. The inevitable recognition scene
between him and Helen is, under the peculiar circumstances, less affecting than such scenes usually are. The big
scene later in which the two effect their means of escape is
a close parallel to the one in *Iphigenia*. Whether the dramatist meant this as self-parody or simply chose to use a
successful theatrical effect twice (as dramatists since him
have been known to do), certainly he was aware of the
parallelism. Furthermore, the ironic jokes on the Egyptian
king are more extensively elaborated than those on the Tau-
rian. Thus, after Helen has explained that the body of her
supposedly dead husband must be buried at sea (a device
for escaping by ship), Theoclymenus turns to the ragged
Grecian (Menelaus, pretending to be the messenger of his
own demise) and says:

> An acceptable message have you brought,
> O stranger.

Menelaus replies (with a wink to the audience, or a tone to
convey it):
> Most agreeable to myself
> And the deceased.[30]

The jesting continues in this vein for some time.

If only a wraith of Helen was at Troy, how futile indeed
was the Trojan War! This ironic reflection impresses one

critic,[31] and it may well have been in the poet's mind; but it would hardly impress an audience. Many of Euripides' contemporaries, however, may have been struck by the fact that this extravagant idealization of Helen was an ironic reversal of the dramatists' usual characterization of her, not to speak of her traditional reputation. They may have wondered whether Euripides, wearied by criticisms against his representations of bad women and accusations of being a woman-hater, deliberately chose a most notorious wanton and rehabilitated her to show what he could do when he tried!

What he usually did with Helen is illustrated from an early scene in *Orestes,* in which that lady, the cause of the Trojan War, is shown returned after its close to her husband and to luxury, while the children of Agamemnon, the king who really won the war, lie in misery.[32] The effectiveness of this ironic contrast is heightened by a touch of satirical comedy when Electra remarks after Helen's exit that in sending a lock of her hair to her sister's tomb Helen has been careful to cut off only the tips!

Anxious of beauty, the same woman still!

SENTIMENTAL IRONY

In the *Ion* the comedy is mixed with much sentiment, notably in the scene before the recognition between mother and son. The famous recognition scene in *Iphigenia in Tauris* is more purely sentimental, because the audience is not sure of a happy ending. Orestes and Pylades, the two shipwrecked youths, are brought before Iphigenia, the priestess, as captives for sacrifice. In the ensuing interview she is much moved at learning that they are Greeks, and talks freely of herself. She has just had a terrifying dream which leads her to fear that her brother Orestes is dead, and she confides her grief unknowingly to the living man himself. It adds piquancy to the situation that she is expected shortly to put him to death and is touched by his unhappy fate.

> Unhappy youths, what mother brought you forth?
> Your father who? Your sister, if perchance
> Ye have a sister, of what youths deprived!

She is eager to learn news of her far-off family, and questions the young men indirectly. These questions give Euripides opportunity for much ironical ambiguity. Of herself, supposedly slain at Aulis, she says, for example:

> Unhappy she! the father too, who slew her!
> ORESTES
> For a bad woman she unseemly died.
> IPHIGENIA
> At Argos lives the murdered father's son?
> ORESTES
> Nowhere he lives, poor wretch, and everywhere.

And when Iphigenia says she must slay him, he exclaims:

> Oh that a sister's hand might wrap these limbs![33]

Far more pathetic than such playings on sentiment is the joyful greeting that Iphigenia gives her father (in *Iphigenia at Aulis*) when she comes to the Grecian camp expecting to be married to Achilles, whereas she is in reality to be slain by her father's own command. First the Messenger exults:

> The marriage-song,
> The sound of flutes and dancing feet should fill
> King's tent and camp.—
> It is a day of glory for the girl.

Then Iphigenia's first speech:

> O mother, blame me not! Let me go first
> And put my arms about my father's neck.

Agamemnon is in agony. She notes that he seems troubled.

> IPHIGENIA
> ... send your cares away!
> AGAMEMNON
> Why, all my cares are only for your sake.
> IPHIGENIA
> Then smooth your face, unknit your brows, and smile!
> AGAMEMNON
> I am as glad as I can be, my child.
> IPHIGENIA
> And all the while the tears are in your eyes!

Later, when Iphigenia has left, Clytemnestra asks:

> When is the bridal?
> AGAMEMNON
>   When the moon is full.
> CLYTEMNESTRA
> And have you slain the victim for the goddess?
> AGAMEMNON
> I shall do so; I must.
> CLYTEMNESTRA
>   The marriage-feast,
> You hold it later?
> AGAMEMNON
>   When I have sacrificed
> What the gods call for.[34]

In praise of Euripides, Browning quotes his wife:

> *The Human with his droppings of warm tears.*[35]

Better than the *Alcestis,* which Browning was then interpreting, the foregoing scene might have served to justify
the exclamation.

TRAGIC IRONY

Euripides is not Sophocles' equal for purely tragic irony.
Much of what various critics call tragic irony in him is, in
my opinion, melodramatic. Admittedly the distinction is
debatable. It is also true that the tone of a play as a whole
modifies the effect of individual scenes and that we must be
on our guard against making too much of these scenes out of
their context. Perhaps the safest course will be to consider
here only plays of generally admitted tragic power and see
what uses are made of irony in them. I shall limit the discussion therefore to four: *Hippolytus, Medea, The Trojan
Women,* and *The Bacchae.*

Of Hippolytus we are told: "That a youth so pure should
be the victim of such a foul intrigue is indeed tragic and
ironic; but all too often in life, as the Nurse points out, he
who refuses to recognize the elemental forces of nature is in
the end overwhelmed by a fate that is unnaturally severe."[36]
"Pure" Hippolytus may be, but he is also conceited and
arrogant; he is guilty of *hybris* toward Aphrodite; and it is
on this human plane that spectators are bound to judge him;
they are unlikely to interpret the goddess, in the critic's
fashion, as a mere symbol of elemental forces.

This critic also finds it ironic that "both Theseus and Hippolytus bemoan the visitation of the sins of the fathers upon
the sons."[37] Like father, like son: they both are guilty of
hybris. This irony also needs thinking out. In the theater, if
we disregard for the time its religious ambiguities, *Hippolytus* seems to me one of the least ironical of Euripides' plays.

In *Medea,* Jason's character is drawn very ironically. His sophistical self-justification, his inflated conceit, his cold selfishness are set off sharply, almost comically, by his pose of pompous magnanimity. He is putting away Medea, the barbarian, to marry a Grecian princess, and yet he has the colossal effrontery to tell Medea that she need not have been exiled if she had kept her temper, not reviled her superiors. "Yet even after all this," says her magnanimous lover, "I weary not of my good-will, but am come with thus much forethought, lady, that thou mayest not be destitute nor want for aught, when, with thy sons, thou art cast out."

To this Medea responds with biting sarcasm. ". . . My case stands even thus: I am become the bitter foe to those of mine own home, and those whom I need ne'er have wronged I have made mine enemies to pleasure thee. Wherefore to reward me for this thou hast made me doubly blest in the eyes of many a wife in Hellas; and in thee I own a peerless, trusty lord." But his egoism is too tough for mere words. She should be thankful, he tells her, that she has had the privilege of living among the civilized Greeks! ". . . Thou dwellest in Hellas, instead of thy barbarian land, and hast learnt what justice means and how to live by law, not by the dictates of brute force."[88]

Such fatuous complacency reminds of Bernick's defense against Lona Hessel after she has condemned him for having married a woman he did not love in order to get hold of her money, and then for having posed as a "pillar of society." "I can honestly say," he tells Lona, "that I have grown happier every year. Betty is good and willing; and if I were to tell you how, in the course of years, she has learnt to model her character on the lines of my own—"

Surely Euripides was satirizing the Grecian assumption of superiority to the *barbaroi*—an assumption in comparison to which the English smugness in the nineteenth century, epitomized by Kipling's reference to "lesser tribes without the law," was almost humble. Euripides was one extraordinary Athenian who could view his fellow citizen's pride of culture with critical detachment. It is no wonder that his popularity was slow in developing.

In the second scene between Medea and Jason the passage in which she pretends that he did all for the best "is full of the grimmest tragic irony." "Her instructions to the children themselves are full of consummate irony, as are her last words."[39] And in the last scene it is "effective dramatic irony" that Jason should say that he "has come to save his children from the vindictive wrath of the kinsmen of Creon."[40] But on the whole the play does not make powerful use of irony unless in the moral ambiguity of its plot—a matter which we shall consider under philosophical irony.

For a modern audience *The Trojan Women,* though far from the most exciting, is unquestionably the most deeply moving of Euripides' plays. Its tragic feeling is undisturbed by melodrama or satire or sentimentality; it does not fall into two or more distinct parts, like *Heracles* or *The Suppliants;* its moral meaning is unambiguous and nobly humane; its ending is not patched up by a god from the machine, but is the inevitable consequence of what has gone before. It is not, to be sure, a normal tragedy of conflict and defeat. I have called it elsewhere[41] a "pathodrama" rather than a tragedy in the Sophoclean sense. But its natural succession of episodes strike us as realistic and believable in a degree greater than is possible, perhaps, for the Sophoclean play of contrived plot. And its impact on a war-wearied audience is, as I can testify from having witnessed it recently, profound.

There is irony in the dramatic situation. "The prologue," we are told, ". . . casts a certain irony over the whole action of the play, for it foretells the eventual punishment of the barbaric cruelty and sacrilege of the triumphant Greeks."[42] To the thoughtful Athenian, conscious of his own city's cruelties in the then raging Peloponnesian War, this irony may well have been double. It is the tragic reverse of the prologue to the *Ion* and the *Alcestis,* for here we are told that those who are enjoying good fortune will suffer. The effectiveness of this irony, however, is much less than it would be if the reversal of fortune were enacted as it is in Sophoclean tragedy. What we hear about is never so impressive as what we see; and after Poseidon's prophecy the whole of what we see is the sufferings of Hecuba and her women. Hence we cannot claim for this irony a notable contribution to the power of the play. It frames the picture, but we look at the picture.

There is no doubt of the tremendous power of *The Bacchae,* and various critics have given it a place equal or nearly equal in tragic rank to *Agamemnon* and *Oedipus the King.* Its excellence of construction makes it exceptional in Euripides' works and justifies its being compared in this respect to the best in Sophocles. Though it is full of strange and terrible effects, its serious tone and underlying significances (however one interprets the latter) raise it above mere melodrama. And the romantic fervor of its lyrics puts it in a place by itself among Greek tragedies.

At the same time, it is ethically the most ambiguous of all Greek plays. Does it subtly attack the Dionysian religion, or overtly praise it? Is Pentheus a hero of Sophoclean type, guilty of *hybris* and brought low by *nemesis,* or is he a well-intentioned mortal in the hands of an implacable deity? The critics cannot agree, and we shall not expect an audience to do better. Hence the quality and degree of irony in the play become uncertain. Most uncertain is the philosophic irony, if there is any, which arises from its theme. We shall consider this later. But even the obvious dramatic ironies which abound in it will affect us differently according as we interpret the play.

When doctors disagree, laymen may choose. My choice is what I think an imaginative and humane spectator would feel, whatever his general interpretation, in seeing this play. I think he would feel these ironies to be inhumanly, even fiendishly, cruel. If the spectacle were done realistically it might well be so horrible as to provoke the revulsion of laughter. Hence, without questioning the high qualities I have enumerated as distinguishing this play in other respects, I make bold to consider it in this respect as melodrama, not tragedy.

MELODRAMATIC IRONY

Melodrama is the drama of thrills. Tragedy may afford thrills, as *Hamlet* does, and thus far may be melodramatic. But tragedy is always more than melodrama, for it primarily affects the higher centers of the brain, not the primitive ape-brain in all of us that relishes gooseflesh and spinal shivers. Tragedy may well build on violence and theatricality, for such things hold audiences and such things may be justified by the logic of the action. But its claim to distinction is that it builds up to something more spiritual and leads us finally, as I have said elsewhere, to the "impassioned contemplation of ultimates."[43]

It will be clear, then, that there may be melodramatic effects in an undoubted tragedy, and that the final judgment of a play as on the whole melodramatic or tragic is not necessarily involved if we call incidental ironies in Euripides melodramatic. I think it clear—though I cannot, of course, prove it—that in the effects to be described the poet was primarily seeking the thrill for the thrill's sake. He often had higher aims for his plays as wholes; perhaps he always did; but we are dealing here with the effects by themselves.

In *Iphigenia in Tauris* we noted the sentimental irony in the recognition scene and the irony developed out of the heroine's deception of Thoas. Kitto finds these ironies melodramatic rather than tragic. "Tragic irony assumes security where there is none, in order to emphasize the hero's blindness; now a state of affairs contrary to the truth is assumed merely to increase the piquancy of the situation."[44] This is well put.

In the *Heracles* the tyrant Lycus, in the hero's absence, has usurped the throne, and as the play opens he is about to slay Amphitryon, husband to Heracles' mother; Megara, Heracles' wife; and Heracles' children. Just in the nick of time the hero returns. After a consultation with his family he goes to lie in wait for Lycus in the palace. Lycus now appears and asks where Megara is. Amphitryon replies that she is sitting a suppliant at the altar.

LYCUS
Imploring them quite uselessly to save her life.
AMPHITRYON
And calling on her dead husband, quite in vain.[45]

After a display of ruthlessness and *hybris,* Lycus goes in to his death. The character and fate of the tyrant here parallel in broad outline those of Agamemnon in Aeschylus, but since Lycus is a melodramatic villain rather than a tragic hero, and since his fate is a preliminary episode, not the catastrophe of the play, the irony is weak.

Matters are otherwise with Heracles himself. He, like a Sophoclean hero, is shown first triumphant, then in downfall and misery, and finally in noble reconciliation with his fate. "To emphasize the profound distress of Heracles most effectively, he must be presented first in the glory of success and victory. Only thus can the great pathos and irony of his fall be appreciated."[46] Madness seizes him after his victory over Lycus, and he slays his wife and children. There is therefore a pathetic irony in the scene in which, on his first arrival, his children cling to him and "he says that his homecoming is fairer to them than his departure."[47]

But as a whole *Heracles* is episodic (it falls in two), puzzling, and melodramatic. We wonder how any critic can rank it with the greatest Greek tragedies. At all events its dramatic irony is of minor importance in its total effect. Of its philosophic irony I shall speak later.

In *Hecuba* a doubly ironic touch is a remark of Agamemnon's when the Trojan queen, after the fall of the city, begs his aid or rather noninterference while she avenges herself upon an enemy. "How," asks the leader of the Greeks, "can the female sex o'er men obtain a conquest?" The audience probably knew that Hecuba and her women would soon give an answer to that question. And they certainly knew that Agamemnon's own wife would obtain a conquest also, over him, on his return to Argos.

Hecuba's enemy is King Polymestor, who, hoping for gain, had put to death one of her sons. The king is unaware that she knows his guilt. She now lures him and his children inside her tent, holding out as enticement the hope of their finding buried treasure. As he enters she says:

> Thou with thy children
> T'accomplish all the dread behests of fate,
> Shalt thither go where thou hast lodged my son.

Once inside, his children are murdered by the women and he is blinded. At the end of the play, after judging between the blind man and his punisher, Agamemnon (no doubt shaking his good Grecian head at such barbaric goings-on) offers the pious prayer:

> May success
> Attend the voyage to our native land!
> And in our mansions may we find all well,
> Freed from these dangers.[48]

After Clytemnestra, in *Iphigenia at Aulis,* has learned that Agamemnon is about to sacrifice their daughter, but before he knows that she has discovered his plot, she says to him:

> Truly, your words are fair;
> Your deeds, how shall I name them?

How indeed!

Electra (in *Orestes*) has been condemned to death by the people of Argos, along with her half-demented brother, for the murder of their mother. Menelaus has failed to protect them. They and Pylades hatch a wild plot to kill Helen. "That," says the faithful Pylades, referring to Menelaus, "would grieve his soul." Electra suggests seizing Cousin

Hermione as a hostage and says she will await the girl while the others go into the palace to slay the girl's mother. Hermione arrives fresh from leaving offerings on Clytemnestra's tomb. In this play she is very unlike her character as drawn in *Andromache;* perhaps for contrast to Electra she is here represented as a kindly person. She expresses sympathy for the condemned pair, whereat Electra humbly begs her to join Orestes inside in supplicating Helen for aid. Perhaps together, she suggests, Menelaus' wife and daughter can persuade him to save the matricides.

> Fall at thy mother's knees—how blest her state—...
> Our woes alleviate, to the trial go:
> My foot shall lead, sweet prop of all our hopes![49]

Though this Euripidean Electra is hardly an amiable character here, she is even less so in the play that takes her name. In the *Orestes* she shows real love and tenderness for her distracted brother, and her intention toward her inoffensive cousin does not go so far as murder. But in the *Electra* she is savage vengeance incarnate.

The Euripidean version of the recognition scene between Electra and Orestes, unlike the Sophoclean, has a long delay before the brother discloses himself, and the rejoicings afterward are very short. This is an unusual procedure for Euripides, who made much of his recognition scenes elsewhere; but if he wrote his play after Sophocles' had appeared, he may have wished to be different. However that may be, the delay in recognition enabled him to exploit a less hackneyed situation for sentimental irony. Electra does not know the stranger, but he knows her. In the course of his cautious questionings this irony is pointed up.

ELECTRA
My mother's blood first shedding might I die!
ORESTES
Oh, were Orestes nigh, to hear these words!

Yet he carefully refrains from saying, "I am Orestes." His caution goes so far that we suspect the author of prolonging the situation just for its own sake. There follow a scene with Auturgus, Electra's peasant husband, a long ode, and a colloquy between Electra and the paidagogos before Orestes appears again and the old man recognizes him. One can hardly agree with the critic[50] who finds this treatment less sentimental than Sophocles', and it certainly is less plausible.

The brother and sister next proceed to plot the murder of their mother and her paramour. Orestes manages the latter deed offstage. Aegisthus, we are told, greets him hospitably as a stranger and invites him to assist at a sacrifice of a bullock. Whereat Orestes takes the sacrificial meat ax, and as the king bends over to examine the beast's entrails, chops him down from behind. The adjective "manful" which one critic[51] applies to this deed hardly seems appropriate. The body of the slaughtered man is then brought onstage and Electra gloats over it in a long tirade.

It is this savage female's next task to get her mother within her savage brother's power, and she manages it by a deceit so base that we would be hard put to it to find its match in all the legends of the deceitful Greeks. She sends Clytemnestra the lying message that she has borne a child. She well knows that her mother, bad as she is, will not fail to come to her under these circumstances. With fiendish irony she uses the motherly tenderness that she knows Clytemnestra is still capable of as a trap to cause her death.

The queen's entrance has a visual irony similar to that of
the king's entrance in *Agamemnon,* for both arrive in splendor, riding in a chariot, with a train of attendants; and both
(as the audience knows) are coming to their death. The
chorus sings to Clytemnestra:

> Hail! Equal with the gods I thee revere,
> Thy riches such, and such thy happy state ...

And the whole subsequent dialogue between mother and
daughter is full of cruel irony. The body of Aegisthus has
been hidden in the hut. Clytemnestra knows nothing of his
murder. She is, in fact, in a softened mood toward her
daughter, regrets the past, and even suggests a reconciliation
with Aegisthus. Electra pretends to agree.

> ELECTRA
> My grief is great: but I will check my rage.
> CLYTEMNESTRA
> And he no longer will be harsh to thee.
> ELECTRA
> High his aspiring; in my house he dwells.[52]

Clytemnestra has come for the purpose of making the
proper sacrifices to the gods, called for by the birth of her
supposed grandchild. She now goes into the hut to perform
this pious task, as she supposes; actually, to be slain by her
son. And as she enters Electra cries:

> You will indeed sacrifice to the gods the sacrifice which you
> should make to them. The ritual basket is at hand, and the sacri-
> ficial knife is whetted. ...

This irony Professor Harsh, putting it mildly, calls "diabolical."[53]

The scene is mercifully brief, and Electra can almost be pitied as the warped product of her parents' crimes. We can offer no such excuses for the cruelty of a god. What, then, shall we call the divine irony of the Dionysus who contrives that his human enemy shall be torn in pieces by his own mother, and as a preliminary amusement plays at length with the destined victim?

The earlier scenes of *The Bacchae,* to be sure, permit Pentheus to choose his course; but once that is decided and his punishment inevitable, the fun begins. I do not mean that what follows is fun for us. We, being human, cannot help feeling much sympathy for the young king, headstrong, puritanical, and arrogant though he is. But it certainly seems to be fun for the god. If he can be taken as psychologically a real person (as dramatically he must), there is no other word more appropriate. Indeed, the situation is the familiar situation of comedy between the *alazon* (Pentheus and the *eiron* (Dionysus).

Pentheus, for what seem to him good reasons, is hostile to the new religion. Thinking the god merely one of its priests, he orders his long hair cut off, his staff snatched away, and himself held prisoner.

DIONYSUS
My Lord
God will unloose me, when I speak the word.

PENTHEUS
He may, if e'er amid his bands
Of saints he hears thy voice!

DIONYSUS
Even now he stands
Close here, and sees all that I suffer.

Sure enough, the god frees himself, and in a later scene he casts a spell on Pentheus (Murray suggests hypnotism) under which the king acts as if drunk, reveals a hidden longing to be a Peeping Tom to the bacchantes on the mountains, and becomes the willing tool of the god. The better to spy, the god dresses him as a woman with long hair (an ironical reversal of the earlier scene) and assures him that he himself will guide him secretly where he can observe all.

DIONYSUS [*to* PENTHEUS]
He who erst was wroth,
Goes with us now in gentleness. He hath
Unsealed thine eyes to see what thou shouldst see.

Pentheus now feels a god's strength within him.

DIONYSUS
Thy soul,
Being once so sick, now stands as it should stand.

Pentheus exults in the expectation of trapping the bacchantes.

DIONYSUS
But on;
With me into thine ambush shalt thou come
Unscathed; then let another bear thee home!

PENTHEUS
The Queen, my mother.

DIONYSUS
Marked of every eye.

PENTHEUS
For that I go?

DIONYSUS
Thou shalt be borne on high!

[Those are indeed ironic lines for listeners who know the end of the play: how Agave will enter carrying her son's

severed head stuck on a stick, and triumphing in the delusion that she has slain a lion with her hands.]

PENTHEUS
That were like pride!
DIONYSUS
Thy mother's hands shall share
Thy carrying.
PENTHEUS
Nay; I need not such soft care!
DIONYSUS
So soft?[54]

Sophocles, in his extant plays, never uses an irony so savage as this. Nor has any other important dramatist. The
nearest approach to it, perhaps, is Seneca's. Atreus has
feasted his brother Thyestes, unknowing, on the bodies of
his own sons. The replete and drunken father expresses a
desire to see his children.

ATREUS
Father, spread wide thy arms, they come, they come.
(*The platter is uncovered.*)
Dost thou indeed now recognize thy sons?
THYESTES
I recognize my brother![55]

Both Sophocles and Euripides had already dramatized this
legend. Seneca probably got this amiable *coup de théâtre*
from one of them. Which is more likely to have been his
model?

Of Agave's exultation when she enters with her son's head
on the stick, a critic says that it "forms perhaps the most
powerful scene of dramatic irony in all tragedy."[56] One
might agree with this opinion if one substituted "horrible"

for "powerful." If this irony is more powerful than that of *Oedipus,* it is so only in being, like a punch in the belly, a shock to the viscera—which the irony of Sophocles is not. The queen tore her son's body apart with her fingers. She probably appeared with her arms still dripping with gore, her garment disheveled, and prancing and staggering like the mad woman she is. This final *coup* is a sight so ghastly that it ought to turn the stomach of anyone not habituated to slaughterhouses. Modern critics who accept the effect with calm admiration are surely not so habituated, and we can explain their sangfroid only by concluding that they do not think of the play as something to be judged on the stage.

Even Gilbert Murray, notwithstanding his interest in the theater, is only concerned, when he comes to this scene,[57] to show how it proves his theory of the origin of Greek tragedy in the "ancient ritual" of the Vegetation God torn apart and resurrected. So delighted is he by the way in which the scene illustrates this "sparagmos" that he does not consider it dramatically at all.

That Euripides' taste ran often to such gruesomenesses is indicated by the plots of some of his lost tragedies. The daughters of Pelias, for example, in the play named from them, are persuaded by Medea to cut their father in pieces and boil him in a pot, thinking Medea will rejuvenate him. When she does not, they have to flee for their lives. An ironic joke on them! Ino, in the tragedy named for her, has twin children, and disappears. King Athamas, her husband, then marries Themis, who also has twins. Ino returns secretly disguised as a slave. Themis, jealous of Ino's twins, plots to murder them and consults with the supposed slave about ways and means. Ino suggests putting white clothes on Themis' children and black on her own, for identification. Of course she does the opposite and Themis kills her own babes. An ironic joke on her![58]

PHILOSOPHICAL IRONY

It is natural to try to explain a great poet's work throughout as the expression of reasoned intention. Even a poet himself may do so after the event, as Poe did in his account of how he composed "The Raven." But no one has ever believed Poe, and if anything is sure about the creative process, it is that the inventive faculty—call it intuition, imagination, "inspiration," or what you will—plays a much larger part in it than analysis or logic. The latter faculties operate chiefly to check and weigh and correct imaginative creations after their setting down.

Thus *a priori* it is improbable that Euripides was so pure a rationalist as Verrall made out. To him the poet was always consistently attacking the Olympians, either as a tongue-in-cheek satirist or as direct polemist, and all the contradictions of the plays are explicable on these terms. "There is perhaps no one among the great writers of Athens," he tells us, "who does not prove himself on occasion a master in the art of hinting. Aeschylus, a man sincere if ever man was, was so exercised in ambiguity that scarcely a modern comes near him, and wields it, as in the person of Clytemnestra, literally like a fiend. The irony of Sophocles, of Plato, of Demosthenes and many others is famous. ... But in Euripides it was the base of the fabric."[59]

We can agree with the last sentence, but not on the ground that Euripides was simply a rationalist. He was

more absorbed than any other great dramatist in the study
of irrational feeling, ranging from nostalgic dream, sentiment, and pathos, to the heroics of self-sacrifice, and on to
the brutalities of savage hate, blood lust, and raving madness. These passions are in his characters, to be sure; but
Euripides, being a poet, had first to feel them in his fancy.
Rationalist in one of his dual natures, he was irrationalist in
the other. I said earlier, "If any poet's soul ever fought a
'civil war in the cave,' this one's did." His deepest irony,
then, is not a cool intellectual irony, but the expression of
this war.

Of his extant plays, those are least characteristic and effective in which he subdues this duality for the sake of propaganda. During the early years of the Peloponnesian War, as
we noted earlier, he seems to have been carried away by
patriotic fervor. The *Heracleidae* and the *Suppliants* glorify
Athens and righteous war with apparently no *arrière-pen-
sées,* and the *Andromache* vilifies Sparta in a spirit of *Gott
straffe England.*[80] If there is underlying irony in these plays,
it is very well hidden. Nor need we assume it, to explain
how he could later on attack all war with such disillusioned
bitterness in *The Trojan Women.* The effect of events on his
sensitive spirit, as the war dragged on and his fellow citizens
descended to every baseness and cruelty, is a sufficient explanation for the change.

Without going all the way with Verrall, however, we can
agree that Euripides' most noted plays generally show skepticism toward the gods, not merely by occasional disparag-
ing remarks, but by an ironic light that colors the entire
action. Furthermore, his skepticism leads him in some to
treat also wicked human characters with what seems in-

dulgence, and good characters with cruelty. "This bewildering shift of sympathy," Murray tells us, "is common in Euripides."[61] It is most striking, as we shall see later, in *Medea* and *The Bacchae,* but it is observable even in his tragicomedies and melodramas.

In *Alcestis,* Apollo has a role of dubious dignity, and the mightiest of Grecian heroes, Heracles, is made to appear on the stage tipsy. *Iphigenia in Tauris* seems superficially to be orthodox in its treatment of the gods, but Verrall makes a plausible case when he insists that it loses much by such an interpretation. "The deepest part, the real substantial *tragic* foundation, is cut away. Properly understood it is not a melodrama, it is a tragedy."[62] "Properly understood" means understood in the study, not in the theater: in the latter place the play is a romantic melodrama with a happy ending. However, even there it has ironical ambiguity enough to impress the sensitive.

To Verrall, brother and sister are victims of a religion in danger. The deceit they play on Thoas, with the theft of the holy image, is shameful, but the real shame falls on the Apollonian oracle that commanded such deeds. There is no dramatic need for the *deus ex machina* at the end, since the Greeks would escape if the poet did not arbitrarily conjure up a contrary wind. This curious ending "acquires a serious meaning only on the supposition that the miraculous conclusion is mere irony and pretence."[63] What shall we think? Certainly the moral issue is dubious, as Goethe felt when he made his sentimental alteration of the plot. And certainly the ending is puzzling.

Helen seems to ridicule not only the legends of old Greece, but oracles also. Apollo's conduct, as described in the *Ion,* is disgraceful, and Verrall of course considers the play an almost open attack on the god. The religious explanation of Ion's birth is to him "completely incredible and inapplicable to the facts," and "is revealed with transparent irony."[64] "It is not too much to say," he concludes, "that on the Euripidean stage whatever is said by a divinity is to be regarded, in general, as *ipso facto* discredited. It is in all cases objectionable from the author's point of view, and almost always a lie."[65] No unprejudiced spectator in the theater would reach so extreme a conclusion. He would find the *Ion* an entertaining romantic comedy or melodrama, with charming lyrics, comic and sentimental scenes, and a happy ending. Its religious and moral irony, therefore, are something for the more thoughtful to note if they will; it is not dramatically or emotionally compulsory.

Euripides, however, is seldom so light in mood when dealing with such matters. In *Heracles,* the hero, after saving his family from being slaughtered by a tyrant, is deliberately driven mad by the gods, so that he slaughters his family himself. This is an ironical reversal indeed; and if we take it with normal sympathies, it condemns the gods by implication as powerfully as anything the author wrote. In *Orestes* we are horrified by the savagery of brother and sister, thrilled by the mad scene, excited by the melodramatic peripeties, weirdly amused and shocked by the Asiatic eunuch who grovels for his life before Orestes, and at the end amazed (flabbergasted is a better word) by the most extraordinary resolution *deo ex machina* in all the poet's works. In this, Apollo makes the following announcements: Helen was not slain by Orestes, but has been snatched off—to heaven, of all places. Menelaus shall forbear his "fiery rage." Bloodthirsty Electra shall be rewarded by marriage with Pylades. Orestes, after ridding himself at Athens of the taint of matricide, shall marry—Hermione! To Verrall this denouement is "transparently perfunctory and ironical."[66] Murray, on the contrary, attempts to justify it by talking of hypnotism and mysticism.[67] If we may take the unscholarly view of an average spectator in the theater, we shall find it, as most critics before Murray have done, artificial and unconvincing. But the role of the god is in any view an unimpressive one; and if Athenians suspected Euripides of ironic implications they may have interpreted the scene as Verrall did.

The conduct of the gods is particularly dubious in *Hippolytus* and *Electra,* and the degree to which the author expects us to sympathize with the protagonists is particularly uncertain. Phaedra is destroyed by Aphrodite merely as a means of revenge on Hippolytus. And the motive for the goddess's revenge is merely that the youth scorns her and prefers to worship Artemis. Make as much as we can of the young prince's *hybris* toward Aphrodite (or, if one prefers a naturalistic terminology, the danger he runs in suppressing a basic instinct), he suffers far beyond his deserts. And if, as the poet has Aphrodite tell us, Phaedra's passion is not her own fault, but solely of the goddess's making, the unhappy queen is even more obviously an innocent victim of a wrangle between two goddesses who are "capricious, vindictive, and jealous of each other."[68] Yet can we be sure that we are expected to condemn the immortal ladies? The action of the play moves on two planes at once. On the human plane, we are likely to find in the prince and his mother-in-law faults enough to give their misfortunes some moral basis, and at the same time to sympathize with them enough to feel a tragic sense at their deaths.

Not so Electra and Orestes; they are almost wholly unsympathetic. Perhaps, as some critics think, Euripides was making a study of extreme villainy similar to the *Medea*,[69] or wished to go counter to Sophocles and condemn blood vengeance.[70] He certainly gave his audience an hour and a half of savage melodrama, and I doubt whether many of them got any moral message out of it.

What critics, on the other hand, can get out of it may sometimes be surprising. One of them tells us that Electra shows "no vindictiveness," that she is not fierce like Sophocles' Electra, and that the play is a "more pleasant" one than those of the elder poets![71] No matter how well founded one may think a judgment about this dramatist, it is possible to find it contradicted by somebody.

The *dei ex machina* who command the resolution of this play are Castor and Pollux. "The Dioscuri end the *Electra*," writes Kitto,[72] "partly because it is so ridiculous for a woman like Electra to have uncles in the sky, partly because it is so damaging for the newest of the divinities to say what these say about Apollo." He generalizes: "Euripides liked to produce gods, especially Apollo, at the end less to cut the knot than to cut their own throats." This sounds like Verrall. Contrariwise, Grube tells us that the contradictions in Euripides between fifth-century religious thought and the facts of the legend are "not deliberate but accidental"; "nor is whatever indirect religious propaganda they may contain a primary concern of the dramatist."[73]

What are we to think? It is better to ask what the Athenian spectator thought. The play was written for him to see and hear. If he was a simple person, he must have taken the resolution as seriously meant; if he was a regular playgoer—and he probably was,—he must have thought it far-fetched. If, like Aristophanes, he believed the poet to be attacking religion, he probably thought much as Kitto does. It is entirely possible that Euripides expected to puzzle some of his audience. The ambiguity of this theatrical situation, with some of the spectators solemn and amazed and others ironically pained and amused, is one of a peculiar double irony. Its only notable parallel elsewhere is the later drama of Ibsen, as we shall see.

Medea is an even more striking case of moral ambiguity—the most striking of all except *The Bacchae*. Jason is selfish, but he is not a fiend. Yet it is the fiend with whom the author induces us to sympathize, and it is the fiend who triumphs, slaughtering not merely her rival but her own children in order to make Jason suffer. And after all, what is Jason's crime? Nothing worse than having put her aside (he was not legally married to her) in order to marry someone else legitimately and better his worldly position. Reno is full of people like Jason, and the public conscience does not think their children and their prospective brides should be slaughtered.

In condemning dramas generally as immoral, Rousseau asked, "What does one learn from *Medea* except how cruel and unnatural a mother can be made by jealousy?"[74] He could have made a stronger case had he pointed out how audiences in the theater are seduced to favor the passionate, no matter how wicked, as against the cold and rational. But of course Rousseau, who said that "cold reason has never done anything illustrious," was on the side of passion. It is a fact, however, that no merely intelligent person can ever be a really appealing hero in a play. Audiences do not care for intelligence. To make a character sympathetic the author must make him emotional about something. Hence Jason is no hero. And it is an ironic treatment indeed that this great hero of Grecian folklore is thus reduced to a mean egotist and a stuffed shirt; that he is more sinned against than sinning, yet we almost rejoice at his misery.

What was Euripides trying to do in *Medea?* Perhaps the strongest case for a tragic interpretation is made by Kitto.[75] Medea to him is not an Aristotelian heroine, for her fault is her whole nature, no mere *hamartia*. And the play is not a mere character study: that is too simple an explanation. "It is not melodrama, for Medea, though extreme, is true, and her character and deeds leave us with something more than the mere excitement of a strong story." "She is tragic in that her passions are stronger than her reason." The tragedy of the play is "that such a character should exist at all." Hence the horrors are justified, as they are not in Sophocles, where tragedy is the ruin of a noble hero. Euripides "asks us to feel terror when we hear of what her passion leads her to do, pity for all who are broken, tragic enlightenment when we see that all are victims of a primitive force."

At the opposite pole from this scholarly interpretation is the effect on average spectators. *Medea* was a highly popular stage play in ancient times, and is one of the most frequently produced of the Greek dramas today. The reason for its popularity is not that it makes a philosophical demonstration of the dangers of primitive forces in human nature, but that it is a violent, spectacular, and thrilling melodrama.

Between these extremes lies the position of thoughtful folk who feel the obvious dramatic effects as the average spectator does, but who are troubled by the way in which their moral sentiments are upset. To them the play is either a perverse product of an immoral genius or the honest statement by a moral genius of a view of the world in which ideals are frustrated and the good in us destroyed by the evil in us. In this last view *Medea* is a projection in dramatic terms of the conflict in the poet's soul, and hence a work of bitter irony.

The Bacchae in its attitude toward religion is the most ambiguous of the plays. Norwood calls it an enigma.[76] We have a choice of explanations. Is it, as Murray finds, "impossible to deny," "a heartfelt glorification of 'Dionysus'"?[77] Or was the poet piously recommending "the acceptance of the national faith and traditions as the only ground of a contented and happy life," and exhibiting "the mischief of an unsound and irreligious philosophy"?[78] Or shall we agree with Wilamowitz' observation: "Nobody can misunderstand Euripides worse than in seeing it [*The Bacchae*] as a conversion to old wives' tales."[79]

Recent critics often argue that Euripides intended this play, like *Medea* and *Hippolytus,* to represent the clash of natural forces with fallible reason. In this view, Dionysus is "the elemental urges of the human heart, the deep passions,"[80] or "the symbol of an ecstasy that is above, or beside, reason, one which the plodding rationalist rejects at his peril."[81] This argument is all very well as an explanation of why Euripides the rationalist should apparently, in his last work, attack rationalism; but it has little bearing on the play as a drama. In the theater the audience will see Dionysus as a man (or as a god with human traits of character), not as a symbol. And we are judging the irony of the play by its effect in the theater.

We may, nevertheless, wonder what Euripides' opinion really was. Norwood insists that he "had a definite opinion about the two questions: Does the god Dionysus exist? Is his religion a blessing to humanity? His opinion could have been written down in a few lucid sentences. Had this not been so, he would have postponed beginning his play until it was."[82] But does every work of art, as this critic insists, spring "from a definite concept held by the artist, some piece of reality clearly understood and sincerely felt"? Clarity was a Greek virtue, but clarity may be the result of seeing reality too simply. Euripides, whatever else he was, was not simple-minded. In his old age he was surely able to see his own self-division and to dramatize it.

The simplest solution to "the riddle of *The Bacchae*" may be acceptance of its complexity as intentional. In this view, Euripides was putting on the stage the war in his own soul. Pentheus is Euripides, and Dionysus is Euripides, and the defeat of Pentheus is the poet's pessimistic commentary on all efforts of reason to explain and govern the world. I cannot believe that the poet had any concern whether the god existed. I think the traditional ritual of the tragic performance which Murray emphasizes as making this "the most formal Greek play extant"[83] simply served his need for a symbolical frame.

If this be the case, there is no play in existence more bitterly and pessimistically ironical than *The Bacchae*. If this be the case, Euripides did not cease to be mindful of the spectators in the theater (for he gives them perhaps the most thrilling and spectacular drama he ever wrote), but he also eased the burden of his soul's torment in terms that few spectators would ever guess. Or that few critics would ever guess. He was not trying to tell the world, though he may have known a few who could read the riddle. He was exorcising his own demons. Hence in Pentheus the poet represents not merely "the plodding rationalist," but his own idealism, his own moral earnestness, his own pride of intellect: and he lets those spiritual qualities be torn limb from limb by the subliminal savagery of human nature—which gave them birth.

"It is then actually the tragedy of his own life that is represented here," says Steiger.[84] Yes, and it is his life tragedy in a deeper sense than the lifelong polemic against traditional beliefs in the gods which Steiger emphasizes. These beliefs could have had no literal meaning to him by then. But the gods could certainly represent forces innate in man: more particularly, in the poet himself. Looking back over his life and over the vicissitudes of his beloved Athens, as he could see them all in perspective from his exile in Macedonia, he must have felt as did the aging Ibsen when he said, through his master builder, "Nothing really built; nor anything sacrificed for the chance of building. Nothing, nothing! the whole is nothing."

CHAPTER IX

Ibsen

I T IS TO IBSEN that we turn last. None who has come after
him has yet proved to be of his stature, and the great
dramatists who preceded him, after the Greeks, were
not ironists as he was.

Shakespeare had his periods of fundamental questioning
when, as Dowden described it, he was "in the depths"; and
such plays as *Measure for Measure* and *Timon of Athens*
are expressions of them. But his great works rest on the
unshaken assumption that human goodness is a reality—
indeed, the only ultimately important reality. Surely this is
what we feel in the darkest passages of *Macbeth* or *Lear;*
and when he ended his career with *The Tempest,* the assurance is serenely manifest. Shakespeare used irony on occasion, but he did not build on it. We have argued against
overemphasizing the irony in *Othello.* The ambiguous
prophecies of the witches in *Macbeth* have ironical consequences which make this play perhaps a better choice for
tragic irony than *Othello;* but even *Macbeth* is ironic only
incidentally. The grim joke that fate, through the witches,
plays on the usurper might have been made central and
essential, but as the play is written there are many other
matters that absorb our attention and rouse us to unironic
emotion. Hamlet is an ironic personality, and there are

ironic elements in his tragedy; but the ironic elements are
not built up for effect, and the prince himself rises above
defensive irony to a spiritual calm and readiness that triumph over fate.

A painstaking search through the plays would undoubtedly discover many excellent lines of verbal irony and incidents involving irony of events; but unless the searcher fell
into the fallacy of finding irony simply because he was looking for it, in speeches and in events that would not strike
an uninvolved playgoer as ironic, or unless he defined irony
in a highly special sense, as did Friedrich Schlegel and his
followers, he could hardly challenge our general impression
that Shakespeare was fundamentally an ironist in his tragedy no more than in his comedy.

We have a like impression of Corneille, the worshiper of
heroic honor. Or rather, it is much stronger, because Corneille never allows himself to be amused by anything when
writing a tragedy, and he often strains the concept of
"gloire" to the verge of absurdity without awareness of the
danger he runs. Shakespeare, had he so chosen, could have
been a great ironist. He lets Falstaff deal with the point of
honor comically, and if he had cared to take a Cornelian
theme for a play—the irresistible force of Love meeting the
immovable body of Honor in head-on collision,—he could
hardly have developed it with the Frenchman's unvarying
solemnity. The Frenchmen of the seventeenth century kept
their tragedy and their comedy in separate compartments.
They were undoubtedly capable of irony, but their dramatic
principles forbade it.

Certainly Racine was capable of it, for by temperament
he was sharply satirical and bitingly critical, and his one

comedy, *Les Plaideurs,* shows what gifts in those directions he had. But he subdued his temperament otherwise to the prevailing pattern of neoclassical tragedy. That forbade any note of comedy; but even so, ironic twists might have appeared, except that his Jansenist morality prevailed over his temperament. Even in his worldly period he was the pious Jansenist in his attitude toward his passionate heroines. As a man he admired them, but as a Christian he condemned them. If he had allowed any ironic doubts about Original Sin and Divine Grace, he could not, as he did, have condemned Phèdre out of hand as a sinner; he would inevitably have been wryly amused by the way she is tricked by life, or fate, or the gods, into becoming evil in spite of herself. Racine treats Athalie with cruel irony, but she is the enemy of righteousness, and his purpose in this play is to exalt Jehovah and His prophets.

Unlike Racine, Ibsen was never able to return to the faith of his childhood, though like Racine he never shook off its influence on his moral thinking. The clash between aspiration and reality was a fundamental conflict in him throughout his life, and as a consequence it is a fundamental conflict in all his plays also. Sometimes it finds expression in earnest tragic utterance, but it is more often conveyed with ironic duplicity.

As we noted earlier, there are striking parallels between Ibsen and Euripides. Steiger[1] lists four principal ones:

1. Both were moralists, attacking outworn ideals or conventions on the basis of a more spiritual concept of morality. Both were inspired by a missionary spirit; both aroused violent opposition; and both remained steadfast.

---

[1] For notes to chapter ix see pp. 269–270.

2. Both put women first in many of their plays, giving them stronger characters than the men. Both dealt with marriage problems in a way that challenged the masculine conventions of their times.

3. Both were concerned for fatherland. Neither was a partisan; both showed love of country by criticizing its faults. Euripides, however, was no such political nihilist as Ibsen was.

4. Both were natural fighters, "fanatics of truth." Both worked for life, not abstract theory; their dramas are not mere problem plays.

These excellent and striking parallels could be extended interestingly, and Steiger gives us many interesting comparisons between particular plays. One can hardly go as far as he does in assuming that a knowledge of the Norwegian poet enables us to explain unknown or uncertain characteristics of the Greek. (I do not claim that my explanation of *The Bacchae* is more than a plausible theory.) But the likeness of the two men is remarkable; and it is so in no feature more than the one central to our discussion—their division of soul or spiritual irony. This is much more fundamental than those which Steiger emphasizes. It is indeed so fundamental in Ibsen that it hides itself behind the immediate subject matter of the plays, and so has been too little noted by criticism. But when we look for it we find it in every play he wrote. Whether, because we are looking for it, we find more of it than the facts warrant may be judged by the evidence I am about to offer.

In dealing with such a theme it is extremely valuable to know the significant facts of the subject's formative years. We know almost nothing about Euripides'. Fortunately we know a good deal about Ibsen's. He was born (1828) in a small town near the southern coast of Norway—an isolated and spiritually narrow community. He felt confined and stifled by it, and later he left Norway entirely in search of spiritual freedom in a larger world. But of course the world of Italy and Germany was not really his, and he never felt at home there. And ironically, when as an old man he returned to Norway to stay, he found it also alien to him. Consider the mournful letter he wrote from Christiania in 1897 to his Danish friend: "Here all the sounds are closed, in every acceptation of the word—and all the channels of intelligence are blocked. Oh, dear Brandes, it is not without its consequences that a man lives for twenty-seven years in the wider, emancipated and emancipating spiritual conditions of the great world. [He had lived mainly in Dresden and Munich.] Up here, by the fjords, is my native land. But—but—but! Where am I to find my homeland?"[2] His spiritual exile gave him extraordinary detachment, but it diminished his happiness.

The motives that pushed him into exile were due to more profound forces than the isolation and narrowness of the town of Skien. His mother and sister Hedwig were ardent pietistic Lutherans who tried to bring the boy into the fold with them. But something in him—probably a combination of the strong individualism and skeptical intelligence he manifests later—kept him aloof. He seems to have harbored a sense of guilt for having refused their loving appeals. It must have been strong and profound; he must have thrust it back almost below the threshold of consciousness. Certainly its existence helps explain both the intense moral earnestness of his mature work and its lack of spiritual assurance; certainly a feeling of guilt becomes manifest in the half-autobiographical plays of his last years, as we shall see later.

He would not have felt such guilt if he had not been very strongly drawn to religion. He had, as I have written elsewhere, "the emotional habit pattern of a Protestant preacher of the most evangelical persuasion, but without the preacher's faith." At first, as he was maturing, he sought a substitute for the faith he could not accept. "Failing, he grew disillusioned and bitter, and at length desperate. But all his life he was the moralist, the stern searcher of souls, the searcher above all of his own soul. He tells us so.

> What is life? a fighting
> In heart and in brain with Trolls.
> Poetry? that means writing
> Doomsday-accounts of our souls."[3]

Particular events of his boyhood added to his spiritual homelessness. His father belonged to one of the town's "better families," and during Ibsen's earliest years was well-to-do, fond of entertaining, and looked up to. But when the boy was eight years old his father went bankrupt and took to drink. From affluence and respect the family were reduced to poverty and social abasement. Ibsen's extreme sensitiveness and pride received hurts that help explain his later financial caution, his suspicions of strangers, and his touchy anxiety for the outward marks of respect and honor, like medals on his frock coat. The "rich Jon Gynt" whom Peer remembers is a sketch of the poet's own father. Probably Ibsen, like Peer, recalled those early sociable times with envy, for his father's failure had shut him out from them, and when he himself was finally rich enough and honored enough to afford them, and far more, he lacked the capacity to enjoy them. ("Where's the lost young man?")

Again, the family was so poor that he could not have a proper education and was forced at fifteen to leave home to earn a living in a distant village as a druggist's apprentice. And from then on he had to struggle against poverty until after the publication of *Brand* in 1866. The struggle developed the dramatist's powers of representing tragic conflict, but it dried up the springs of lightheartedness. He was thirty-eight when it was over.

Temperamentally he was compounded of contraries. He was shy, yet assertive; introverted, yet moved by evangelical impulses; timid and even—in a physical sense—cowardly, yet as a dramatist undaunted by the harshest criticism; thin-skinned, yet satirical; idealistic and poetic, yet keenly observant of things as they are; self-critical, yet vain; stiff and reclusive toward society, yet hungry for love and affection; without a faith, yet deeply religious. These contraries can be ranged on two opposing sides as belonging to two antagonistic persons or natures which dwelt and fought in his soul.

One of the two was domestic. Like all thoroughly masculine men, he longed for love not merely in a narrowly sexual sense, but in the sense that includes romantic idealizations of women, desire for mutual tenderness, and yearning for home and children. Other great dramatists have felt such desires, but none has worked them into the substance of his plays as Ibsen did. Shaw, indeed, in his almost total lack of such feelings, is in this fundamental sense Ibsen's opposite, incapable of appreciating one whole side of his master's character. I have elsewhere called Ibsen a "poet of

love"; and so he is—not of the easy romantic love that popular movies exploit, but of love denied or destroyed by
egotism.

The egotist was the other of his two personalities. He
was intensely ambitious and had impulses to ruthless self-
assertion, not simply in the fashion of Peer Gynt, who when
the ship founders drowns the cook to save himself—for this
is the expression of a mere animal instinct,—but more profoundly in the pursuit of a selfish ambition. Peer lay under
the hedge and dreamed of being emperor. Almost all of
Ibsen's male characters drive themselves (or are driven) by
some such egotistical dream. (Notable exceptions are Dr.
Wangel in *The Lady from the Sea* and Dr. Stockman, who,
though vain and ambitious for applause, is warm-hearted
and generous). This dream is what moves Catiline, hero of
the play Ibsen wrote at the age of twenty-one, and Rubek,
hero of *When We Dead Awaken,* which he wrote fifty
years later. There are Skule and Haakon and Bishop Nicholas (Skule and the bishop remarkable results, in part, of
self-analysis) in *The Pretenders.* There is Brand, the missionary with more ambition than love in his heart. There
are the Emperor Julian, Bernick, Helmer, Ekdal, Rosmer
(a subtle study of unconscious egotism), Tesman, Solness,
Allmers (a pious fraud), and Borkman. The last wanted to
be a Napoleon of finance; in his delusion of grandeur, after
his failure and imprisonment, he even assumes the Napo-
leonic pose awaiting the arrival of an imaginary delegation
of humble bankers. Ibsen himself wanted to be a Napoleon
of poetry. In a poem of the late 'fifties, "On the Heights,"
he describes how the young artist learns to live "above life's
line of snow" and watch his home burn down, his mother

buried, his sweetheart wed to another, without emotion except for the esthetic effect of the pictures.

The point to remember always about these partial self-portraits is that their egotism represents only one side of Ibsen's nature. "The ambivalence of ambition and love in Ibsen's mind ... is indicated by the strange and ironical ending [of "On the Heights"]:

> Parched are the veins where a flood tide ran,
> And I surely find, when my heart I scan,
>   All symptoms of petrifaction.

Yet:

> Up here on the fells must be freedom and God,
> Men do but grope, in the valley."[4]

The tender, altruistic Ibsen is much less exemplified in his men than in his women. He could on occasion exhibit a female egotist—a Hilda Wangel, a Hedda Gabler; and after Solveig of *Peer Gynt* he ceased to represent the Romantic dream girls of the youthful plays and always drew his women realistically. But it is the women who love unselfishly and deeply. There is a beautiful brief study of such a woman in *The Pretenders:* Margrete, Earl Skule's daughter, who marries Haakon and by her love saves his soul from the sin that destroys his rival. There is Agnes, of course, in *Brand:* a full-length portrait, believable and moving, though greatly idealized. *Pillars of Society* has three such women: Mrs. Bernick, Martha, and Lona Hessel. Nora was intended, at least, to be another, and at the end of the play she may have become one. Mrs. Alving is one of the noblest studies of the type in all drama. Dr. Stockman's wife and daughter are others; little Hedwig in *The Wild Duck;* Rebecca West, as she becomes at the end; Rita Allmers (at least in comparison to her fatuous spouse); and Ella Rentheim.

Ella (in *John Gabriel Borkman*) is Ibsen's judge. When Borkman tells her that though he had loved her he had nevertheless married her sister for money, Ella calls it "your great, your terrible crime ... that crime for which there is no forgiveness." "The great, unpardonable sin," she concludes, "is to murder the love-life in a human soul." It is true that in a much earlier play Bernick commits the same sin and wins forgiveness; but the ending of *Pillars of Society* is Ibsen's one weak yielding to theatrical convention. Bernick belongs in prison, and probably would have been sent there if Ibsen had ever revised the play. Instead he wrote *Borkman*. And elsewhere he shows time and again that this sin brings destruction. Because of it Skule loses the kingdom to Haakon and meets death. Brand is overwhelmed by the avalanche because, as the Voice tells him, he had forgotten that God is the God of love. Rosmer, too weak to rise to love, commits suicide. Solness, made temporarily insane by the Nemesis his egotism has aroused, falls to death from the tower. Borkman climbs in the snow to die of the cold in his heart. Rubek and the woman he has injured climb the mountain to die together.

That Ibsen took this sin with such profound seriousness may seem strange to more lighthearted persons. But he grew up in an atmosphere of extreme pietistic Protestantism, and his nature was permanently bent in the mold of Protestant idealism and soul searching.

A genuine Protestant is a person of religious earnestness who refuses to yield his will to a priest and who insists on the responsibility of the individual to his own conscience.

He cannot lighten the burden of his own guilt by laying it on another's shoulders through confession and penance. He sees society as an aggregate of individuals each engaged in a never-ending struggle between good and evil in his own soul. Each must fight for his own salvation, and each has the duty to help his fellows. To refuse such help—to disobey the command of his conscience—is a mortal sin. But to follow this imperative may sometimes require of him an exercise of will beyond human power. Brand, whom Ibsen called "myself in my best moments," is an idealized projection of this heroic will. Yet Brand is at the end condemned for lacking love. The austerity of Protestant morality in its emphasis on will, and its egotism in its emphasis on individual conscience, are both mitigated in its best exemplars by the spirit of Christian charity. In Ibsen there was not so much mitigation as a clash.

In his youth his Protestant moral heroism was also colored by the Romanticism of the period. Thus the heroes of his early plays were noble-souled vikings or Schilleresque rebels; the heroines, strong-minded Valkyries or patient Griseldas. But even in the earliest play, if we look beneath the Romantic *décor,* we can see something else which is not Romantic; and in *Love's Comedy,* his eighth play (published 1862), no one can miss it. Here the poetic hero and the idealistic heroine decide not to marry, but to part, so that their love may remain unspotted by petty domesticity. This Romantic paradox (later a favorite of Browning's) is so far-stretched as to be ridiculous, and we suspect that Ibsen was almost aware of the fact. He was by then himself happily married; and he was certainly not in a serious Romantic mood in bringing into the play, as an awful example of the effect of domesticity, a clergyman saddled with twelve children and expecting more, who used to be a poet and is now a windbag.

The satirical Ibsen is always lurking behind the youthful plays of heroics; here he comes boldly into the open. Yet the theme of the play is the theme of Protestant idealism: the hero has a mission and must sacrifice everything to it, even, if need be, his love and happiness.

The satirical Ibsen existed in the druggist's apprentice at Grimstad whose pranks, he says, "brought down upon me the ill-will of all the respectable citizens," as for example making a drawing which represented a local gentleman drunk and embracing his horse under the impression that he was kissing his sweetheart. This satirical Ibsen became the disillusioned realist of the 'eighties who saw the whole race of man no longer idealistically, as God's children, but biologically, as an animal species with ineradicable traits of the beast. And it is the same Ibsen who in his last play, *When We Dead Awaken* (1899), speaks through the sculptor Rubek. Behind his popular portrait busts, says the sculptor, "there is something equivocal, something cryptic. I alone can see it. And it amuses me unspeakably.—On the surface I give them the 'striking likeness,' as they call it, that they all stand and gape at in astonishment,—but at bottom they are all respectable, pompous horse faces, and self-opinionated donkey muzzles, and lop-eared, low-browed dog skulls, and fatted swine snouts—and sometimes dull, brutal bull fronts as well."

If the poet had grown up in an environment of faith like that of his early years he might have been spared this violent disillusionment. But his era, like that of Euripides, was a time of widespread doubt and religious disintegration. Though he was essentially a dramatist, interested in concrete personalities rather than abstract thought, he was profoundly affected by the philosophical currents of his time. Hence the idealist in Ibsen continued to strive with the satirist in an unavailing search for what his Emperor Julian calls "the third empire"—a religion that could satisfy modern man both emotionally and intellectually.

"He never reconciled these impulses in himself, but he objectified them in his characters and made them fight to more definite conclusions. Hence his plays are fiercely dramatic. They show us people who will, passionately and with high seriousness, and who struggle unremittingly."

"Viewed as a whole, as recorded in the plays it [this struggle] has two phases like a tragic plot: the rising action, in which Ibsen strove to find a religious reconciliation, and which culminated [in *Emperor and Galilean*, 1873] in climactic failure; and the falling action, in which he faced the bitterness of his defeat and turned from the poetry of ultimate ideals to the prosaic analysis of particular falsities in the relationships of men and women. This analysis, unsustained by faith, led him gradually to such disillusionment and spiritual desolation that his courage in facing them directly, and his mental power in preserving his sanity and objectivity, are alike extraordinary."[5]

Thus far I have tried to sketch the nature of Ibsen's self-division in broad outline so that when we turn to concrete ironies from particular plays they may take on coherence. We have now to consider the plays in detail.

One might begin with *Catiline*, written in Grimstad when Ibsen was an ill-schooled youth. He had decided to try for the university and had been boning up his Latin. It is characteristic of his ironic temper that in reading Cicero he sympathized with the object of the orator's invective, the rebel against Order and Respectability. The Catiline he draws is unintentionally absurd, but it is significant that, like his creator, he is torn between ambition and love, which are symbolized by the two opposing types of woman, strong-minded temptress and faithful wife, between whom he vacillates.

This conflict, which underlies almost all of Ibsen's twenty-five plays, is not in itself ironical, of course; it becomes so only when Ibsen sees it with grim humor, realizing both the pain and the comedy of it. But since it was his temper to do just that, we might reasonably expect such an underlying irony in many of the plays where it has seldom been noted.

An irony that is not noted, even by a scholar, is not, speaking strictly, a dramatic irony, for it certainly will not make an effect on an average audience. There is much in Ibsen that an audience misses. But with subtle dramatists like Euripides and Ibsen we are forced to go beyond the dramatically obvious. In time, audiences also grow more subtle. There was little comprehension of *The Lady from the Sea* in 1888; but when it was played in Oslo in 1928, according to a biographer,° it was very fresh and significant, for by then psychoanalytical literature had enlightened the spectators to appreciate its meaning. Moreover, a director who is aware of the subtleties in his script can often project them dramatically through his actors. Other plays than *The Lady from the Sea* may gain new life and freshness in revival if produced with such understanding. At all events, we cannot really understand Ibsen's irony, even his striking surface irony, without going beyond the theatrically evident. We shall limit ourselves to the most striking instances.

The Pretenders has been too much neglected in the theater outside Scandinavia, for it is a great play. With judicious cuts (for its last acts drag), it should powerfully move any intelligent audience, provided actors could be found equal to the main roles. The central theme is the struggle between Skule and Haakon for the kingship of Norway. Skule fails because, in the final analysis, he has denied love for ambition. Haakon is saved in time from a like sin. Skule's failure is tragic, for he has noble qualities. But he is a divided soul, whereas Haakon is a healthy extrovert, sure that he is doing the Lord's will. Skule (and here lies the double irony of the theme) is also in large measure the Ibsen of 1863, an apparent failure at poetry; and Haakon is also Ibsen's friend and successful rival, Björnstjerne Björnson. Of course there is no hint of this personal application in the play, but that it was in Ibsen's mind cannot be doubted. And with what dispassionate fairness to his happy rival, and stern objectivity toward his own weaknesses, does he set forth the opposing natures of the two men!

There is a little of Ibsen himself also in the emotional frustration of Bishop Nicholas, the third of the central figures. From an actor's point of view, the bishop is one of Ibsen's most enticing creations. And in a study of irony he is extraordinarily interesting. His superstitious ignorance is in sometimes grotesque contrast to his sly cunning; his malevolence, to his humor. In the temporary successes of his diabolical machinations he reminds us of Iago, though he is old and effeminate whereas Iago is young and virile.

He is also a fully rounded character with understandable motivation, not a stage villain.

Here is Nicholas speaking on his deathbed: "Ay, I have hated much; hated every head in this land that raised itself above the crowd. But I hated because I could not love. Fair women—oh, I could devour them even now with glistening eyes. I have lived eighty years, and yet do I yearn to kill men and clasp women; but my lot in love was as my lot in war: naught but an itching will, my strength sapped from my birth; dowered with a seething desire—and yet a weakling! So I became a priest: king or priest must that man be who would have all might in his hands. [*Laughs.*] I a priest! I a churchman! Yes, for *one* churchly office Heaven had notably fitted me—for taking the high notes—for singing with a woman's voice at the great church festivals. And yet they up yonder claim of me—the half-man—what they have a right to claim only of those whom they have in all things fitted for their lifework!" And to one of the two pretenders: "Neither of you shall add the other's height to his own stature. If that befell, there would be a giant in the land, and here shall no giant be; for I was never a giant!"

The central theme of *Brand* (1866) is so solemn that on a first reading many overlook its vigorous and almost lighthearted satire. Satire is of course much more obvious in *Peer Gynt* (1867), and it is the whole substance of the prose comedy, *The League of Youth* (1869). But *Brand* has plenty of it. The Mayor and the Dean are the special butts of Ibsen's ridicule. The former comments, when Brand risks his life to bring spiritual help to a dying murderer:

> Well, 'tis opposed to all routine
> To labor in a strange vocation,

> Intrusively to risk one's skin
> Without an adequate occasion.—
> *I* do my duty with precision,—
> But always in my own Division.

And the Dean, advising Brand in the duties of a parish priest, says he should serve the state as well as the church:—it pays to do so.

> Souls do not grow more hard to save
> Because the Country profits too;
> With due discretion and despatch
> Two masters' bidding you may do . . .

The good cleric objects to Brand's emphasis on individualism, since what the State needs is a conformity which makes like progress for all in the fashion of soldiers on the march, never too slow or too fast. Brand's ironic jeer at this is the author's own:

> Kennel the eagle;—and let loose
> On empyrean flights the goose.

Behind the Mayor and the Dean are the Norwegian people whom Ibsen lashed out at for being petty, cowardly, mean-souled, and selfish, yet proud of themselves because their distant ancestors were piratical ruffians. "I may," says the Mayor complacently,—

> I think, without a touch of vanity,
> Point backward to the stir we made
> In the great Age long since decay'd,
> And hold that we indeed have paid
> Our little mite of Fire and Fray
> Towards the Progress of Humanity.

This rendering (Herford's) conveys the metrical effects of the original with great fidelity. That these four-beat

rimed verses are much better adapted to satire than to tragedy has troubled more solemn critics, who would like to
justify what they clearly fear to be a lack of poetic ear on
the author's part by the assumption that Norwegians must
find the meter less jiggety than we do. Unfortunately for
such a theory, the original, equally with the translation,
lacks the majesty of tragic style. Thus, the two lines,

> *I* do my duty with precision,—
> But always in my own Division

read in the Dano-Norwegian:

> Jeg gør bestandig og min pligt,—
> men altid indom min distrikt.

It is more reasonable to assume that Ibsen chose his meter
deliberately for its satirical effect. He was a skilled versifier,
as is obvious to any reader of his lyrical poetry. He had used
blank verse in early plays, but chose not to do so here.

Even apart from the metrical effects, the verbal ironies in
these passages are sharp and clear. The dramatic irony in
Brand is less obvious, yet it is more fundamental. The hero
has set up for his parish a standard of "All or Nothing," and
declares that "the devil is compromise." Time comes for
him to apply this standard to himself. Either he can take
his family south to save his child's life, thus deserting his
mission, or he can remain—and let his child die. That is
his cruel dilemma. What finally decides him to remain is
not noble and unselfish motives, though these influence
him also, but vanity. To put it crudely, he is afraid that
folks will say he did not practice what he preached! The
poet intended him to be a genuine spiritual hero after the
pattern set by Kierkegaard's intransigent preachments, yet

ironically, when the poet came to deal dramatically with
the concrete motives that influence his hero as a human
being, he shows him to be more concerned with what the
mad girl, Gerd, will say of him if he leaves than he is with
saving his child's life. And in the last act it is the example
of the mad fanatic Einar which tips the scales for Brand
and decides him to act with no less inhuman fanaticism.
Brand is determined not to be outdone by a man he despises!
Our hero's aspiration has dwindled from the greatness Ibsen
conceived for him into megalomania.

When the poem appeared, people generally took it to
be a ringing call to strenuous will and uncompromising
idealism, a pious work suitable for a confirmation gift.
Ironically enough, Ibsen undoubtedly began it in exactly
this spirit and was himself not wholly aware of how far he
had altered his attitude by the time he finished it. Or rather,
the idealist (and egotistical) Ibsen refused to recognize the
ironical realist Ibsen who lurked behind him as he wrote.
By the time of *The Wild Duck* the latter's bitter laughter
cannot be ignored, but in the earlier work he keeps almost
out of sight. Almost, but not quite. Brand built an immense
church for the little parish and then discovered it to be an
empty shell. He threw the key away and took himself into
the mountains, intending to worship instead on a glacier.
Ibsen the idealist built a colossal structure of heroism, but
before the structure was completed Ibsen the ironist came
and showed it to be hollow.

The converse of this irony is that of *Peer Gynt*. Ibsen
first conceived of Peer as representing certain outstanding
weaknesses of Norwegian character: vanity, selfishness, sub-
stitution of daydreaming for reality, acting on whim rather

than purpose. Peer was to be a horrible example of a character almost the exact opposite of Brand. Yet ... before he
finished this second dramatic poem, Ibsen had come to
know his Peer intimately, and, I think, grudgingly to be
much fonder of him than he thought the rascal deserved,
even as he probably got sick of his Brand long before he destroyed him. At any rate, he gives Peer another chance.
Critics have said that it is the love of faithful Solveig that
reprieves Peer. A more plausible suggestion is that Peer's
heart has not, like Brand's, been wholly hardened. But most
likely the ending is indecisive because the cross currents of
Ibsen's divided sympathies forbade a decision. Probably he
is enigmatic because he could not decide which answer to
his enigma was the right one.

The Emperor Julian is essentially a character like Brand
who seeks an ideal religion uncompromisingly and fails because his refusal to compromise turns him into an inhuman
fanatic. As we noted earlier, *Emperor and Galilean* is Ibsen's
climactic failure in his search for a faith. On Julian's death
the "third empire" remains an unrealized dream. Indeed, the
emperor, in his uncompromising ruthlessness, has turned
it into a nightmare of cruel tyranny.

After that, Ibsen gave up grandiose plays of seeking
idealists. The realistic satirist in him got the upper hand
and kept it for the rest of his life. Yet it is significant of the
enduring vitality of his idealistic half-nature that seeking
idealists are central in almost all his realistic plays to the
end. The tone is different now: there is no real hope of
victory for them and they are usually treated with a subtle
scorn (really ironic self-condemnation) because their seeking, as the old poet came to view it, is essentially selfish. But

the Ibsenite hero is always the same willful individualist, the same protestant against the world as it is, the same aspirer to a better one, the same unconscious egotist whose failure arises from his selfishness. They all climb, and they all fall. This symbol of the climb and fall "obsessed Ibsen's imagination throughout his life,"[7] from the poem "On the Heights" to the last play he wrote. Brand, Solness, Borkman, Rubek, all climb to death.

From *Pillars of Society* onward, the satirical Ibsen is dominant. In the middle period of *Ghosts* he is savagely indignant; gradually he becomes coldly sardonic; but always he casts the glare of disillusionment over the action. Hence, from *Pillars of Society* onward, ironic contrast is always implicit and often strikingly evident.

In dealing with the later Ibsen it is particularly important not to neglect the comic aspect of his irony. His reputation for gloom is so widespread, and the surface impression of these plays so well supports it, that many people find difficulty in crediting him with a sense of humor at all. But if we realize that his comic vision is always mixed with the painfulness of ironic disillusionment, we shall not be surprised that it is not evident to those who judge by surface impressions only.

Pillars of Society has minor characters satirically caricatured like those in *Brand* and *Peer Gynt* and like almost everyone in *The League of Youth*. But the most effective irony of character is in the study of Bernick, that chief "pillar of society" whose fatuous egotism was noted in the last chapter when we compared him to Jason.

A more celebrated example of male vanity is Helmer. What irony that Nora should expect a miracle of self-sacrifice from *him!* Yet he is not a rascal like Bernick; he is honest and loving. What if his honesty is mixed with priggishness, his love with vanity and sensuousness? How many of us mortals are better? Contrariwise, Nora is not a tragic heroine, despite the fact that star actresses always like to play her as one. She is, to be sure, loving and idealistic; and at the end of the play she grows up—with a suddenness that would surely be unbelievable in real life. But prior to that transformation she is a spoiled child, an accomplished liar, and so adept at feminine wiles that when in need of money she is perfectly ready to seduce her husband's best friend for it—so long as the friend does not embarrass her by becoming openly amorous. She wants, in short, to get the money without paying for it. She merely play-acts the tragic heroine.

With such protagonists as these *A Doll's House* cannot be purely tragic even though Ibsen originally conceived it so. Actually, the relations of the two are often those of high comedy.[8] Ibsen the idealist was too intensely in earnest at the time about his theme of female subjection to let Ibsen the realist develop this comedy fully; yet—ironically—it is there nevertheless! Nora's door-slamming no longer shocks us as a symbol of revolutionary significance, but a more realistic interpretation of this famous play than is customary should prove that as a bitingly ironic comedy of character it has an enduring vitality.

Ghosts also, in spite of its reputation for unmitigated gloom, has many moments of ironic comedy. A recent production which interpreted the text without *parti pris* proved this by the frequent smiles and occasional laughter that it evoked. Indeed, Engstrand, that hypocritical rascal, and

Pastor Manders, that "big baby," are almost too comically caricatured to fit the hard realism of the piece. Even Regina affords amusement as we watch her single-mindedly "gold digging" at any available male, as in her scene with Manders in Act I. Viewed with such a background, the central tragic theme gains a peculiar ironic poignancy which it lacks when the play is done in the customary gloomy fashion.

This tragic action is one of unmatched power in its complex employment of dramatic irony. The sins of the father are transmitted to the child in spite of his mother's heroic sacrifices. Mrs. Alving's hard-won emancipation from superstitions ("ghosts") is yet superstitiously expressed by her building of an orphanage with Chamberlain Alving's tainted money—a propitiation to the gods! And Engstrand burns the orphanage down so as to get the money for an "Alving Home" for sailors where Regina, Alving's bastard, will assist in profitable vice! Manders' moral refusal of Mrs. Alving when she ran away from her husband to him brings immorality and insanity to Alving's children and tragedy to her. Her generous goodness of heart makes her a victim, where a harder, more selfish woman might have dominated the evil around her.

The irony with which Ibsen treats even his heroine's noble struggle to free herself from the clinging prejudices of her society is nowhere more cruelly illustrated than in the scene with Oswald in the last act. She has not wholly freed herself from illusions, for she still thinks that children should always honor their parents, as the Ten Commandments bid. Hence she brought Oswald up away from his father and never let him know the kind of man his father was. (Of course, ironically, the son on his return has acted just like his father by making love to the servant, his half sister.) At last, events force Mrs. Alving to reveal the terrible secret to her son, and he merely says, "After all, I don't know that it matters much to me." Naturally she is shocked. "But surely a child should feel some affection for his father, whatever happens?" Oswald: "When the child has nothing to thank his father for? When he has never known him? Do you really cling to that antiquated superstition?"

What irony there is in the famous ending! The rain that has been the gloomy background of the whole play now stops and the sun comes out ("Then came the dawn"!). Oswald, sinking into imbecility, cries out for the sun like a baby. Mrs. Alving, the woman who did what a wife should do and stayed with her husband, now faces "a dilemma which is possibly the cruelest in dramatic literature: killing her son, or sparing him to live a paretic idiot."[9] The Manderses of the world, having learned nothing, will continue to minister to the ghosts that haunt it; and the Engstrands will continue to make profit out of the simplicity of the Manderses. And behind the scene the author's tight lips curl in a grim sardonic smile as if to ask, "Well, you respectable people, you who blamed my Nora for running away, how do you like *this?*"

Ghosts was nevertheless dominated by the mood of indignation. The thwarted preacher in Ibsen has here his clearest expression, though he is evident enough in *Pillars of Society* and *A Doll's House*. Ibsen's attitude seems to have been that even if ultimate ideals are unattainable, at least the falsities in society deserve excoriation. But the mood could not logically last. If men are merely animals, what use is there in being angry at them?

Dr. Stockman, in his next play, is vastly indignant at the sink of civic corruption he uncovers, but his creator, as though half conscious of something futile in the mood but unwilling to admit it, makes the doctor more of a "character" than a hero, amusingly vain, impulsive, boyish, and not a little unreasonable. *An Enemy of the People* is one of Ibsen's most comic plays in spite of its theme.

To view men biologically required a major revolution in the religious spirit of the poet, and no wonder it was difficult for him to take it lightly. After all, he grew up in the Christian tradition that considered mankind the chief creation of God, with immortal souls engaged in a cosmic drama that led to eternal salvation or to hell. It was not easy to make an adjustment so radical and so destructive of the ideals dearest to the poet's heart. The moral indignation of his middle period may be taken as a surface symptom of the spiritual struggle going on beneath it—a "defense mechanism," so to speak.

But with *The Wild Duck* Ibsen capitulates and the revolution is complete. "All my life," he seems to say, "I pictured men and women as free souls who have the power of choice between good and evil, and whose struggle and decision are of tragic significance. But those pictures were false! Men are merely animals, and most of them tame, domestic animals at that! Very well, then! A sculptor whose statues dissatisfy him takes the hammer to them. Shall a dramatist be less ruthless? I shall review my idealistic plays from the new point of view. I shall make grim fun of all that I have written. It will be a salutary self-discipline. Of course, the critics, not to mention the public, will be puzzled. The Ibsenites in particular will be upset. That will be amusing."

On the surface *The Wild Duck* is a realistic story, intricately but convincingly plotted, about an odd group of heterogeneous characters loosely connected by old Werle's misdeeds in the past and his efforts to set things right. The play ends unhappily, but it has many passages that are full of comedy. On the surface, as the casual playgoer sees it, it is troubling because the death of little Hedvig is deeply pathetic yet leads to no spiritual regeneration of her parents such as would justify it sentimentally and as was to be expected in any properly constructed play. But the casual playgoer finds the play fascinating nevertheless—or would, if he could see it well done.

Playgoers with no further knowledge will also be impressed by a new quality, or at least a quality less emphasized in earlier plays—its mysterious and haunting symbolism. Some, of course, have been less impressed than exasperated. Sarcey, for instance, when he saw the play at the Théâtre-Libre in 1891, was almost driven wild. "Ah, that Wild Duck!" he exclaimed. "Nobody in the world, nobody in the universe, not you who have heard the play, nor Lindenlaub and Ephraim who translated it exactly, nor the author who wrote it, nor Shakespeare who inspired it, nor God, nor the devil—nobody will ever know what that wild duck is, nor what it is doing in the play, nor what it means, nor what it rimes with!"[10]

Sarcey's model of dramatic art was the work of Dumas *fils* and he had got spiritual hardening of the arteries from years of reviewing the Paris stage of the late nineteenth century; his state of mind is understandable. One needs some poetry in his soul to respond to the suggestive magic of the symbols in this play.

At the same time, there is no need to take them in the vague mood of Maeterlinckian mysticism. When we view them in terms of Ibsen's thoughts in writing the play, they have quite definite meanings. The only trouble about them is that they have too many for easy assimilation. To a logical rationalizer who is discontented unless he can reduce all meanings to one, the wild duck is indeed troublesome. That crippled bird has analogies with Gregers, with old Ekdal, with Hjalmar, with Hedvig, with Ibsen himself, and with "all lamed enthusiams of mankind." It stands for "the surrogate happiness by which people console themselves . . . for their defeat in the contests of life."[11] It is a symbol of false and self-deceiving Romanticism.[12] And we need not limit its significance to one of these meanings. Ibsen was not writing a fable like Aesop's. The bird has each of these meanings and all of them together.

But the title unduly focuses our attention on the wild duck alone. The bird is, after all, but one of a little menagerie of animals assembled in the Ekdal attic. And the attic that contains them, as the childish Ekdal males see it, and as dreamy Hedvig sees it, is not a dusty space under the eaves, littered with gear and smelling of rabbit droppings, but a world of make-believe. We who see it and them objectively see it as the realm of illusions by which weak mortals live, those illusions that Relling cynically and pitifully called "life-lies" (*livsløgner*). We can see the attic at once with the amused scorn of Ibsen the realist and the tragic pity of Ibsen the idealist. We see it finally, if we can fuse the complex ironies it involves into a unity, with the eyes of a third Ibsen, above and beyond his usual duality—an Ibsen whose presence is seldom so strongly felt as here,—

Ibsen the poet, who sees the beauty of the dreams, the pity of Hedvig's vain though heroic sacrifice, the pathos of all futile mortals who would like to soar but whose wings are clipped from birth.

The discordant moods may blend in this higher unity. Certainly they grow more and more compelling the better we understand this extraordinary play. But they remain discordant, and the dominant one is that of self-satire. "In *The Wild Duck* the cynic suddenly gets the upper hand and turns in ironic scorn on all that the idealist had previously held up for admiration. Brand had gone about among the cottagers making the claim of the Ideal, but in *The Wild Duck* such claims when made by Gregers Werle are both absurd and pernicious. Lona Hessel had declared solemnly that Truth and Freedom were the pillars of society; *The Wild Duck* demonstrates that lies and subservience make the world run smoothly. In *A Doll's House* a 'true marriage' is shown to be possible only when based on complete sincerity; but here the marriage of one contented couple is ruined by the discovery of the truth, and the projected marriage of an aging rascal with a clever courtesan promises to be secure and happy on the basis of what Hjalmar Ekdal describes as 'complete confidence, entire and unreserved candor on both sides'—a devastatingly ironical distortion of Nora's ideal. In *Ghosts* the sins of the father are visited upon the innocent child; in *The Wild Duck* the father remains prosperous and the child (little Hedvig) is happy in spite of her heredity until her busybody of a half brother insists on preaching Ideals at her. In *An Enemy of the People,* Doctor Stockman, the hero, campaigns to drain 'the swamp of deception' in society; but here the revelation of truth brings merely the child's futile self-sacrifice and declamatory speechifying from her foster father."[13]

Is it any wonder that Graham Wallas exclaimed, "When I came to the end of the play, the bottom fell out of the universe"?[14] No language but that which involves the contradictions of irony can describe the effect. "Where shall I find an epithet magnificent enough for 'The Wild Duck'!" cried Shaw, writing as dramatic critic of the *Saturday Review* in 1897. "To sit there getting deeper and deeper into that Ekdal home, and getting deeper and deeper into your own life all the time, until you forget that you are in a theatre at all; to look on with horror and pity at a profound tragedy, shaking with laughter all the time at an irresistible comedy; to go out, not from a diversion, but from an experience deeper than real life ever brings to most men, or often brings to any man: that is what 'The Wild Duck' was like last Monday at the Globe."[15] "The curtain falls on a scene unparalleled anywhere in its mixture of tragedy and humour—unless it be in real life," writes A. E. Zucker. *The Wild Duck*, "like no other drama in the world, views with irony and pity Destiny's 'little children stumbling in the dark.' "[16]

After observing the double and triple ironies of this play, to concern ourselves with those of the later plays, powerful and subtle as they are, may seem an anticlimax. But actually they take us even deeper into the poet's self-division. In these late plays he seems not to challenge but to respect conventional moral assumptions. This respectful manner has almost universally fooled playgoers. They do not see the mockery beneath. A good many critics have also been taken in, particularly those who had to judge the plays soon after

they were written. Time has given us a perspective that
Ibsen's contemporaries could not have.

As a dramatist Ibsen ought not to have played such tricks
on the public! We shall grant that; we shall grant that since
these ambiguities fail to affect many in the theater, they are
not dramatic. Perhaps we should call them hyperdramatic.
At any rate, we cannot afford not to study them. Indeed,
they are extraordinarily fascinating, and perhaps a more
general appreciation of them may change the public feeling
toward the plays when produced, and the methods directors
use in interpreting them.

As for Ibsen himself, by this time he no longer needed to
appeal to the wide public. He was still the dramatist and
wanted his plays produced; but he also wanted to express
his biological view of mankind honestly and fully. The
latter wish put him in a dilemma. The limits that hedge a
dramatist's plain speaking on such matters are always narrower than those of a novelist, for people will be willing
to read about many things they will refuse to see. And the
limits for the dramatist were far narrower in the 'eighties
and 'nineties than they are now. Ibsen preferred not to meet
the difficulty by direct attack, as he did in *Ghosts;* perhaps
he was tired of fighting. He avoided the difficulty by making
his plays conventional on the surface, while underneath
"there is something equivocal, something cryptic. I alone
can see it. And it amuses me unspeakably!" Beneath the
masks of respectable gentlemen he carved the donkey's
nose, the dog's muzzle, the pig's snout.

These plays when seen thus may repel the tender-minded.
It is true of Ibsen, as of Euripides, that although he rouses
strong admiration in some, he rouses strong dislike in

others, and seldom love. The ironist may feel as deeply as any unironic poet, but his treatment of his material chills sentiment. It is his fate, as one who sees without illusions, to antagonize all the worthy people who live by illusions.

It is peculiarly ironic, therefore, that hidden behind Ibsen's repelling exterior was a sensitive poet who longed for love and domestic affection and—even lighthearted merriment. This side of him was well hidden; it was withdrawn from the sight of the world by intense repressions and an abnormal shyness. "I know it to be a defect in me that I am incapable of entering into close and intimate relations with people who demand that one should yield one's self up entirely and unreservedly. I have something of the same feeling as the Skald in *The Pretenders;* I can never bear to strip myself completely."[17]

He was also driven away from such relations by a strong compulsion. Very early he centered his life exclusively on writing plays and sacrificed everything that interfered with it. This zeal was too intense to be explained merely by selfish ambition. The essentially religious spirit of his work makes it fairly clear that his devotion was psychologically similar to that of a missionary answering a Call. Was his lifework an unconscious effort to propitiate heaven with a substitute for the faith he had refused in his childhood? Certainly playwriting was not an adequate substitute for religion; and as he grew old it seemed to him, in spite of fame and fortune, hollow and vain.

It is Ibsen himself, pretty clearly, who speaks through Solness in the last act of *The Master Builder:*

... You see, I came as a boy from a pious home in the country; and so it seemed to me that this church-building was the noblest task I could set myself.... He wanted to give me the chance of becoming an accomplished master in my own sphere—so that I might build all the more glorious churches for him. At first I did not understand what he was driving at; but all of a sudden it flashed upon me.... Then I saw plainly why he had taken my little children from me. It was that I should have nothing else to attach myself to. No such thing as love and happiness, you understand. I was to be only a master builder—nothing else. And all my life long I was to go on building for him.

But Solness defied the Lord. In spite of his vertigo he climbed to the top of the tower to shout his defiance:

Hear me now, thou Mighty One! From this day forward I will be a free builder—I, too, in my sphere—just as thou in thine. I will never more build churches for thee—only homes for human beings.

Such defiance brought its punishment; the Lord's "turn came."

Building homes for human beings—is not worth a rap, Hilda. ... Men have no use for these homes of theirs—to be happy in. And I should not have had any use for such a home, if I had had one. (*With a quiet, bitter laugh.*) See, that is the upshot of the whole affair, however far back I look. Nothing really built; nor anything sacrificed for the chance of building. Nothing, nothing! the whole is nothing.

Ibsen's conscience seems to have troubled him for his wife's sacrifices in devoting herself to his career. They had had one child, but they had never had a real home, living as they did abroad in furnished flats among foreigners. Suzanna Ibsen had a rich nature that needed wide contacts and warm human relations. She gave her life up mainly to protecting her difficult husband from such contacts, so that he could wrap himself up in his work. And he, too, needed such contacts, though he repelled them. Something, he felt, had almost died in him for want of them.

His strong domestic yearning is suggested in an early lyric which—surprisingly enough—brings to mind that very different poet, Longfellow, and his "Children's Hour"! Ibsen's verses are called "A Home Study" ("Fra mit husliv"—From my home life) and were written in 1864. The poet is sitting at evening by the lamp when the dream children come in.

> They came, my dream-winged children, a band
>   Of romping girls and boys.
> Fresh-cheeked as after a bath—oh, grand
> Was the race we started through fairyland,
>   With the maddest, merriest noise.

"Grave Alice, and laughing Allegra"! But at this point the fancies of the two poets diverge. Ibsen was the poet of love defeated or denied. His own warring nature defeats it and denies it.

> But just as the fun was at topmost rate,
>   I chanced to look in the mirror.
> And there stood a stranger, grave, sedate,
> Close-buttoned, with eyes of the grey of slate,
>   And slippers, or I'm in error.
>
> With that, my madcaps were stricken dumb;
>   One stands like a block of wood,
> Another falls to sucking his thumb;—
> You know how the boldest boys turn mum
>   If a stranger but intrude.[18]

To win greatness, Ibsen buttoned himself up close. He achieved his end, but only at a price.

Solness is not Ibsen, for Ibsen thoroughly objectified and individualized him. But between his career and that of his creator there is a parallel too close for accident. They both were self-made men. Solness at first built churches; Ibsen at first wrote idealistic plays full of religious aspiration. Solness turned to building "houses for people to live in"; Ibsen, to domestic drama. Solness has vertigo on high places; Ibsen was physically timorous. Solness and Ibsen both felt that they had been chosen by God for a special mission; both refused the Call and revolted against their "sickly conscience." Now both saw old age coming and felt the challenge of "youth knocking at the door." Both had a sense of futility in their achievements; both mourned the lack of a real home; both felt guilty toward their wives. Solness received no real recognition until his home burned down; Ibsen, until he had exiled himself from Norway.[19]

Therefore in everything Solness says or does Ibsen must have seen an ironic self-criticism. Solness is an extremely egotistical man, hindered from ruthlessness in gaining his ends by that "sickly conscience" of his. He hankers after young girls; he fears the rivalry of younger men; he is weary of his doleful wife. But he stops short of acting fully on his inclinations. He is neither a hero nor a villain; he is, in fact, a good deal of a fraud. It could not have been unintentionally that Ibsen made him not a trained architect but a self-made "master builder."

When Hilda breezes into his life, full of hero worship and sex attraction, he loses his head completely. Her ecstatic admiration, which on a natural plane can only be interpreted as perverse and psychopathic, intoxicates him. He would rather risk death than let her see through him. His fall is in large part the consequence of insane vanity, and makes a ridiculous end to a life that was never anything but false and hollow. He is another Brand, seen without any illusions.

This is the grim ironic joke that Ibsen plays upon himself. And he plays another on the public—one which most of them have never suspected. To most of them Solness may be a queer sort of fellow but nevertheless a man of superior powers and even noble aspiration—a genuine Ibsenite seeker, in short, who sins in a heroic way and suffers retribution. On the very day when he defied God's command to go on building churches he kissed Hilda and woke in her the nemesis of his act of *hybris*. And the irony of the situation, thus viewed, is that he actually receives Hilda with delight as a source of spiritual rejuvenation. *The Master Builder* on the surface, then, follows a familiar tragic formula; and its protagonist appears to be a tragic hero. But Ibsen knows better and smiles inwardly at the way his hearers are fooled.

Let us, then, look with suspicion on the other male "heroes" of this period. I find no irony in his treatment of Dr. Wangel (in *The Lady from the Sea*), for though a weak man he is an honorable one, and he is not an egotist. *Hedda Gabler,* of course, is a special study of the way in which feminine character can be perverted by unhealthy social conditions. Its male characters are secondary. In *John Gabriel Borkman* and *When We Dead Awaken* the protagonists are condemned directly and overtly. But *Little Eyolf* has a protagonist who at first glance seems noble. Is he?

Let us view the "surface likeness" first. Noble sentiments certainly roll from Alfred Allmers' lips. He is as moralistic as a preacher, though actually he is a young scholar who on marrying money retired from teaching, and who, like his creator, has lost all his early religious beliefs. According to the "surface likeness," he married Rita and her extensive real estate largely for the sake of his half sister Asta, whom he loves tenderly and who has been dependent on him since their parents' death. According to this view, Rita seduced him by her beauty and at first their love was passionate. During one lovemaking they left their baby Eyolf lying on a table. He fell off and injured his leg so badly that he became a cripple and had to hobble about with a crutch. In remorse Alfred withdrew from his wife and buried himself in his study to write a monumental book on Human Responsibility (*Det menneskelige ansvar*). Rita felt that the child had come between her and her husband and out of jealousy neglected him. Asta, who was almost an inmate of the home, tended to take the mother's place with the boy.

Ten years later, just before the opening of the play, to cure a persistent cough Alfred went on an extended walking trip into the mountains. He went alone. He lost his way and for a time actually feared death. He experienced a mystical vision that made him realize his neglect of his son, whom he had treated in the manner of a schoolmaster. When he found his way, he hurried home determined to be a real father to Eyolf. In this mood, the night before the opening of the play, he refused to make love to Rita.

In Act I the child becomes fascinated by a weird old woman, the "rat wife," and when she rows off on the fjord, he tries to follow her, falls in, and is drowned. Sensual Rita is now consumed by remorse, for at the very moment that the boy is drowned she wishes him out of the way because he has come between her and her husband. In the later course of the play Alfred brings her round to a more spiritual view of life, and at the end they both resolve to devote themselves to good works hereafter by helping the poor children in the village.

How a good critic could be taken in by the surface likeness of this play is indicated by Edmund Gosse's comments.[20] "If we turn from the technical virtuosity of *Little Eyolf* to its moral aspects, we find it a very dreadful play, set in darkness which nothing illuminates but the twinkling sweetness of Asta.... In Rita jealousy is incarnate, and she seems the most vigorous, and, it must be added, the most repulsive, of Ibsen's feminine creations."

Let us see now what the case is if we look beneath the surface.

In this view, Allmers is, like Hjalmar Ekdal, a spoiled child grown up, emotionally immature because dependent on female adoration and care but in his own opinion vastly superior to all women; full of noble sentiments but essentially weak and selfish; boastful of creative achievements but actually sterile. Hjalmar's uncut scientific journals and Alfred's pile of blank paper (brought back from his journey) are similarly symbolic. In short, both men are empty windbags. We are told that Alfred got articles published before his marriage, but since then he did not, of course, need the money (any more than Hjalmar did, living on old Ekdal's bounty). He merely pretends to be writing his great book, just as Hjalmar pretends to be working on a "great invention." The only essential difference between the two men is that Alfred is less easily seen through. Of course neither wife nor sister sees through him.

His mother died when he was an infant. His father then married a woman much younger than he, and a little later she bore a daughter, Asta. When Alfred was in his adolescence and Asta still a child, Allmers Senior and his second wife both died. For several years thereafter the two young people lived together while Alfred was going through the university and starting his career. Their relationship during this period must be pieced together from their reminiscent talk in the play, but it is clear enough. Asta worshiped Alfred, and he became to her, emotionally, both father and husband. So strong was this emotional fixation that years after his marriage to Rita, at the time of the play, Asta cannot respond normally to her manly and ardent suitor, Borgheim.

Alfred also developed an unhealthy fixation upon Asta. He liked to pretend that she was a boy, he called her his "little Eyolf," and he even sometimes dressed her in boy's clothes! Why? We suggest that subconsciously he was aware of incestuous feelings toward her and the pretense helped to hide them from his consciousness. The incestuous nature of his attitude toward her during the play is indubitable. He named his son Eyolf; he cannot bear that Asta should marry; he wants her always on hand. After the child's death, he finds moral excuse to blame Rita and decide on leaving her; his strong unconscious motive is that he wants to live with Asta as in the old days. He asks her if she will return to him. She cannot do such a wrong to Rita, and forces herself to reveal a secret about her birth which she has only recently learned from reading old letters of her mother's. This secret is that she is illegitimate— and therefore of no relation to Alfred at all.

This revelation should stop any honorable man's mouth, one would think. Not Alfred's. In Act III he is still planning to leave Rita and hoping to get Asta away from Borgheim for himself. In talking to the two of them he says that he dreads being alone. "The thought of it runs like ice through my blood." Perhaps that will make Asta feel sorry for him. He is really glad that she has definitely refused Borgheim and that the latter must take his journey alone. (Borgheim is going off into the mountains to build roads, not to moon.) "You see," Alfred tells the engineer, "you can never tell whom you might happen to meet afterwards—on the way.... The right fellow traveller—when it is too late—too late." Alfred is really talking to Asta, and she understands. "Alfred! Alfred!" she cries (*"softly, quivering"*). In other words, he reproaches her for abandoning him, as though her duty still were to live for him alone—even now! And later, when Rita urges Asta to stay on with them, he joins her plea: "Remain—and share our life with us, Asta. With Rita. With me. With me—your brother!"

That word "brother," spoken under the circumstances, is profoundly shocking to Asta. Though Alfred refuses to face the facts, she cannot; intuitively she is horrified at the desires she senses in herself and in him. She turns to Borgheim and asks him to take her with him. Ironically, it is the blind selfishness and egotism of Alfred's infatuation that saves her for what may well be yet a normal womanhood.

And it is a final irony that very soon afterward Alfred has worked himself round full circle into accepting life once more with Rita. So long as he has an adoring female to keep him from feeling loneliness "like ice" in his blood.

... In plainer words, his empty soul craves flattery to give it the sensation of being full.

In this view, furthermore, Rita speaks truly when she cries to Alfred, "I am a warmblooded being! I don't go drowsing about—with fishes' blood in my veins." He, like so many other Ibsen "heroes," committed "the unpardonable sin" by marrying her for her money, though he pretends that he did it for Asta's sake, and though, to be sure, he was also attracted by her beauty. Rita, on the contrary, genuinely loved *him,* with the warm love of a healthy, normal woman. When she began to sense his lack of response, her love became sharpened at times into passionate solicitations. He was at least normal enough to be carried away by these, until the accident to their baby gave him a respectable excuse for evading the marital duties he was not quite man enough to want, and for hiding in his study. His book on "Human Responsibility" is ironically named, as it is really a fiction to enable him to escape from his own responsibilities as a husband and as a father.

At first Rita loved the child as a mother should, but when she found Eyolf apparently a barrier between her husband and herself she was torn between conflicting loves. In the deep frustration of her passion for Alfred, after his trip, she expresses a momentary wish that the boy might be ... At that very moment, apparently, the boy falls into the fjord. Her horror at herself for wishing his death so works upon her that in the last act she finally comes to an unselfish and redeeming resolve. The poor boys in the village who jeered at Eyolf and who failed to rescue him—they also need love and care. She will give her life to *them.* This is a genuine resolution to her conflict, and her salvation.

Alfred's attitude toward his son lacks Rita's excuse of unresolved emotional conflict. In his case it is simply an egotistical withdrawal. He could be a schoolmaster to the child, and pretend that he was doing his duty. On his trip he had no high mystical experience; he was simply scared of death. Never spiritually mature and independent, he could not bear to be alone; and then to be lost! Naturally, he could not admit to himself that he had been simply frightened out of his wits, so he developed a romance about receiving a message from on high. He comes home full of the moral afflatus of his new role and pompously refuses his wife's still loving advances.

But he is so little touched, really, by altruistic love of children that after Eyolf's death he wishes that the poor people's hovels might be torn down and the boys who failed his son might all be drowned! He also romances a little about committing suicide: it is a good way of winning feminine sympathy. When he is "gone," he says, Rita should "have the whole place down there razed to the ground."

All this is mere pose. As soon as Rita expresses her determination to help the poor boys, he comes promptly round to joining her. After all (not to mention suicide), it is one thing to talk pompously about leaving one's erring wife; it is quite another to do it, especially when doing so means poverty and discomfort and loneliness. Allmers and Hjalmar both take the same pose and act on the same motives: both decide to stay. And both quickly discover creditable motives for so doing.

"The truth is," says Alfred, looking thoughtfully at Rita, "we have not done much for the poor people down there." He had never dreamed of doing anything for them until she suggested it; he had wanted them all drowned. A little later, "Perhaps, I could join you? ..." And at the final curtain he is his old self again: he has transformed Rita's loving mission into a theme for fatuous grandiloquence. "Upward—toward the peaks. Toward the stars. And toward the great silence." ("Opad,—imod tinderne. Mod stjernerne. Og imod den store stilhed.") What a satire on the Ibsen who wrote *Brand!* "The great silence" indeed! Silence is one thing there would never be with Alfred Allmers around.

Yet almost everyone who has seen and read the play has taken that windbag at his own valuation. Ibsen laid his trap very cleverly indeed. The problem of interpreting this play on the stage, for a director who sees the trap, may actually be insoluble. Yet it ought to be a fascinating one. Suppose a modern audience could really share the author's ironic point of view? What a startling play *Little Eyolf* might be! And could one find any recent drama, written with benefit of the Freudian Enlightenment and all the discoveries of modern psychiatry, that could match it in subtlety of psychological analysis of perverse and subconscious motives?

Lastly, what shall we think of the noble Rosmer, whose moral influence, according to the received notion, converts the wicked Rebecca into a self-sacrificing penitent? Well, there are certainly two ways of looking at him!

The "surface likeness" shows Rebecca as bad enough in heredity, in upbringing, and in disposition, to deserve the condemnation of all right-thinking people. She was the bastard of an atheistical libertine, Dr. West. And she had been his mistress also! (To be sure, she had not known that she was his child. This shocking fact, by the way, is so quietly indicated in the play that many readers never guess it at all.) She had, as she tells us, a pagan spirit and a ruthless will. When she arrived in Rosmersholm, she fell passionately in love with its master and set to work to get him to herself. She managed this without violence because Beata, his wife, was hysterical. Lies were enough; Beata went and drowned herself.

Rosmer, on the other hand, has always led a blameless life; and no wonder, for he comes of a noble race. He has been a clergyman, and though he has laid aside the cloth and even ceased to profess Christianity, he retains the moral habits of a priest. At the beginning of the play, he is planning to serve men in an active way by joining the Radical Party. Under his spiritualizing and ennobling influence Rebecca is gradually tamed and converted to the Rosmer way, and at the end she atones for her sins by "going the way Beata went."

The ironic view, on the contrary, sees Rosmer as a feeble soul, his virility depleted by aristocratic inbreeding. In this view, his "spirituality" and "purity" are merely the infantilism of a man too undersexed to be male either in sin or in heroism and too morbidly introverted to be really concerned with anyone but himself. Hence he is initially responsible for his wife's hysterical illness. Beata was no doubt inclined to neuroticism to begin with, but she had normal adult passions like Rita; and when she found that she could never become a mother and that her amorous advances to her husband filled him with a holy distaste, she was easy prey to Rebecca's insinuations: Rosmer was losing his faith; he really loved Rebecca; Rebecca was pregnant by him; the only way to save his happiness was to throw herself into the millrace.

Rosmer is subconsciously uneasy about his responsibility for the suicide, for he can never cross the bridge from which Beata jumped, but goes roundabout. He has mourned his wife properly, of course; but aside from the one uneasiness he is relieved by her death. At the opening of the play, he is content in his dreamy way to moon about Rosmersholm, doing nothing except to avoid unhappy memories by walking away from them. It is Rebecca who prods him into announcing his conversion to radical views. It is she, indeed, who without his knowing it brought about this conversion. She has missionary zeal.

Pushed on by her, Rosmer actually tells his brother-in-law, Headmaster Kroll, a Conservative zealot, that he has gone over to the hated Radicals. Kroll's friendship is now changed to bitter political hatred, and he lets loose upon Rosmer through the party newspaper all the scurrility that he can think up. And his animosity is more than merely political. Kroll had been in love with Rebecca and jealous of Rosmer; he had long suspected an intrigue between them, especially after his sister Beata had hinted at it. For political reasons he had done nothing, even when Beata in her desperation came to him for help, and after her suicide he felt guilty for his neglect.

Rosmer all his life had relaxed in the warm bath of admiration and respect. Suddenly to be abused, and with such horrible vindictiveness, in the journal where formerly he had received nothing but adulation, proves too much for the delicate nerves of this moral dilettante. He can't stand it. To be a turncoat after a public declaration of a new faith, to abandon Rebecca without compunction after their close relationship, to eat his own words and prove himself a spiritual coward, are matters that do not weigh with him at all in comparison with his need of the admiration bath. He returns to the fold without a struggle.

Rebecca has wasted her love on this weakling; but what is worse from her point of view, she has wasted her ideals on him. For Rebecca is a strange Ibsenian paradox, a bad person who is at the same time an aspiring idealist in the tradition of Brand, ready to risk all in her ambition to make Rosmer, like herself, emancipated and progressive. What is nowadays called the "ideology" of her ideal is vague, but its details are dramatically unimportant. What is important is that it is the chief thing in life for Rebecca. It is so important to her that, when she sees Rosmer sinking helplessly into bondage to the past, and when he asks her to marry him not from his own free choice and love but in the hope that she can intoxicate him into forgetting the past and thus "take Beata's place," she refuses him. Rather death than marriage on such terms!

Such excessive idealism from the lady who committed murder to marry him is a bit strange. This is one of the few occasions in Ibsen's great works when the motivation of a principal decision seems inadequate. It is hard to believe in such an extremity of zeal for perfection, even in a saint; and Ibsen has been careful to show that Rebecca is no saint; on the contrary. How she could be so passionately in love with him, when we come to think of it, is also strange, considering that his idea of perfect love is "a sort of sweet, secret child love—desireless, dreamless." But—we must take her as Ibsen drew her.

Rebecca will not marry Rosmer to be a nurse for his neuroticism, but when he is threatened by public scandal on

account of his wife's suicide she is ready to sacrifice herself
for him by taking the blame. Her confession, before Rosmer
and Kroll, requires such heroic devotion that surely any
man of spiritual discernment, not wholly wrapped up in
himself, would recognize its true worth. Not Rosmer. She
sacrifices her reputation, her position, her hopes, her love,
almost her life, to restore his peace of conscience, even
though it means giving him back to the Conservative crowd
whom she despises. The act makes no real impression on
him. And he still avoids the bridge over the millrace.

Not merely that. After a visit to the Conservative crowd
to make up with them, he comes back to call Rebecca a liar
and accuse her of using him for selfish ends. When she tells
him that she had acted out of a passionate love for him, this
confession also makes no impression on him. He has now
become fascinated with a lust stronger than any sexual
desire—the perverted lust for death. A psychoanalyst should
have an interesting time speculating on the buried compul-
sions behind it: a sense of sin born of infantile auto-
eroticism, perhaps; a craving to punish himself and Rebecca
for his failure as a man; and obviously also a desire to make
symbolic sacrifice to propitiate the gods whom his intellect
no longer believes in but whom his irrational self still fears.
Rebecca is not alone guilty toward Beata; his own guilt is
much more profound, and because he cannot admit it consciously it is intolerable. Hence his speech has extraordinary
irony when he says, "Your past is dead, Rebecca. It has no
hold on you any more—it is no part of you—as you are
now." He is talking really of himself, as he would like to be!

The upshot is that he proposes first a marriage ceremony
for them (being ghost-ridden by priestly tradition, he needs

ceremonies), and then suicide together, off the bridge "the same way that Beata went." Here the irony is direct: Rosmer now exerts over her the same power of suggestion that she had exerted over Beata. But Rebecca is not befuddled; she dies clearsighted. Her life and her ideals have failed utterly; there is nothing to live for. If he wants it this way, why not?

So viewed, *Rosmersholm* might better be called *Ghosts* than the play of that name, for its attack on outworn and unreal ideals of morality is even more fundamental. In the earlier play they were dealt with openly and viewed as existing outwardly in social tradition. In this play they are implicated with the most inward and hidden motives of the human soul. And in view of all that we now know of Ibsen, can we doubt which of the two interpretations he really meant?

We find it impossible to deal adequately with the later plays without employing terms of psychiatry and psychoanalysis. When Ibsen wrote the plays, "certain medical practitioners interestsd ... in the study of psychiatry were beginning to explain mental illness in terms of disturbances below the threshold of consciousness."[21] Yet no evidence has been offered to show that Ibsen was familiar with such researches; and even if he had been, they could never have given him the insights he possessed into the secret places of the human heart. These are an achievement of genius—an achievement too little recognized by the world at large.

So also is his irony. The more we study him, the more clearly we see it as a dominant quality of his drama. He not only employs the familiar forms of dramatic irony with great power, but he has devised a new form of irony—one which so far as I know is unique in him,—the irony which uses a complete dramatic action to contrast the "surface likeness" and the hidden truth. If any dramatist other than Sophocles deserves to have a type of irony named after him, Ibsen does. "Ibsenian irony." We have guessed that Euripides did something like this, but we cannot be sure. We know enough of Ibsen to be sure. The term is certainly better deserved than "Sophoclean irony."

Of all the great dramatists, we have found not Sophocles but Euripides and Ibsen to be the chief ironists. And we shall hardly be wrong if we say that not even Euripides used irony as Ibsen did—with such power and depth, such subtlety and complexity, such relentless soul searching.

CONCLUSION

CHAPTER X

The Limitations of Irony

THROUGHOUT this study I have tried not to be like Sir
Thomas Browne with his quincunxes, seeing irony
everywhere because I was looking for it. I have tried
steadily to maintain my definition of irony as an incongruity that rouses both pain and amusement, and to apply
it only when a disinterested person would feel those conflicting emotions. Hence I have refused to treat as irony
mere tragic anticipation of calamity or merely comic contrast. But I may well have enlarged the meaning of irony
to which the reader is accustomed, in applying the term to
men of divided mind and self-derisive temperament. The
enlargement, however, seems justified: these men do not
merely *use* irony; they *live* ironically; and irony is as a consequence basic in their view of the world.

We set out to understand the ironic spirit as it manifests
itself in drama, and our purpose does not require us also to
evaluate it in comparison with other ways of seeing the
world. But immersion in any special study is likely to produce a distortion of values. We might easily be led, for
example, to romanticize a Euripides or an Ibsen into a person superior to other men because he is supreme in irony.
As Arnold observed, the scholar is prone to overrate his
subject "in proportion to the trouble which it has cost him."

Therefore we may need to pause before we end our book and ask ourselves just how important and valuable the ironic view really is in literature and in society.

Some writers have, in my opinion, greatly overrated it. Randolph Bourne, for example, in an essay called "The Life of Irony,"[1] goes so far as to assert that the ironic life is better than the religious life! It "has the courageous spirit, the sympathetic heart and the understanding mind, and can give them full play, unhampered by the searching introspection of the religious mind that often weakens rather than ennobles and fortifies." On the contrary, if our study of Ibsen, not to mention the Romantics, has shown anything, it has shown that it is exactly the ironic spirit which encourages introspection. And it is the deep and undivided conviction held by great leaders of religion which strengthens and fortifies them. Mr. Bourne speaks of irony as "in its best sense . . . an exquisite sense of proportion"—which is so broad and undifferentiating a definition as nearly to equate irony with wisdom itself. Hence perhaps my disagreement with him is due to his use of the term in a special and private sense. If that is so, he should have made it clearer that he was ignoring the usual meaning of the word. And at all events, when he writes of his ideal ironist that "he cares too much. He is feeling the profoundest depths of the world's great beating, laboring heart . . . ," I confess that I am reminded of Alfred Allmers.

Another example is a lengthy philosophical study written in French by a Vladimir Jankélévitch.[2] Under such metaphorical headings as *Les Visages de l'Ironie* and *Des Pièges de l'Ironie* Mr. Jankélévitch treats irony as though it were

---

[1] For notes to chapter x see pp. 271–272.

CONCLUSION 249

almost a Platonic Idea with a supernal existence separate
from and above individual human beings. Such treatment,
at least to one who prefers the Aristotelian approach and believes that such terms have no meaning except as derived
from concrete instances, becomes excessively abstract; and
its abstractions are not lessened by a style which amplifies
each thought by an outpour of dogmatic metaphorical generalization. He will tell us, for example, that "irony is the
somewhat melancholy gaiety which the discovery of a
plurality inspires in us."[3] This is a suggestive observation
and calls for thought. But Mr. Jankélévitch gives us no time
to figure out why a plurality should inspire both gaiety and
melancholy; after a colon he amplifies as follows:

Our sentiments, our ideas, must renounce their seigneurial soli-
tude for humiliating neighborhoods; they cohabit in time and
space with the multitude; novelties avow their old age and turn
to the confusion of the naïve; the universe grows animated but
the particularity atrophies; and there is in the world at the same
time more variety and less fervor.

In time, sentences of this sort, where every clause is an
apophthegmatical metaphor, are wearing. It may be that
I have missed some important matters in Mr. Jankélévitch's
book; I read it through conscientiously, but I was overwhelmed by it. At any rate, I am sure of one thing: he considers irony a high attribute of the rare philosopher. His
concluding paragraph, for example, is as follows:

Irony, like Eros, is a demonic creature. Amorous irony, serious irony, always midway between tragedy and levity. Almost
nothing is as grave as we fear nor as futile as we hope. The masks
that madly throng the corso, in the carnival of Hoffmann, have
learned the good news: thought has destroyed "contemplation,"

but self-consciousness, in offering it its own image, renders it to its true fatherland; and thought breathes freer when it is recognized, dancing and grimacing, in the mirror of reflection. That is to say that humor is not without love, nor irony without joy, and hence that lucidity will not be lacking to those who will have loved with all their heart.[4]

Lucidity would be less lacking to us who read if the meaning of this passage had been less involved with gods and carnivals and mirrors. But its manner, at all events, conveys plainly enough the author's admiring sentiments.

We find overvaluation of irony even in the unemotional environment of a philosophical journal, and in an essay generally helpful because the writer, Georges Palante,[5] is primarily interested in analysis and explanation, not laudation. He notes, for example, that although laughter and irony have a like source, irony is at the same time "douloureuse" because to find reason falsified by fact is painful. Again, he considers the most frequent source of irony to be "the dissociation that is set up in a soul between intelligence and sensibility." His citations and examples are also helpful, though he seems at times to identify all irony with the Romantic variety. But his emotional bias in favor of irony becomes manifest when he praises it as a useful counterweight to evangelism and dogmatism, and especially when he quotes with approval from Proudhon's *Confessions d'un Révolutionnaire* a passage (the concluding paragraphs of that fervid plea for socialistic reform) which does nothing less than deify irony. This passage is so amazing that I quote it in full, including matter omitted by Mr. Palante.

Liberty, like reason, exists and manifests itself only in the incessant disdain of its own works; it perishes when it admires itself. This is why irony has always been the character of philo-sophical and liberal genius, the seal of the human spirit, the irresistible instrument of progress. Static folk are always solemn folk; the man of the people who laughs is a thousand times nearer reason and liberty than the anchorite who prays or the philosopher who argues.

Irony, true liberty! it is thou who deliverest me from the ambition of power, from the servitude of parties, from the respect for routine, from the pedantry of science, from the admi-ration of great persons, from the mystifications of politics, from the fanaticism of reformers, from the superstition of this great universe, and from self-adoration. Thou revealedst thyself long ago to the Sage on the throne when he cried in view of that world in which he figured as a demigod, *Vanity of Vanities!* Thou wert the familiar spirit of the Philosopher when he un-masked at the same time dogmatist and sophist, hypocrite and atheist, epicurian and cynic. Thou consoledst the dying Right-eous One when he prayed on the cross for his executioners: *Father, forgive them, for they know not what they do!*

Gentle Irony! thou alone art pure, chaste, and discreet. Thou givest grace to beauty and seasoning to love; thou inspirest charity by tolerance; thou dissipatest homicidal prejudice; thou teachest modesty to woman, audacity to the warrior, prudence to the statesman. By thy smile thou appeasest dissensions and civil wars; thou makest peace between brothers, thou curest the fanatic and the sectary. Thou art mistress of Truth; thou servest as providence to Genius; and Virtue and thou, O Goddess, are one.

Come, sovereign: pour upon my fellow citizens a ray of thy illumination; light in their souls a spark of thy spirit: that my confession may reconcile them, and that the inevitable revolution may be accomplished in serenity and joy."

Perhaps we shall be forgiven if we differ from Proudhon by not considering irony a goddess. Certainly the great ironists will forgive us: they were men with a strong sense of the ridiculous. One can imagine the reaction of a Voltaire or an Ibsen if he had been told that he felt "the profoundest depths of the world's great beating, laboring heart," or that his painful amusement at the discrepancies of things made him virtuous, or that it was his spirit that Jesus felt on the cross.

A scholarly and profound, but even more mystical, valuation of irony appears in the earliest work of the Danish moralist philosopher, Søren Kierkegaard—a doctoral dissertation accepted by the University of Copenhagen in 1841, the full title of which is *The Concept of Irony, with Constant Reference to Socrates.*[7] As this title indicates, Kierkegaard based his concept of irony upon the character of Socrates, which in the first part of the work he studies through its different representations in Xenophon, Plato, and Aristophanes. In this study he makes clear that, as he uses the term, irony is not merely a figure of speech or conduct, but the capacity to view existence from contrasting points of view. "Irony oscillates between the ideal ego and the empirical ego; the former would makes Socrates a philosopher, the latter a sophist; but what makes him more than a sophist is that his empirical ego has universal validity."[8]

For our purposes it is perhaps unnecessary to ask exactly what the "ideal ego" and the "empirical ego" mean. They certainly suggest a German metaphysics; and in the second part of the dissertation Kierkegaard's indebtedness to Hegel, along with certain qualifications and disagreements, is acknowledged. "A definition that runs through all irony is that the phenomenon is not being but the contrary of being."[9] Hegel was correct in saying that irony is "infinite absolute negativity."[10] In Hegel's view, individuals are standard-bearers in the conflict of ideas that constitutes world history. An idea is valid for a time, but must then be supplanted by a new idea. The first individual who represents the new is a sacrifice to it, a tragic hero.[11] For him the old has lost its validity; he denies it, knowing that the new is coming; but he does not possess the new. Hence his negativity. This is infinite because he does not deny this or that phenomenon;[12] it is absolute because that which causes the denial does not yet exist. John the Baptist denied Judaism without knowing Christianity. This act made him the objective form of world irony. But for a full development of this irony it is necessary that the individual be aware of his irony and enjoy his negative freedom in it. "Irony is the infinite nimble play with Nothing that will not be terrified by it but puts its head again into the storm. . . . It is serious with Nothing so far as it is not serious with Something."[13]

If one understands this correctly, one gathers that irony means to Kierkegaard an awareness of metaphysical opposites, both in oneself and in the world. The aspect of comic amusement at the painful, which has been emphasized in the present study, is hardly suggested further than in such words as "play" and "enjoyment," employed occasionally in connection with this philosophical awareness. From this view it is explicable how Kierkegaard can agree with Friedrich Schlegel that Shakespeare is the grand master of irony because he is above his work.[14]

But Kierkegaard condemns Schlegel's and Tieck's Romantic irony on the ground that it is Fichtean subjectivity—subjectivity "of the second power":[15] the ego observing the ego; that it is essentially critical of reality itself and turns historical fact into myth; that its choice of truth is whim; that consequently its poetry is empty. The true irony is a controlled force (*beherrschtes Moment*), as in Goethe, not whim; it is "a spirit that serves the poet."[16] "What doubt is for science, irony is for personal life. Therefore, as the scientists affirm that no true science is possible without doubt, so with equal right one can affirm that no true human life is possible without irony."[17] "Irony limits, terminates, bounds, and hence gives truth, reality, substance; it chastises and punishes and hence gives support and consistence. Irony is a taskmaster feared only by one who knows him not, but loved by one who knows him."[18]

Since the same term is employed here for a high philosophical awareness, and in general usage for an amused and detached sense of painful contrasts in the phenomenal world, there is danger of confusion between them, though actually there is little in common between them. In practice, in his extraordinary pseudonymous works, Kierkegaard employed the ordinary irony constantly for controversial and religious ends. But what he calls by the name irony is not amusing or painful, but simply a detached understanding superior to the object of its regard. Only in this sense can a critic find Shakespeare the "grand master of irony." And in this sense, of course, irony can be exalted as a guide to spiritual progress. Irony in the ordinary sense can make no such august claims.

Let us, then, refrain from thinking the ironist a more important force in the progress of civilization than the evidence warrants. Socrates alone, among supreme ironists, has been an immense positive force upon morality; and it is not his irony which brought that influence to bear. Indeed, as

I suggested earlier, his irony, delightful as it is to us as readers, could only have antagonized his fellow citizens who were its victims and hindered the acceptance of his doctrines.

There could hardly be an assertion more contrary to the truth than Proudhon's that "static folk are always solemn folk." Ironists and humorists, are, next to the merely lazy, the most likely folk to be static, for they relieve their feelings by their mockery. Solemn folk have no such outlet. It is solemn folk who instigate revolutions, win battles, rule the world. Even if a dictator has a sense of humor, as sometimes happens, it is a luxury that he must forego in a crisis. Countries in which liberty and general well-being prevent revolutionary passions from developing extensively sometimes produce a Disraeli or a Franklin Roosevelt; but the men who rule mankind are mostly stern Romans—when they are not paranoiac Hitlers. Even more is unironic seriousness the rule among those who found religions.

No, the ironist is generally a passive person who looks on as the world goes by. He is not indifferent to it, but whenever he has an impulse to act he reflects that reform is hopeless and rebellion perhaps worse ultimately than submission. Futility and vanity are his final terms for human effort. To those who understand his hidden ironic meaning, his view of life is more discouraging even than outspoken pessimism. It cannot be laughed aside like the gloom of an Ecclesiastes, because it laughs itself and forestalls the mockery of an unwilling hearer. And the final consequence of its disillusioning vision is the despair of an Ibsen or a Swift.

Because of his clear vision of things as they are, the ironist can see evils and point them out to others. By so doing he

often assists reform. But his laughter rounds upon his pity
or his indignation and stultifies it in himself. Thus Ibsen
wrote in 1884: "I gave up universal standards long ago, because I ceased believing in the justice of applying them. I
believe that there is nothing else and nothing better for us
all to do than in spirit and in truth to realise ourselves."[19]
Ibsen's own self-realization, to be sure, was full of struggle
because his nature was protestant and dramatic; but the
outcome of his self-realization was frustration and despair.

On a lower plane than his, irony becomes self-conceit and
self-indulgence rather than self-realization. Mr. Chevalier,
writing of Anatole France, observes: "Irony, which origi-
nates in an awareness of incongruity, becomes readily a
superior satisfaction, a conscious pleasure in such awareness.
In actual experience, Irony characterizes the attitude of one
who, when confronted with the choice of two things that
are mutually exclusive, chooses both. Which is but another
way of saying that he chooses neither."[20]

Irony "tends to neutralize all passions and to turn all men
into spectators of the human comedy," writes Mr. Worcester. Further, it "offers an escape from mental pain, as mor-
phine." The habit of irony, like the drug habit, "is an escape
from responsibility." Finally, "irony is negative in its nature.
It reaches the height of its electric force only when it is used
for a positive, creative purpose. Lacking such purpose, romantic irony and cosmic irony at their most extreme convey
an impression of megalomania and frustration—of weakness, not of strength."[21]

Even when used as a positive weapon, irony has its obvious limitations. In its higher forms it is understood by few
and fully appreciated by fewer. The majority, when they be-

come aware of it, are repelled. And of those who understand it and feel it, many are themselves of the self-indulgent ironic type, mere dilettanti who will never in the world put any lesson it teaches into useful practice. The bitterest arraignment of evil becomes to them merely another mildly titillating esthetic effect. Aldous Huxley's early novels, for example, did no more to many of us who read them in the 'twenties than give us pleasant shocks. The author himself, however, employed irony to express a desperate horror at the world he saw around him; and since then, because he could not rest in desperation, he has gone on to religious faith and unironic sermonizing. Whenever an ironist acquires a genuine faith and a genuine desire to establish it, he stops being an ironist and preaches.

The cosmic despair of the late nineteenth century left a spiritual vacuum in the place of traditional religion; and into that vacuum rushed all the gaseous isms generated in our miasmatic modern society. In the anarchy that followed the First World War, these isms could take bodily shape in oppressive and revolutionary new governments. But we Americans ignored the dangers and made whoopee until we had a Depression, and a Second World War, to sober us. We might have saved ourselves and all civilization from at least the last horrible holocaust if we had had a solid faith and acted on it. Instead, we descended in the 'twenties into our lowest depths of materialism, cynicism—and irony. The Nasty 'Twenties were an era of ironic disillusionment. It remains to be seen whether the 'fifties will be less spiritually blighted—or more.

We conclude that spiritual ironists are sick souls, and that irony as a weapon is usually a method of destruction. But the reason that the ironist's soul is sick is that he has visions of a better world than the existing one, and the destruction of present evil gives opportunity for future good. Hence the estate of irony is honorable even through its existence is evidence of the terrible imperfections of human life.

NOTES

A FOOTNOTE ABOUT FOOTNOTES

FOOTNOTES used to be frankly what they are called—notes at the bottom of the page; and in strictly professional monographs they still are. Indeed, there is much to be said for putting them where the eye can glance them over in an instant. But if a book is intended to be read even partly for pleasure, such a practice is esthetically objectionable. Hence mine are put at the back of the book. At the same time, I wish to assure the reader of one thing: he need never consult them unless he wishes quotations in the original or purely bibliographical references. They consist of those and nothing else. Whenever I wanted to qualify or amplify, I have done so in the text. Would that every writer who hides his notes in the back would do likewise!

NOTES TO CHAPTER I: THE FORMS OF IRONY
(Pages 3–14)

[The epigraphs preceding chapter i are from the following: Plato, *Symposium*, transl. Jowett; Max Eastman, *Enjoyment of Laughter* (New York, 1936 and 1939), p. 204; David Worcester, *The Art of Satire*, p. 141; Anatole France, *On Life and Letters*, third series (London and New York, 1922), p. 32 (essay on Rabelais).]

[1] Otto Ribbeck, "Ueber den Begriff des εἴρων" (*Rheinisches Museum*, Band 31, 1876), pp. 381–400; J. A. K. Thomson, *Irony*. Sedgewick, *Of Irony*, reviews this topic clearly and briefly.

[2] A. C. Bradley, quoted in *Webster's New International*.

[3] Article [signed "C. T."], "On the Irony of Sophocles," *Philological Museum*, Vol. II, pp. 483–537.

[4] Worcester, *The Art of Satire*, p. 78.

[5] Job, 12:2.

[6] *Pudd'nhead Wilson's Calendar*.

[7] Quoted in *More Invective*, ed. Hugh Kingsmill (New York, 1930).

[8] Edgar Johnson, ed., *A Treasury of Satire* (New York, 1945), p. 319.

[9] *Micromégas*, ch. i; my translation.

[10] Anatole France, *Penguin Island* (London, 1909), p. 137.

[11] *Ibid.*, p. 52.

[12] Plato, *Euthyphro;* Jowett's translation.

[13] France, *On Life and Letters* (*La Vie littéraire*) (London and New York, 1922), Pref., p. viii.

[14] *The Short Stories of Saki* [H. H. Munro] (New York, Viking, 1937), "Sredni Vashtar."

[15] France, *Penguin Island*, p. 318.

[16] *New Yorker*, issue of September 8, 1945.

[17] Kant, *Critique of Aesthetic Judgement* (Oxford, 1911), p. 199.

[18] Max Eastman, *The Sense of Humor* (New York, 1921), chap. xi.

[19] Eastman, *Enjoyment of Laughter* (New York, 1936).

[20] I review the main theories of comedy at greater length in *The Anatomy of Drama*, chap. v. All references to that book are to the first edition.

[21] *A Treasury of Satire* (New York, 1945), Introd., p. 6.

NOTES TO CHAPTER II: EMOTIONS THAT CLASH
(Pages 15–48)

[1] Cited by David Worcester, *The Art of Satire*, p. 78, from *The Arte of English Poesie*, 1589.

[2] Vladimir Jankélévitch, *L'Ironie* (Paris, 1936), p. 100.

[3] My translation from the *Théâtre complet* of Becque (Paris, n.d.), T. 2.

[4] Biographical notes in *The Short Stories of Saki*, p. 695.

[5] I Kings, 18:27.

262   NOTES

[6] *Spectator* for May 2, 1896 (Vol. LXXVI), p. 627.
[7] I discuss this imaginative participation at length in *The Anatomy of Drama,* chaps. iii and iv.
[8] "A la comédie comme à la tragédie nous venons pour voir souffrir." Faguet, *Drame ancien, drame moderne* (Paris, 1903), p. 5.
[9] *The Anatomy of Drama,* p. 131.
[10] Lines 443 ff., quoted by Ribbeck; my translation. The original reads:

εἴπερ τὰ χρέα διαφευξοῦμαι
τοῖς τ᾽ἀνθρώποις εἶναι δόξω
θρασὺς, εὔγλωττος, τολμηρὸς, ἴτης,
βδελυρός, ψευδῶν συγκολλητής,
εὑρησιεπής, περίτριμμα δικῶν,
κύρβις, κρόταλον, κίναδος, τρύμη,
μάσθλης, εἴρων, γλοιός, ἀλαζών . . .

[11] F. M. Cornford, *The Origin of Attic Comedy* (London, 1914), esp. pp. 132 ff.
[12] Cf. Cornford's synopses of the plays, pp. 222 ff., scenes marked AL.
[13] Thomson, *Irony,* p. 26.
[14] *Ibid.,* p. 33.
[15] *Ibid.*
[16] Cf. *The Anatomy of Drama,* chap. iii, esp. p. 99.
[17] See Kierkegaard's views, pp. 252–254 above. Also Paul Friedländer, *Platon* (Berlin and Leipzig, 1929), Vol. I, ch. vii. Professor Friedländer is free from Hegelian metaphysics, but gives Socratic-Platonic irony hardly a lower valuation than does Kierkegaard.
[18] Worcester, *op. cit.,* p. 118.
[19] G. G. Sedgewick, *Of Irony, Especially in Drama* (Toronto, 1935), p. 251.
[20] Thirlwall, "On the Irony of Sophocles," p. 508. Cf. the digest of his essay above, pp. 143–148 f.
[21] Worcester, *op. cit.,* p. 118.
[22] Cornford, *op. cit.,* p. 35.
[23] Sedgewick, *op. cit.,* p. 26.
[24] *Ibid.,* p. 29.
[25] *Ibid.,* p. 30.
[26] *Ibid.,* p. 75.
[27] *Ibid.,* p. 94.
[28] Max Eastman, *Enjoyment of Laughter,* p. 203.
[29] Lines 245 ff.; Campbell's translation. Italics mine.
[30] Note by Sir Richard Jebb, *The Oedipus Tyrannus* (Cambridge, Eng., 1927), p. 36. The passage quoted is as he gives it in this note, condensed from lines 261–262.
[31] Lines 1068 ff. The words which I have italicized are as follows in the Greek:

. . . ἐμαυτὸν παῖδα τῆς τύχης νέμων . . .
τῆς γὰρ πέφυκα μητρός . . .

Τῆς is clearly emphasized here by position.
[32] S. K. Johnson, "Some Aspects of Dramatic Irony in Sophoclean Tragedy," *Classical Review,* Vol. 42 (December, 1928), pp. 209–214.

[33] Lewis Campbell, *Tragic Drama in Aeschylus, Sophocles, and Shakespeare* (London, 1904), p. 170, quoting a statement published in 1872.

[34] *Ibid.*, p. 57.

[35] By Joseph Kesselring. I quote from *S.R.O.* (New York: Doubleday, Doran, 1944).

[36] I condense material from chap. iii of *The Anatomy of Drama.*

[37] *The Anatomy of Drama,* pp. 83–84.

[38] Aristotle, *Poetics,* ch. v.

[39] Jankélévitch observes this parallel, *op. cit.,* p. 33.

Notes to Chapter III: The German Sources
(Pages 51–64)

[The epigraphs preceding chapter iii are from the following: Jean Paul Richter, *Sämtliche Werke* (Weimar, 1930), 1. Abteilung, 5. Band, p. 328—I am indebted to my colleague, Professor Edward V. Brewer, for locating the source of the quotation; Pirandello, *L'Umorismo* (Florence, 1920), p. 186.]

[1] Edwin H. Zeydel, *Ludwig Tieck, the German Romanticist* (Princeton, 1935), p. 89.

[2] Many of these allusions are explained by Alfred Edwin Lussky, *Tieck's Romantic Irony* (Chapel Hill, 1932), chap. vii.

[3] "...so wurde gezankt, gescholten, gegrämelt, gebrummt, gemault, gegrollt, geschmollt, gekeift, gebissen, gemurrt, geknurrt und geschnurrt..." Influence of Rabelais? Sterne?

[4] "...alle die Pappeln und Thränenweiden, und der goldene Mondenschein hineinweinend, und dann das murmelnde Gemurmel des murmelnden Giessbachs..."

[5] Tieck, *Schriften* (Berlin, 1828), Vol. I, p. xxi.

[6] "O Herr des Himmels! Erde?—Was noch sonst?
Nenn' ich die Hölle mit?"

[7] "Das Gesetz ist aufgefressen! Nun wird ja wohl der *Tiers état* Gottlieb zur Regierung kommen."

[8] Zeydel, *op. cit.,* p. 91.

[9] Fritz Ernst, *Die romantische Ironie* (Zürich, 1915), pp. 52–53; my translation.

[10] In a speech of Jeremias, Act. IV of *Zerbino.*

[11] Zeydel, *op. cit.,* pp. 90 f.

[12] *Schriften,* Vol. I, pp. viii, xiii.

[13] Cornford, *The Origin of Attic Comedy,* p. 123.

[14] Philip Whaley Harsh, *A Handbook of Classical Drama* (Stanford University Press, 1944), p. 268.

[15] *Ulysses of Ithaca,* Act. I, Sc. 3, from Robert Prutz's German version (*Ludwig Holberg, sein Leben und seine Schriften*, Stuttgart and Augsburg, 1857). This is the only translation of any of Holberg's burlesques that I have found available.

However, Tieck considered this play Holberg's masterpiece in that kind (Prutz, p. 207).

[16] Hedwig Hoffmann Rusack, *Gozzi in Germany* (New York, 1930), chap. vi.

[17] Zeydel, *op. cit.*, p. 80; Lussky, *op. cit.*, chap. iv.

[18] Cf. Helen Walden, *Jean Paul and Swift* (New York University, 1940), chap. i.

[19] Lussky, *op. cit.* In the preceding paragraph I have followed Professor Lussky's analysis of Schlegel's theory.

[20] "...im frohen Genusse ihrer selbst nur aus reiner Willkür und Laune, absichtlich ohne Grund oder wider Gründe." Quoted by Ernst, p. 3, from *F. Schlegel's Prosaische Jugendschriften* (1882), I, 13, 20.

NOTES TO CHAPTER IV: THE PIRANDELLIAN UNIVERSE
(Pages 65–79)

[1] *Rousseau and Romanticism* (Boston and New York, 1919), chap. vii.

[2] "Mir ist immer in meinem Bewusstsein als wär' ich doppelt, als wären zwei Ich in mir: ich höre mich in Innern reden." Jean Paul Richter, *Werke* (Weimar, 1927), II, 5, p. 59; quoted by Walden, p. 51.

[3] Walden, *Jean Paul and Swift*, p. 53.

[4] Jean Paul Richter, *Vorschule der Aesthetik*, §36.

[5] "...zerteile mein Ich in den endlichen und unendlichen Faktor und lasse aus jenem diesen kommen. Da lacht der Mensch, denn er sagt: 'Unmöglich! Es ist viel zu toll!' Gewiss! Daher spielt bei jedem Humoristen das Ich die erste Rolle; wo er kann, zieht er sogar seine persönlichen Verhältnisse auf sein komisches Theater, wiewohl nur, um sie poetisch zu vernichten. Da er sein eigener Hofnarr und sein eigenes komisches italienisches Maskenquartett ist, aber auch selber der Regent und Regisseur dazu..." *Vorschule der Aesthetik*, §34.

[6] "...mit der Entstehung des Theaters entsteht auch der Scherz über das Theater, wie wir schon im Aristophanes sehen, es kann es kaum unterlassen, sich selbst zu ironisiren, was der übrigen Poesie ferner liegt und noch mehr der Kunst, weil auf der Zweiheit, der Doppelheit des menschlichen Geistes, dem wunderbaren Widerspruch in uns, seine Basis ruht." Tieck, *Phantasus* (1812–1816).

[7] Babbitt, *Rousseau and Romanticism*, p. 266.

[8] *Don Juan*, Canto II.

[9] *Ibid.*

[10] Jankélévitch, *L'Ironie*, p. 134.

[11] France, *On Life and Letters*, 3d ser., p. 9.

[12] *Ibid.*, 4th ser., p. 46.

[13] "Nature's Questioning," from *Collected Poems of Thomas Hardy* (New York, Macmillan, 1926).

[14] *Ibid.*, "Hap."

[15] *Ibid.*, "Freed the Fret of Thinking."

[16] *A Shropshire Lad*, LXII.

[17] *Ibid.*

[18] Quoted by Chevalier, *The Ironic Temper*, p. 30.

[19] Cf. Richard Gordon Lillard, "Irony in Hardy and Conrad," *P.M.L.A.*, Vol.

L, No. 1 (March, 1935), and A. R. Thompson, "The Humanism of Joseph Conrad," *Sewanee Review* (April, 1929).
[20] A. R. Thompson, review of *Brave New World,* in the *Bookman,* Vol. LXXIV, No. 6 (March, 1932).
[21] *The Waste Land.*
[22] Pirandello, *L'Umorismo* (1908). I cite the second edition (Florence, 1920).
[23] *L'Umorismo,* p. 178.
[24] "... da quel avvertimento del *contrario* [la riflessione] mi ha fatto passare a questo *sentimento del contrario.* Ed è tutta qui la differenza tra il comico e l'umoristico." *Ibid.,* pp. 178–179.
[25] *Ibid.,* p. 205.
[26] "brancolar nel vuoto," *ibid.,* p. 195.
[27] *Ibid.,* p. 214.
[28] "un nostro inganno per vivere," *ibid.,* p. 216. Cf. above, p. 223.
[29] *Ibid.,* p. 217.
[30] *Ibid.,* p. 218.
[31] "L'umorista non riconosce eroi," *ibid.,* p. 223.
[32] *Ibid.,* p. 16.
[33] *Ibid.,* p. 17.
[34] *Ibid.,* p. 18.
[35] *Ibid.,* note, p. 212.
[36] Domenico Vittorini, *The Drama of Luigi Pirandello* (Philadelphia, 1935), p. 21.
[37] By Vittorini, p. 7.

Notes to Chapter V: Molière
(Pages 83–102)

[1] John Palmer, *Molière* (New York, 1930), p. 423.
[2] London, New York, Toronto, 1943.
[3] Campbell, *Shakespeare's Satire,* p. 217.
[4] *Lettre à d'Alembert sur les spectacles,* 1758.
[5] Harsh, *A Handbook of Classical Drama,* p. 316.
[6] L. A. Post, introduction to *The Girl from Samos* (Oates and O'Neill, *The Complete Greek Drama,* New York, 1938, Vol. II, p. 1123).
[7] Harsh, *op. cit.,* p. 322.
[8] *The Complete Roman Drama,* ed. George E. Duckworth, translator anonymous (New York, 1942), Vol. II, p. 422.
[9] Palmer, *Molière,* p. 200.

Notes to Chapter VI: Shaw
(Pages 103–127)

[1] Preface to *Major Barbara.*
[2] Quoted by Hesketh Pearson, *G. B. S.: A Full-length Portrait* (New York and London, 1942), p. 366.

³ Quoted by Pearson, p. 4.
⁴ Henderson, *Bernard Shaw, Playboy and Prophet* (New York and London, 1932).
⁵ Preface to *The Shewing-Up of Blanco Posnet.*
⁶ Quoted by Henderson, p. 599.
⁷ Pearson, p. 198. (The preceding quotations from Shaw are taken from p. 199.)
⁸ Quoted by Henderson, pp. 615, 616.
⁹ Preface to *Three Plays for Puritans.*
¹⁰ Preface to *John Bull's Other Island.*
¹¹ Preface to *Fanny's First Play.*
¹² Sequel note to *Androcles and the Lion.*
¹³ A. E. Morgan, *Tendencies of Modern English Drama* (New York, 1924), p. 45.
¹⁴ Eric Bentley, *The Playwright as Thinker* (New York, 1946), pp. 170–172.
¹⁵ Preface to *Three Plays for Puritans.*
¹⁶ Preface to *Major Barbara.*
¹⁷ Preface to *On the Rocks.*
¹⁸ *Euripides and Shaw, with Other Essays* (London, 1921).

NOTES TO CHAPTER VII: AESCHYLUS AND SOPHOCLES

(Pages 131–150)

[Epigraphs preceding chapter vii are from the following: Pascal, *Pensées,* §§418, 412; Ulrich von Wilamowitz-Moellendorff, *Euripides Ion* (Berlin, 1926), p. 17; Ibsen, *Lyrics and Poems from Ibsen,* transl. F. E. Garrett (London and New York, 1912). The stanza quoted reads, in Henrik Ibsen's *Samlede Værker* (Copenhagen, 1899), p. 433:

> At *leve* er—krig med trolde
> i hjertets og hjernens hvælv.
> At *digte,*—det er at holde
> dommedag over sig selv.

In its original German form, as given in Brian W. Downs, *Ibsen: The Intellectual Background* (Cambridge, Eng., 1946), p. 137, note:

> Leben, das heisst bekriegen,
> In Herz und Hirn die Gewalten;
> Und dichten; über sich selber
> Den Gerichtstag halten.]

¹ Emerson, "Ode Inscribed to W. H. Channing."
² Ibsen, *Letters* (New York, 1905), p. 200.
³ Herbert Weir Smyth, *Aeschylean Tragedy* (Berkeley, 1924), p. 15.

[4] H. D. Kitto, *Greek Tragedy* (London, 1939), pp. 66, 109, 106.

[5] *Ibid.*, p. 38.

[6] *Ibid.*, p. 59.

[7] *Ibid.*, p. 51.

[8] Smyth, *op. cit.*, p. 140.

[9] Campbell's translation.

[10] Harsh, *A Handbook of Classical Drama*, p. 68.

[11] Edith Hamilton's translation, in *Three Greek Plays* (New York, 1937), p. 232. Italics mine.

[12] Cf. T. B. L. Webster, *An Introduction to Sophocles* (Oxford, 1936).

[13] Quoted by Webster, *op. cit.*, p. 15, from Phrynichus.

[14] Cf. Thirlwall, "On the Irony of Sophocles" (see pp. 143–148, above); Kitto, *op. cit.*, pp. 139 f; Abby Leach, "Fate and Free Will in Greek Literature," in *The Greek Genius and Its Influence,* ed. Lane Cooper (New Haven, 1917).

[15] See note 32 to chap. ii.

[16] Kitto, *op. cit.*, p. 122.

[17] Jebb, "The Genius of Sophocles," an undated lecture in *Essays and Addresses* (Cambridge, 1907), pp. 29–33.

Notes to Chapter VIII: Euripides

(Pages 151–195)

[1] William Nickerson Bates, *Euripides, a Student of Human Nature* (Phiphia, 1930), pp. 28, 51, 69–70, 77, 118, 145.

[2] G. M. A. Grube, *The Drama of Euripides* (London, 1941), pp. 51,

[3] A. E. Haigh, *The Tragic Drama of the Greeks* (Oxford, 1896), p.

[4] Kitto, *Greek Tragedy,* esp. chap. ix.

[5] R. B. Appleton, *Euripides the Idealist* (London and Toronto, chap. iv.

[6] A. W. Verrall, *Euripides the Rationalist* (Cambridge, 1895), esp. *Essays on Four Plays of Euripides* (Cambridge, 1905); *The Bacchants of Euripides and Other Essays* (Cambridge, 1910).

[7] J. T. Sheppard, *Greek Tragedy* (Cambridge, 1920), esp. pp. 130 f.

[8] F. L. Lucas, *Euripides and His Influence* (Boston, 1923).

[9] Werner Jaeger, *Paideia* (transl., Oxford, 1939), Vol. I, Bk. 2, chap. iv. Quotations on pp. 341, 329.

[10] Paul Decharme, *Euripides and the Spirit of His Dramas* (transl., New York and London, 1906), pp. 57, 76.

[11] Gilbert Norwood, *Greek Tragedy* (London, 1920), p. 311.

[12] Gilbert Murray, *Euripides and His Age* (New York, 1913), p. 195.

[13] Max Pohlenz, *Die Griechische Tragödie* (Leipzig and Berlin, 1930), pp. 166–167, 273, 321–322, etc.

[14] Hugo Steiger, *Euripides* (Leipzig, 1912), pp. 2 f.

[15] Decharme, *op. cit.*, pp. 95 f.

[16] Steiger, *op. cit.*, p. 10 and chap. vi.

[17] Kitto, *op. cit.*, p. 276.

[18] Whitney J. Oates and Eugene O'Neill, Jr., *The Complete Greek Tragedy* (New York, 1938), Vol. I, General Introduction, p. xxxi.

[19] Donald Clive Stuart, *The Development of Dramatic Art* (New York and London, 1928), p. 91.

[20] A. W. Schlegel, *Lectures on Dramatic Poetry* (transl. Bohn), pp. 111, 113, 115 f.

[21] *Euripides the Rationalist,* p. 2.

[22] Murray, *op. cit.,* p. 242.

[23] Verrall, *Euripides the Rationalist,* p. 100.

[24] Harsh, *op. cit.,* p. 170.

[25] Kitto, *op. cit.,* p. 313.

[26] Harsh, p. 165.

[27] Aldington's translation.

[28] Grube, *op. cit.,* p. 327.

[29] Verrall, *Essays on Four Plays,* pp. 51 f.

[30] Wodhull's translation.

[31] Harsh, *op. cit.,* p. 226.

[32] *Ibid.,* p. 235.

[33] Potter's translation.

[34] Stawell's translation.

[35] *Balaustion's Adventure,* last section. Mrs. Browning: *Wine of Cyprus.* I am indebted to Professor L. A. Post for telling me that it was Mrs. Browning, not her husband, who was first responsible for this characterization.

[36] Harsh, *op. cit.,* p. 183.

[37] *Ibid.,* p. 184.

[38] E. P. Coleridge's translation.

[39] Grube, *op. cit.,* pp. 158, 160.

[40] Harsh, *op. cit.,* p. 179.

[41] *The Anatomy of Drama,* p. 124.

[42] Harsh, *op. cit.,* p. 210.

[43] *The Anatomy of Drama,* p. 273. I discuss this distinction between melodrama and tragedy at length in the chapter from which I quote.

[44] Kitto, *op. cit.,* p. 329.

[45] E. P. Coleridge's translation.

[46] Harsh, *op. cit.,* p. 200.

[47] *Ibid.,* p. 201.

[48] Wodhull's translation.

[49] Potter's translation.

[50] Harsh, *op. cit.,* p. 214.

[51] *Ibid.,* p. 216.

[52] Wodhull's translation.

[53] Harsh, *op. cit.,* p. 215. The translation is his.

[54] Murray's translation.

[55] *Thyestes,* Ella Isabel Harris's translation.

[56] Harsh, *op. cit.,* p. 243.

[57] Murray, *op. cit.,* p. 180.

[58] Plots from Decharme, *op. cit.,* Pt. II, chap. ii.

[59] Verrall, *Euripides the Rationalist*, p. 91.
[60] Cf. Harsh, *op. cit.*, p. 192.
[61] Murray, *op. cit.*, p. 185.
[62] *Euripides the Rationalist*, p. 193.
[63] *Ibid.*, p. 197.
[64] *Ibid.*, p. 138.
[65] *Ibid.*
[66] *Essays on Four Plays*, p. 256.
[67] Murray, *op. cit.*, pp. 159–160.
[68] Oates and O'Neill, *op. cit.*, Vol. I, p. 762.
[69] Cf. Kitto, *op. cit.*, pp. 333 f; Grube, *op. cit.*, pp. 302 f.
[70] Steiger, *op. cit.*, pp. 20 f.
[71] Bates, *op. cit.*, pp. 89 f.
[72] Kitto, *op. cit.*, p. 227.
[73] Grube, *op. cit.*, p. 57. Grube italicizes these assertions.
[74] *Lettre à d'Alembert;* my translation.
[75] Kitto, *op. cit.*, pp. 193 f.
[76] Norwood, *op. cit.*, p. 281.
[77] Murray, *op. cit.*, p. 186.
[78] I. T. Beckwith, introduction to *Euripides Bacchantes* (Boston, 1888), p. 1.
[79] "Es kann niemand den Euripides ärger verkennen, als wenn er in ihnen eine Bekehrung zum Glauben der alten Weiber sieht." Quoted by Steiger, *op. cit.*, p. 113.
[80] Grube, *op. cit.*, p. 419.
[81] Kitto, *op. cit.*, p. 382.
[82] Norwood, *op. cit.*, p. 281.
[83] Murray, *op. cit.*, p. 182.
[84] "Ist es doch geradezu die Tragödie seines eigenen Lebens, die hier zur Darstellung kommt." Steiger, *op. cit.*, p. 116.

NOTES TO CHAPTER IX: IBSEN
(Pages 197–244)

[1] Steiger, *Euripides*, pp. 6 f.
[2] *Letters of Henrik Ibsen*, translated by John Nilsen Laurvik and Mary Morison (New York, 1905), p. 447.
[3] *The Anatomy of Drama*, p. 320. I devote a section of chap. ix—from which I quote—to a general discussion of Ibsen as a dramatist. Since there is a necessary repetition here of much that I wrote there, I have thought it suitable to quote the earlier study at times rather than to paraphrase myself.
[4] *Ibid.*, p. 329. The transl. of "På vidderne" is from Fydell Edmund Garrett, *Lyrics and Poems from Ibsen* (London and New York, 1912). The original passages read:

> det flommer ej længer i årens elv,
> og jeg tror jeg mærker i bringens hvælv
> alleslags tegn til forstening.
>
> heroppe på vidden er frihed og Gud,
> dernede famler de andre.

⁵ *The Anatomy of Drama*, pp. 321–322. I am indebted for much of this analysis of Ibsen's Protestant psychology and moral conflict to Janko Lavrin, *Ibsen and His Creation* (London, 1921).

⁶ Halvdan Koht, *The Life of Ibsen* (New York, 1931), Vol. II, p. 248.

⁷ *The Anatomy of Drama*, p. 329.

⁸ Cf. Herman J. Weigand, *The Modern Ibsen* (New York, 1925), chap. ii.

⁹ *The Anatomy of Drama*, p. 291.

¹⁰ Quoted by André Antoine, *"Mes Souvenirs" sur le Théâtre-Libre* (Paris, 1921), pp. 231–232; my translation.

¹¹ Otto Heller, *Henrik Ibsen* (Boston, 1912), p. 220.

¹² Koht, *op. cit.*, Vol. II, p. 206.

¹³ *The Anatomy of Drama*, pp. 177–178. My footnote there reads: "For much of this analysis I am indebted to H. J. Weigand's admirable study, *The Modern Ibsen.*"

¹⁴ Quoted by Henderson, *Bernard Shaw*, p. 314.

¹⁵ Shaw, *Dramatic Opinions and Essays*, Vol. II, p. 97.

¹⁶ A. E. Zucker, *Ibsen, the Master Builder* (New York, Holt, 1929), p. 207.

¹⁷ In a letter to Björnson, 1864; from *Letters of Henrik Ibsen*, p. 77.

¹⁸ *Lyrics and Poems from Ibsen*, p. 17. This gets the meter of the original, and is reasonably accurate in translation.

> De kom, mine vingede børn, på rad,
> viltre gutter og piger
> med kinder blanke, some efter et bad.
> Hej, hvor lege gik yr og glad
> gennem alle de dejlige riger.
>
> ⬦   ⬦   ⬦
>
> Men just some legen gik allerbedst,
> jeg traf til at se mod spejlet.
> Derinde stod en adstadig gæst
> med blygrå øjne, med lukket vest,
> op med filtsko, hvis ej jeg fejled.
>
> Der faldt en vægt på min viltre flok;
> én fingren i munden putter,
> en anden stå som en klodset blok;—
> i fremmedes nærhed, véd De nok,
> forknyttes de raskeste gutter.

¹⁹ I follow Weigand, *op. cit.*, chap. ix, in this parallel. See also Theodore Jorgenson, *Henrik Ibsen* (Northfield, Minn., 1945), p. 465.

²⁰ Gosse, *Henrik Ibsen* (New York, 1908), pp. 196–197.

²¹ Jorgenson, *op. cit.*, p. 417.

NOTES TO CHAPTER X: THE LIMITATIONS OF IRONY
(Pages 247–258)

[1] In *Youth and Life* (Boston and New York, 1913).

[2] Jankélévitch, *L'Ironie* (Paris, 1936). Cited also in chap. i. My translation.

[3] Jankélévitch, *op. cit.*, p. 29.

[4] *Ibid.*, pp. 148–149. "L'ironie, comme Eros, est une créature démonique. Ironie amoureuse, ironie sérieuse, toujours moyenne entre la tragédie et la légèreté! Presque rien n'est aussi grave que nous le craignons, ni aussi futile que nous l'espérons. Les masques qui déambulent follement sur le corso, dans le carnaval de Hoffmann, ont appris la bonne nouvelle: la pensée a détruit la 'contemplation, mais la conscience de soi, en lui proposant sa propre image, la rend à sa vraie patrie; et la pensée respire plus légèrement quand elle s'est reconnue, dansante et grimaçante, dans le miroir de la réflexion. Cela veut dire d'abord que l'humour n'est pas sans l'amour, ni l'ironie sans la joie, et ensuite que la lucidité ne manquera pas à ceux qui auront aimé de tout leur cœur."

[5] "L'Ironie. Étude psychologique," *Revue Philosophique de la France et de l'Étranger*, T. LXI (Paris, 1906), pp. 147–163; my translation.

[6] P.-J. Proudhon, *Les Confessions d'un Révolutionnaire pour servir à l'histoire de la Révolution de Février* (Paris, 1868), pp. 292–293. "La Liberté, comme la Raison, n'existe et ne se manifeste que par le dédain incessant de ses propres œuvres: elle périt dès qu'elle s'adore. C'est pourquoi l'ironie fut de tout temps le caractère du génie philosophique et libéral, le sceau de l'esprit humain, l'instrument irrésistible du progrès. Les peuples stationnaires sont tous des peuples graves: l'homme du peuple qui rit est mille fois plus près de la raison et de la liberté, que l'anachorète qui prie ou le philosophe qui argumente.

"Ironie, vraie liberté! c'est toi qui me délivres de l'ambition du pouvoir, de la servitude des partis, du respect de la routine, du pédantisme de la science, de l'admiration des grands personnages, des mystifications de la politique, du fanatisme des réformateurs, de la superstition de ce grand univers et de l'adoration de moi-même. Tu te révélas jadis au Sage sur le trône, quand il s'écria à la vue de ce monde où il figurait comme un demi-dieu: *Vanité des Vanités!* Tu fus le démon familier du Philosophe quand il démasqua du même coup et le dogmatiste et le sophiste, et l'hypocrite et l'athée, et l'épicurien et le cynique. Tu consolas le Juste expirant, quand il pria sur le croix pour ces bourreaux: *Pardonnez-leur, ô mon Père, car ils ne savent ce qu'ils font!*

"Douce Ironie! toi seule es pure, chaste et discrète. Tu donnes la grâce à la beauté et l'assaisonnement à l'amour; tu inspires la charité par la tolérance; tu dissipes le préjugé homicide; tu enseignes la modestie à la femme, l'audace au guerrier, la prudence à l'homme d'État. Tu apaises, par ton sourire, les dissensions et les guerres civiles; tu fais la paix entre les frères, tu procures la guérison au fanatique et sectaire. Tu es maîtresse de Vérité, tu sers de providence au Génie, et la Vertu, ô déesse, c'est encore toi.

"Viens, souveraine: verse sur mes concitoyens un rayon de ta lumière; allume dans leur âme une étincelle de ton esprit: afin que ma confession les réconcilie, et que cette inévitable révolution s'accomplisse dans la sérénité et dans la joie."
[End. 1849.]

[7] It has been necessary to use the German translation, *Der Begriff der Ironie mit ständiger Rücksicht auf Sokrates,* transl. Wilhelm Kütemeyer (Munich, 1929), from which the following quotations are translated into English.

[8] Kierkegaard, *The Concept of Irony,* p. 130.

[9] *Ibid.,* p. 253.

[10] *Ibid.,* p. 261. No source for this quotation is given.

[11] *Ibid.,* p. 268.

[12] *Ibid.,* p. 269.

[13] *Ibid.,* pp. 278–279.

[14] *Ibid.,* p. 335.

[15] *Ibid.,* p. 284.

[16] *Ibid.,* p. 336.

[17] *Ibid.,* p. 337.

[18] *Ibid.,* p. 338.

[19] Ibsen, *Letters,* p. 383.

[20] Chevalier, *The Ironic Temper,* p. 79.

[21] Worcester, *The Art of Satire,* pp. 141–142.

INDEX

INDEX

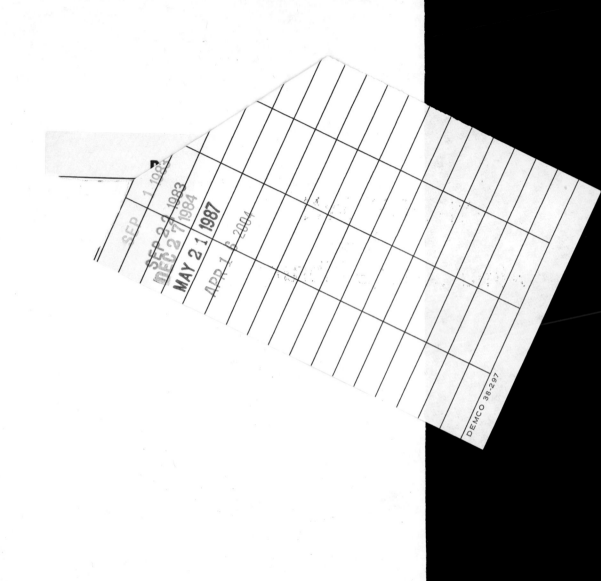